How the Other Half Laughs

HOW THE OTHER HALF
LAUGHS

THE COMIC SENSIBILITY IN AMERICAN CULTURE, 1895–1920

JEAN LEE COLE

UNIVERSITY PRESS OF MISSISSIPPI / JACKSON

The University Press of Mississippi is the scholarly publishing agency of the Mississippi Institutions of Higher Learning: Alcorn State University, Delta State University, Jackson State University, Mississippi State University, Mississippi University for Women, Mississippi Valley State University, University of Mississippi, and University of Southern Mississippi.

www.upress.state.ms.us

The University Press of Mississippi is a member of the Association of University Presses.

Copyright © 2020 by University Press of Mississippi
All rights reserved
Manufactured in the United States of America

First printing 2020
∞

Library of Congress Cataloging-in-Publication Data available

LCCN 2019034310
ISBN 9781496826527 (hardback)
ISBN 9781496826534 (trade paperback)
ISBN 9781496826541 (epub single)
ISBN 9781496826558 (epub institutional)
ISBN 9781496826565 (pdf single)
ISBN 9781496826572 (pdf institutional)

British Library Cataloging-in-Publication Data available

To my family

Contents

Acknowledgments
ix

INTRODUCTION
The Comic Sensibility
3

CHAPTER ONE
The Comic Grotesque
29

CHAPTER TWO
Rising from the Gutter
67

CHAPTER THREE
Illustration and the Narrative Quality of Appeal
93

CHAPTER FOUR
The Black Comic Sensibility
119

Coda
149

Notes
159

Works Consulted
177

Index
189

Acknowledgments

This book was a long time coming and has been pushed along with the help of many people. I will acknowledge a few of them here.

My colleagues in the Department of English at Loyola University Maryland have supported this project in myriad ways. Brian Norman and Mark Osteen have given me persistent encouragement and guidance over the years and also provided much-appreciated opportunities to share my work with colleagues in and out of the department. Nick Miller and I discovered our common interest in visual culture on different sides of the Atlantic; his thorough reading and erudite comments on several key chapters, as well as his role as "accountability buddy" over several summers and a sabbatical research leave, helped me stay on course. I hope I have helped him do the same. And Melissa Girard is a wonderfully generous interlocutor, with or without a glass of wine.

Other Loyola colleagues, especially Kerry Boeye and Matthew Mulcahy, alerted me to sources and scholarship in other disciplines. Participants in Loyola Faculty Writing Retreats have been congenial and intelligent sounding boards throughout the life of this project. Richard Blum provided translation help when I needed it. The Department of Academic Affairs materially supported this project with several Summer Research Grants and a Dean's Supplemental Grant, and the Office of Research and Sponsored Programs provided funds for a last-minute research trip to the William Glackens Collection at Nova Southeastern Museum of Art. I shall be eternally grateful for the cheerful, prompt assistance of Nicholas Triggs and Zachary Gahs-Bucchieri in the interlibrary loan department at the Loyola-Notre Dame Library; their ability to track down incomplete references and obscure publications on microfilm, in digital archives, and in local libraries amazed me over and over again. And thanks to Kate Figiel-Miller, Erin O'Keefe, and other colleagues in Loyola's Center for Community Service and Justice for being a reliable source of moral support and genuine enthusiasm during the final stages of the project.

I am especially grateful to Jared Gardner for his encouragement, and the example he sets as a scholar, editor, and teacher. I also thank Alex Beringer for reading my work and sharing his. I was lucky to be on a panel several years ago with Andreá N. Williams, whose work on the visual culture of the progressive era black press provoked me into new lines of thinking at an opportune moment. Michael Tisserand promptly answered my random questions about George Herriman and generously shared his copious research on that enigmatic artist; thank you. Jennifer Harris, Lori Harrison-Kahan, Mary Chapman, Ellen Gruber Garvey, Jennifer Tuttle, and Karen Skinazi have all contributed to this project, in ways I know of and in ways I suspect I don't. The sisterhood is strong.

I also want to acknowledge Gary Totten, editor of *MELUS: Multiethnic Literature of the United States*, Priscilla Walton of the *Canadian Review of American Studies*, and Keith Newlin, editor of the *Oxford Companion to American Realism and Naturalism*, for publishing earlier versions of several chapters. Brendan O'Neill, former acquisitions editor at Oxford University Press, encouraged this project early on; he and the anonymous readers there helped shape its final form. At the University Press of Mississippi, Katie Keene, Mary Heath, and Valerie Jones have been thoughtful and efficient in bringing the book to completion; many thanks to the readers there, as well, for providing valuable suggestions and enthusiasm for the work.

Most of all, I want to express my overwhelming gratitude to all of the archivists, curators, and collectors who have preserved the base materials that made this work possible at all. Digitization efforts at the Library of Congress's Chronicling America website as well as newspapers.com have enabled research in newspaper comic strips in ways that were impossible only ten years ago. And the openness and generosity of the Library of Congress, Nova Southeastern Museum of Art, the Delaware Museum of Art, and, most of all, the Billy Ireland Cartoon Library & Museum made it possible to include a large number of illustrations in this volume, which gave me the opportunity to develop and model the close reading of comics and tabloid fiction. Thanks especially to Aleesha Ast, Heather Coyle Campbell, Rachael DiEleuterio, Mary Holahan, Susan Liberatore, and Marilyn Scott for their help in locating materials in these collections. Comics bloggers and websites—especially Allan Holtz's Stripper's Guide—are essential if frustratingly ephemeral resources; I fervently hope that standards and methods for preserving digital records and archives will be established before they are lost in the ether.

Finally, love and gratitude to Matt for literally living with this project, like a houseguest who has long overstayed their welcome, for so many years, and for knowing when to say it was enough—or too much. You still make me laugh every day; I'm more grateful for that than I will ever be able to say.

If the images and words contained between these covers—whether they belong to me or to others—offend, I regret the pain they may cause but do not apologize for their existence. Any mistakes, however, are my own.

How the Other Half Laughs

INTRODUCTION
The Comic Sensibility

> A great flow of simple gaiety and humor roared over the dam from which the floodgates of respectability had suddenly been released.
> —Colton Waugh, *The Comics*[1]

Consider two images (see figures 1 and 2). The first presents a family grimly engaged in a scene of tedious, menial labor. Mama and Papa face away from their children, who are likewise disengaged from both them and each other. The children, one in the foreground, one in the background, one fading into obscurity off the right side of the image, each stare blankly at the photographer's camera, but appear unaware that the others are doing so. They are all turned away from the windows, perhaps because they well know that their expectations of light, much less a view, will be frustrated by the brick wall only feet from the panes. A jumble of objects populates the room—a barrel, a hat, a mirror too high on the wall to be of use, random pieces of furniture and manufacturing equipment. The caption accompanying the image, "Bohemian Cigarmakers at Work in Their Tenement," identifies this family as a group of laborers. We now realize that the oldest child in the foreground holds a tobacco leaf, perhaps in order to prepare it for his parents' workbench: not what you call child's play.

This image appears in chapter 12 of *How the Other Half Lives* (1890), Jacob Riis's damning exposé of overcrowding and inhumane working conditions in Gilded-Age New York City. Lest the viewer misinterpret this image or its caption as a portrayal of honest thrift and industry, Riis explains in the accompanying text, "Men, women and children work together seven days in the week in these cheerless tenements to make a living for the family, from the break of day till

Figure 1. *Bohemian Cigarmakers at Work in Their Tenement.* Jacob A. (Jacob August) Riis (1849–1914) / Museum of the City of New York. 90.13.4.150 U

far into the night. Often the wife is the original cigarmaker from the old home, the husband having adopted her trade here as a matter of necessity, because, knowing no word of English, he could get no other work." Unable to speak the language that would enable them to engage in more fruitful labor, they are virtually enslaved; Riis writes of the husband, "he has in nine years learned no syllable of English . . . In all that time he has been at work grubbing to earn bread."[2]

Figure 2 also presents a domestic space, but to much different effect. Here, the dingy clutter of the cigarmaker's flat has been replaced by a spare, clean room. In it, the family matriarch sits in a soft, cushioned chair. She is not working, but reading. Her children dote on her. They ask if they might bring her closer "by der window" so that she can have more light by which to see. "Dot iss plenty," she says as she is pulled out of the frame. "Tank you." This apparent solicitude, however, masks a more devious purpose: Mama is in fact made the butt of a joke, as her chair has been attached to a large spring that recoils when the children release her, causing her to crash into the wall of the flat. The joke is then turned on the children, as Mama spanks them in punishment. This early *Katzenjammer Kids* strip from 1902, drawn by Rudolph Dirks, makes the ethnic American household a site of slapstick comedy, mispronunciation and malapropism, cheeky insouciance—"I could die waltzing," Fritz says to

Figure 2. Rudolph Dirks, *The Katzenjammer Kids* ("Bang! Ach!"), *New York Journal*, January 19, 1902. Library of Congress.

Hans as they watch their mischief bear fruit—and corporeal violence. Yet even though the children are beaten at the end of the strip, they would return next week with another prank to play. Readers did not weep, for they knew that the boys' tears were fleeting.

Riis and Dirks depict similar people occupying similar spaces, but they do so in very different ways. Riis's representation is grittily, shockingly photographic, his prose poignant, verging on purple, as he explains how "a proud race" has been subjugated to "a slavery as real as any that ever disgraced the South."[3] The cigarmakers are shown at their labors, unspeaking, unsmiling, emotionally blank. They appear to be, as Theodore Dreiser wrote of his German American heroine, Carrie Meeber, "waifs amid forces," passive and silent as they are crushed by the effects of urbanization and the weight of poverty. Throughout *How the Other Half Lives*, Riis underscores the fact that it is the environment, not the poor themselves, that is responsible for their misery: "In the tenements all the influences make for evil," he wrote; "they touch the family life with deadly moral contagion."[4]

Yet all was not evil in the tenements. While Dirks's Katzenjammers were certainly full of mischief, they also were full of fun. Throughout the new Sunday comic supplements, as well as in popular fiction and theater, advertising, and even painting, writers and artists did not just focus on the oppressions of urban life but also displayed its exuberant, streetwise whimsy. They showed that the

Other Half did not simply live, simply endure: they also laughed—at times, uproariously. They laughed at reality, and laughed within reality, engaging in what I describe as the comic sensibility. In referring to it as a *sensibility*, I am returning the word to its etymological origins, meaning that it is a visceral appeal to the senses, the sort of humor that is meant to be physically felt rather than intellectually appreciated. Rather than exhibiting the "*delicacy* of imagination" or calling forth the "finer emotions," as Hume wrote of sensibility in the eighteenth century,[5] the *comic* sensibility taps into the guttural, vulgar, violent, and excretionary. Firmly rooted in ethnic and racial humor, in all of its different forms it combines the performative aspects of vaudeville, burlesque, and blackface minstrelsy, the verbal improvisations of dialect fiction, and a multivalent approach to caricature that originated in nineteenth-century comic weeklies such as *Puck* and *Judge*.

The comic sensibility is an interpretive framework that connects a performative act (a gesture, a grimace, a joke, a drawing) to a physiological response (laughter). The physiological convulsions of laughter, which are so often unbidden and sometimes irrepressible, are a byproduct of the comic sensibility; and comic strips, vaudeville, the joke, and comic forms of modernist theater, poetry, and art all seek to produce it. Yet laughter alone does not fully capture the comic sensibility. As Freud noted in his definition of tendentious humor—and as we see in a great deal of ethnic and racial caricature and dialect fiction—laughter can express hostility and cruelty as well as amusement. But as Daniel Wickberg notes in his aptly titled *The Senses of Humor*, the "subjective humor" that developed in the nineteenth century contrasted with the denigrating laughter at the deformed and marginalized described by Aristotle and Hobbes—what came to be known as the "superiority theory" of laughter—and also constituted a departure from the coldly intellectual display of wit that developed in the courts and coffeehouses of the eighteenth century. Instead, emerging from "a middle-class culture of benevolence, sensibility, and sympathy," humor became associated not simply with bodily functions (the origin of the word "humor," of course, coming from the bodily fluids that regulated human character, disposition, and behavior) or with intellect, but with feeling—in particular, common feeling.[6] In this vein, Thomas Carlyle wrote of humor that "its essence is love," a love that was fundamentally associated with a "wholesome," embodied sensibility: "the playful teasing fondness of a mother to her child."[7] Epitomized by the genial humor of Artemis Ward, the shaggy dog story of Mark Twain, and the "smiling aspects of life" that William Dean Howells advocated as the ideal subject for realist writers, subjective humor could lay bare the commonly shared incongruities of lived experience, a "laughing with the other man," as an *Atlantic Monthly* commentator put it in 1907, rather than a "laughing at him."[8]

The comic sensibility is comic in the classical sense of undermining authority, using laughter as expressions of solidarity, commiseration, and communal empowerment. The laughter that I identify with the comic sensibility results from what Freud's predecessor and mentor Theodor Lipps called *einfuhling* (in-feeling, often translated as empathy), and what philosopher Ted Cohen more recently has described as an attainment of "intimacy ... the shared sense of those in a community."[9] Thus the comic sensibility is a performative act producing a physiological rather than intellectual response and eliciting feelings of solidarity and community among the marginalized.

It may be difficult to see how a strip like this early *Katzenjammer Kids* example results in feelings of belonging, much less intimacy. The tendentious aspects of the strip, in contrast, are easily identified. We might laugh at slow-witted Mama for falling prey to Hans and Franz's trickery. We might also laugh at Hans and Franz as a result of the misspellings and mixed syntax of their German American dialect. The laughter, in both of these cases, responds to stereotypical traits of Germans. Yet we also laugh with Hans and Franz as they carry out their devious mischief. And we may laugh simply at the incongruity of seeing the crudely handwritten letterforms and primitive misspellings of "dot" and "iss" and "vas" in a national print publication.

This identification with transgression—in the sense of rebellion but also in the sense of trespass—is the source of comic solidarity in this strip. Rudolph Dirks, the creator of the *Katzenjammer Kids*, was himself a German immigrant, and his strip was an easily recognizable adaptation of the well-known *Max und Moritz* stories produced by caricaturist Wilhelm Busch for a mainstream American audience. Reflecting the demographics of much of the northeastern and midwestern United States, over 30 percent of New York City's entire population in 1890 was either an immigrant from a German-speaking country or descended from one, and tens of thousands of recent immigrants from Eastern Europe and Russia also could understand rudimentary German, due to its close relationship to Yiddish.[10] It seems clear, in retrospect, that the popularity of the *Katzenjammer Kids* may have been at least partly due to the audience's recognition of Dirks's crude "translation" of Busch's work into an urban American context, a translation that may have elicited equal portions of delight and dismay.[11]

For Cohen, the power of much ethnic humor resides in the fact that the ethnic audience shares knowledge with the humorist and laughs with him even as they also laugh at themselves. The humorist, in this case, seeks not to express superiority over his audience, but rather offers his joke to establish a common bond, to establish empathy, or even a communal intimacy, by enabling the recognition of common knowledge and understanding. The empowerment of the audience comes from the fact that they hold the power to laugh—or remain silent.[12] The power of laughter remains with the audience regardless of their position in society or their relation to the humorist.

In the case of the works I study here, the desire to create mass appeal in an era when the audience for mass culture was increasingly multiethnic and multiracial meant that comic artists and writers had to make "the Other Half" laugh. I focus my investigation on the newspapers published by William Randolph Hearst and Joseph Pulitzer and mass-market magazines such as *Cosmopolitan*, *McClure's*, the *Saturday Evening Post*, and *Collier's*. These periodicals revolutionized the practice of journalism and developed a huge mass readership. At the time, Matthew Arnold described the sensational, insistently topical style of the news media as the "New Journalism," and mostly critical commentators inveighed against the "New Humor" emerging in the comic weeklies and the variety stage, which privileged the joke over the comic storyteller, slapstick violence over witty repartee. These "new" modes merged in the comic sensibility. Both the New Journalism and the New Humor displayed a breezy, urban (if not necessarily urbane) irreverence, full of ethnic dialect and comic caricature, and were packaged in eye-catching typography, vibrant color, and dynamic page design.

These publications shared many writers and artists, including Rudolph Dirks, George Luks, Rudolph Block, Richard Outcault, Theodore Dreiser, William Glackens, and George Herriman, many of whom came from immigrant and working-class backgrounds.[13] In fact, some were hired specifically to help these publishers cultivate an ethnic, working-class audience. This loose confederacy of culture workers worked together, sometimes literally elbow to elbow, in the art rooms and news offices of the great newspapers and mass-market magazines. Although these publications competed fiercely with one another, the writers and artists they employed moved quite easily between them, often switching back and forth between rival publications or working for them simultaneously. Historians have generally focused on the intense competition between Hearst and Pulitzer, but the continuities between their publications may in fact be of greater significance. The people who worked for Hearst and Pulitzer not only worked together, but they also socialized with one another, attending the same parties and frequenting the same watering holes. Their interactions with one another within and across different social circles, occupations, and even city blocks enabled the development of the comic sensibility.

To illustrate the complex, layered, and multi-nodal interconnections between work, occupation, social setting, and familial bonds that knit together those who developed the comic sensibility in print and performance at the turn into the twentieth century, one might look at the associations that can be traced from a single moment: the café scene depicted in William Glackens's painting, *At Mouquin's* (1905; see figure 3). The painting appears to depict a moment of introspection (or, at least, dissociation) in a very public setting, a sumptuously dressed young woman looking either bored or pained by her plump male companion. Even though the identity of the painting's central figure is unconfirmed—some speculate that she is Marie Grandjean, wife of Mouquin's owner Henri Mouquin; others believe her to be modeled on an actress, chorus girl, or prostitute—an astounding array of relationships can nevertheless be traced through this image, and especially, to the Café Mouquin itself.

The identity of the woman may be disputed, but that of her leering male companion is not: he is James B. Moore, bon vivant and owner of the Café Francis, just a few blocks away from Mouquin's, which also catered to the bohemian set in New York City from which so much comic energy irradiated. The figures reflected in the mirror behind the couple are also known: the woman, only the back of her head visible, is Edith Dimock Glackens, the painter's wife; and seated across from her, his face a blur but still recognizable, is Chas Fitzgerald, art critic of the *New York Evening Sun*, a stalwart promoter of Glackens and other members of The Eight, and eventually, the husband of Edith's sister Irene. Members of The Eight, including Robert Henri, John Sloan, George Luks, Everett Shinn, Arthur Davies, and Maurice Prendergast, also frequented Mouquin's, as did their wives and lovers. Several of these women, including May Wilson Preston (wife of painter James Preston and close friends of the Glackenses) and Florence Scovel Shinn, were artists and performers too; women were not simply artistic muses but propelled the development of the comic sensibility in their own right.

Mouquin's also attracted other artists, including George Bellows and Walt Kuhn; Kuhn, in turn, was employed as a cartoonist for the *New York World*, where George Luks (and William Glackens, briefly) had also worked as a cartoonist. At the time Glackens painted *At Mouquin's*, Kuhn, at the *World*, befriended Marjorie Organ, the only woman on the *New York Journal* comics staff; at the *Journal*, Organ met Rudolph Dirks, who originated the *Katzenjammer Kids* and worked for Rudolph Block, who edited the comics supplement and also published some one hundred stories as Bruno Lessing, featuring, at different points, illustrations by Glackens and Sloan. (Block would also be the longtime editor of George Herriman, who joined the *New York Journal* staff in 1910). Kuhn introduced Organ to the ideas and work of Robert Henri, and Dirks introduced her to Henri himself—at Mouquin's—in 1908; the two were married after a secret, whirlwind courtship the same year, after which Marjorie Organ Henri joined the social set of The Eight, including Edith Dimock Glackens and the Prestons. Kuhn, meanwhile, would eventually

Figure 3. William Glackens, *At Mouquin's* (1905), Art Institute of Chicago. Creative Commons CC0 license.

organize the infamous Armory Show of 1913, where William Glackens served as head of the committee on American Art and where works by both Glackenses, Kuhn, Henri, Luks, Sloan, Everett Shinn, Prendergast, both Prestons, Bellows, Dirks, and other comic artists including Gus Mager, joined the works of European modernists including Pablo Picasso and Raoul Dufy.

At Mouquin's captures in a single, frozen moment a whirlwind of associations that functioned as a vortex of the comic sensibility. This book will explore a few of its vortices and the ways in which they twisted around and rubbed up against one another. Frequent, repeated contact in a range of environments and contexts fomented improvisation and creativity, while the fundamentally social aspect of these interactions made the comic sensibility a collaborative and communal endeavor. Those who adopted the comic sensibility did not just laugh at their audience out of a sense of superiority. They also laughed with them, in sympathy, identification, and self-awareness. And they also recognized the power of laughing despite—that is, laughing in the face of a cosmic realization of the cruel ironies of modern urban life. The mixture of different verbal registers and sometimes grotesque renderings of ethnic, racial, and social difference resulted in expressions of ambivalence, resignation, and protest even as it elicited chuckles or outright guffaws. Stereotype and caricature certainly were used to make fun of those who were relegated to Other Half, but also, to engage in pointed sociopolitical critique.[14] The comic sensibility poked fun at the Other Half in a way that enabled group identification and succeeded in attracting a huge working-class audience.

I begin this book with the comic grotesque of George Luks in the closing years of the nineteenth century. I then explore the influence of the early comic strip on the fiction of Bruno Lessing, the writing persona of Rudolph Block, who edited the comics section for the Hearst papers for decades, and then, the integration of visual and textual forms of the comic sensibility in the "ghetto stories" that frequently appeared in early twentieth-century magazines, focusing on the author-illustrator pairing of Irish-Jewish writer Edward Lipsett and William Glackens. I end the book by exploring the possibility of a "black comic sensibility" in the work of Jimmy Swinnerton and George Herriman. How did these artists access and transform the comic sensibility to create alternate modes of meaning and opportunities for laughter? Throughout, I show the close interactions between writers, artists, and editors and the interconnections between journalism, literature, art, and performance. I also restore to the record of literary history several important but long-neglected writers of ethnic fiction. Writers such as Bruno Lessing, Myra Kelly, and Edward Lipsett demonstrate that the immigrant experience was not just an unending round of sorrow, oppression, and poverty. Their fiction also empowered both writer and reader through flights of imagination, wit, and sheer ribaldry.

Recognizing the comic sensibility and its impact requires us to reorient our view of this period of American cultural history. When we think of the 1890s and early 1900s, we think about American literary realism—what William Dean Howells described as "nothing more and nothing less than the truthful treatment of material," characterized by a sometimes obsessive fidelity to physical description and the dramatization of mundane, everyday situations.[15] We also think about the emergence of photography and film, forms of representation that would come to compete with, and perhaps, transcend realism itself. We talk about earnest reformers seeking to elevate the concerns of the common man to high tragedy. We talk about commitment to aesthetic principles, technique, and the depiction of the complex workings of human psychology or individual consciousness. The newspaper comic strip and other comic cultural forms can be usefully contextualized within, alongside, and against realism and photography as forms of representation that responded, like realism, to the forces and phenomena of modernity. Liminal and transgressive, the comic sensibility provided a solution to some of the representative conundrums of realism, disrupting its smooth, impermeable surfaces and thumbing its nose at determinism. It created a space for human agency, for expressions of simultaneous surprise and comprehension, for revelatory incredulity, that helped propel modernist revolutions in language, representation, and meaning.

We often take laughter for granted. We forget that it is a fundamental—perhaps defining—aspect of human existence. We laugh not only when we're happy, but also when we're sad or even in despair. We laugh when we're nervous or confused. We sometimes laugh to mock or demean others; at other times, we laugh to express friendship and love. Philosophers including Aristotle, Hobbes, Bergson, and Freud have attempted (and largely failed) to explain why we laugh. While I do not propose to explain *why* we laugh, I do hope to restore the vital presence of laughter to a period of American history that is viewed with deadly seriousness by historians, art historians, and literary critics. Laughter, regardless of the form it takes, is an assertion of presence. The comic sensibility enabled its audience to laugh on their own terms, and thus become co-creators of meaning. The bridge between artist and audience created by the comic sensibility provided an alternative to realist approaches like that used by Riis, which depicted the Other Half as sentimentalized objects of pity, as faceless hordes, or both.

The Problem with Realism

Jacob Riis's photograph of the Bohemian cigarmakers demands to be taken seriously. He dares one to look—and then to look away. The seemingly unorchestrated composition of Riis's image, the visible detritus of everyday life, and the expressions of dull resentment or outright surprise on the children's faces all convey a sense of immediacy, the capture of a single moment in time, what

Susan Sontag described as a "miniature of reality." It exemplifies, in many ways, Sontag's characterization that "a photograph—any photograph—seems to have a more innocent, and therefore more accurate, relation to visible reality than do other mimetic objects."[16] Throughout *How the Other Half Lives*, Riis uses photographic documentation to substantiate his written descriptions of the tenement districts. Frequently shifting into second-person point of view, he treats the reader like a companion on his tour of the slums. "Be careful, please!" he warns readers as he invites them into a dilapidated building on Cherry Street. "You can feel your way, if you cannot see it. Close? Yes! What would you have? All the fresh air that ever enters these stairs comes from the hall-door that is forever slamming, and from the windows of dark bedrooms that in turn receive from their stairs their sole supply of the elements God meant to be free."[17]

A typical purveyor of late nineteenth-century American realism, Riis offers a mimetic representation of contemporary reality in order to spur social reform. In his preface to *Children of the Poor* (1892), a follow-up to *How the Other Half Lives*, Riis explains his method clearly and emphatically: "Ours is an age of facts. It wants facts, not theories, and facts I have endeavored to put down on these pages.... My aim has been to gather the facts," he insists, for others "to build upon."[18] In *How the Other Half Lives*, Riis had declared that the poor remained poor because the better-off half of the world did not know, and "it did not know because it did not care." Riis implies that now that knowledge has been foisted upon us, we cannot continue in a state of apathy or inaction. "What are you going to *do* about it?"[19] he demands.

Most realist writers were less explicit than Riis in connecting representation and action, but taken as a whole, David Shi writes, "American realism revolved around a moral axis.... The most conspicuous social ideal promoted by American realists was the creation of a more democratic culture."[20] Yet in promoting that ideal, realists often spoke from a position of moral—and frequently social—authority, morally superior to their readers, who were often assumed to be from the educated, moneyed classes, and socially superior to the Other Half whose lives they represented. Shi continues: "In giving artistic representation to long-ignored social classes and groups, realists could adopt a patronizing tone that turned subjects of description into objects of condescension."[21] Riis himself found that his efforts to expose the reality of life in the slums were not always appreciated. In his autobiography, he wrote, "It is not too much to say that our party created terror wherever it went." Months after he had photographed one slum, he returned to find "the recollection of our visits to Stanton Street hanging over the block like a nightmare."[22]

Riis conveys an awareness, if not an understanding, of the power dynamics that made him (and, especially, his camera) terrifying phantasms to his photographic subjects. Yet in depicting them from a position of superiority, he also turned them into receptacles of aestheticized pity, fetishes of philanthropic desire. By 1896, Riis, whom Theodore Roosevelt dubbed New York's "most useful citizen," had succeeded in a variety of reform activities, including the cleaning up of New York's water supply and the establishment of Mulberry Bend Park in the place of tenement slums. Perhaps as a result of these accomplishments, the genteel *Century Illustrated Magazine* published a series of pieces from Riis that looked back fondly on the "old alleys." In "The Passing of Cat Alley" (1898), he recalls locations featured prominently in *How the Other Half Lives:* Bottle Alley, Bandits' Roost, Gotham Court. "Three years of reform wiped them out," he reports, and replaced them with "shrubs and trees and greensward." "It is well," he says of these transformations. Yet he goes on to reminisce, for the next half-dozen pages, about the former denizens of Cat Alley, remembering "much kindness of heart and neighborly charity," the delight of the children at the sight of flowers. All in all, he concludes, "Cat Alley, with all that belonged to it . . . had its faults, but it can at least be said of it, in extenuation, that it was very human."[23]

In another piece, he recalls watching snowball fights and sledding with the street children "going down . . . With mighty whoops"; he writes that these children played "just as the dainty little children in curls and leggings were doing in the up-town streets, but with ever so much more zest in their play."[24] The fact that *Century* published these pieces in their December issues, alongside beautifully illustrated sentimental verse, short fiction on holiday subjects, and edifying profiles of historical figures testifies to the extent to which Riis's audience now saw the Other Half as a source for poignant sentiment rather than an impetus for change—or perhaps, anything real at all. For what was left to reform? The slums, after all, were no more.

Because places like Bone Alley and Cat Alley no longer existed, because they had, as Riis puts it, "passed out of my life," he implies that the people who once lived there have also vanished.[25] As a result, they can be known only through Riis's mediation. Riis's language is evocative and vivid, placing you practically at the threshold of Old Barney's former haunts, or in the midst of Italian immigrant family celebrations. But Riis is firmly in control of what we see, placing us within his memory of the scenes, not the scenes themselves. Jay Hambidge's illustrations provide a visual parallel to Riis's narrative (see figure 4). Like Riis, Hambidge takes great pains to show the variety of individuals who once occupied Bone Alley. In contrast to the blank, unseeing stares and often blurry expressions that characterize the flash photographs of *How the Other Half Lives*, Hambidge portrays a collage of individual portraits or vignettes taken from different perspectives. At the same time, he arranges these portraits against a backdrop, rather than depicting an actual street scene. While each portrait conveys strong verisimilitude, the assembled composition could never exist. The very care with which Hambidge assembles his portraits points to the artist as the central observer. Both depictions, the textual and the visual, are clearly mediated representations rather than "miniatures of reality." Indeed, the very carefulness of arrangement, dictated by the artist, might be counted as one of the technical touchstones of realism, where the "artist needs always to make choices about which details to include and which to exclude, as well as how details should be arranged and presented."[26]

Riis's illustrated *Century* pieces are examples of what Carrie Tirado Bramen has called the "intra-urban walking tour": an urban version of local-color realism. The intra-urban walking tour provided middle- and upper-class readers "a sense of contact with the 'other half,' cross-cultural encounters that the new technologies of mobility were making more difficult to experience directly and meaningfully."[27] They used realistic techniques of depicting places and people to provide a "sense of contact," a vicarious experience of reality. Like local color (examples of which occur throughout the issues of the *Century Illustrated Magazine* in which Riis's pieces appeared), it "undertakes to locate some little-known place," as Richard Brodhead has written, "and make it visitable in print."[28] Bramen argues that the intra-urban walking tour "offered a much needed aesthetic vocabulary for middle-class inhabitants of the city who did not resist otherness but actively pursued it," and thus helped create a sense of American identity that was cosmopolitan, transnational, and heterogeneous.[29] Ironically, however, it also enabled middle-class city dwellers to remain at a remove—aesthetically, if not necessarily geographically—from the "charming" and "quaint" ethnic populations they read about in the magazines. They could claim to know them without actually having to get to know them; they could go slumming without guilt.

Realism provided readers and viewers access to a "little-known place," while relieving them of the need to experience it at first hand. As Phillip Barrish writes, "literary realism helped middle-class Americans in particular adjust to social change in the sense that realist works sought to make even wrenching changes legible, comprehensible, almost literally containable between two book covers."[30] In doing so, realism also framed a paradoxical relationship between the artist and the subject of his representation. Riis and Hambidge exhibit an acute desire to both manipulate and separate themselves from the world of the slums, by simultaneously bringing the Other Half closer to the reader while imposing a mediated distance between them. Matthew Frye Jacobson claims that even for reform-minded writers like Riis, "immigrant ghettos were populated not by individuals, who might speak for themselves and whose

Figure 4. Jay Hambidge, *Bone Alley*, illustration for Jacob Riis, "Light in Dark Places," *Century Illustrated Magazine* 53.2 (December 1896): 248.

recognizable humanity might make a claim on our sympathies, but by crowds, throngs, masses of unindividuated and unspeakably odd folk whose very numbers overwhelmed the capacity for empathy."[31]

Certainly, the bewildering onslaught of sound and image, the cacophony of tongues, and the sheer numbers of people who confronted the urban American at the turn into the twentieth century inspired alienation as often as empathy, even if one sincerely desired to connect. No one expressed this sense of frustrated sympathy more forcefully than Henry James. After having lived abroad for more than twenty years, he described the effect of a visit to Ellis Island in 1904:

> he comes back from his visit not at all the same person that he went.... He had thought he knew before ... the degree in which it is his American fate to share the sanctity of his American consciousness, the intimacy of his American patriotism, with the inconceivable alien; but the truth had never come home to him with any such force.... it shakes him—or I like at least to imagine it shakes him—to the depths of his being; I like to think of him, I positively *have* to think of him, as going about ever afterwards with a new look, for those who can see it, in his face, the outward sign of the new chill in his heart.[32]

These immigrants are so alien to James that they make him question his notion of nation itself; they have so violated the "sanctity" of his conception of American consciousness that he speaks of himself in the third person. Elsewhere in *The American Scene*, he refers to immigrants as the "'ethnic' apparition," a horrific phantasm in their own right who have literally replaced "a visible Church, a visible State, a visible Society, a visible Past" in America; "those of the many visibilities, in short, that warmly cumber the ground in older countries."[33]

As Jonathan Crary has written, the end of the nineteenth century witnessed a crisis in perception. Rather than being rooted in a stable, objective notion of truth, the act of perception came to be located in the unpredictable and ultimately fallible capacities of human physiology. Perception itself, then, came to be questioned: what, exactly, *does* one perceive? What *can* one see? Feel? Know? Advances in optical technologies (including the portable camera and flash powder used by Riis), the spectacular nature of urban modernity, and the rapid transformation of the American social fabric only exacerbated anxieties about the possibility of accurate representation and perception. Riis's intrusive, overbearing use of the second person, Hambidge's detailed and ordered renderings of the slum residents, and James's obsessive turn inward are all "anxious attempt[s] to reconsolidate a cohesive visual field" even as they acknowledge the impossibility of doing so. Works like these, Crary writes, represent "the larger problem of realism ... where realism is no longer a question of mimesis but of the tenuous relation between perceptual synthesis and dissociation."[34]

Realism, then, becomes one way to respond to the "shock of the new," a response that many theorists, from Benjamin to Baudrillard, have claimed reflected a sense of dissociation and alienation, as noted by Crary. Crary argues, however, that this new, urban, spectacular, technological world also provided opportunities for the creation of a "newly modern individual autonomy," the possibility of "a sovereign awareness of the intimate singularity and creative mutability of the self."[35] The heterogeneity of late nineteenth-century urban spaces and the stress on exchange and consumption might unmoor traditional systems of affiliation and identification, but these aspects of modernity also enabled "permeability and mobility,"[36] as we have seen in Glackens's *At Mouquin's*. Crary locates this recognition of modernity's double edge in late realist and modern painting, but notes that painting simply participates, along with other cultural artifacts, behaviors, and practices (including technology and mass culture, for example), in both demonstrating and producing new forms of subjectivity.[37]

The Comic Sensibility

The comic sensibility, perhaps as much as the modernist modes of expressionism and abstraction, illustrated a "sovereign awareness of the intimate singularity and creative mutability of the self." It was dominated by expressive modes seemingly far removed from realism such as caricature, stereotype, and the grotesque; it frequently transformed the mundanity of everyday existence into spectacle. Yet the turn to the comic did not constitute an escape from reality. In many ways, it provided opportunities for artist and audience alike to more deeply engage with those realities, imaginatively, intellectually, and even physiologically.

In his 1905 work *The Joke and Its Relation to the Unconscious*, Freud noted that jokes, like dreams, function as eruptions of the id within the ego's conscious mind. The difference between the two, he wrote, is that while the *dream* remains contained within the individual mind, the *joke* only exists if it is recognized as such by another—that is, if it makes someone laugh. Thus, the joke is inherently social. The uncontrollable abdominal convulsions of laughter, the quick intake of breath and its noisy, spontaneous exhalation, constitute nonverbal expressions that establish a social relationship between the laugher and the joker. Laughter is an expression of comprehension, and thus an affirmation of shared perception.

The shared perception accessed through the joke, of course, is frequently a recognition of incongruity. Freud wrote that jokes were able "to bind into a unity, with surprising rapidity, several ideas which are in fact alien to one another both in their internal content and in the nexus to which they belong."[38] This ability to bind distinct or "alien" ideas into unities can be seen in all kinds of wordplay, including puns, malapropisms, double entendres, and portmanteaus. The joke, then, both confirms social relations in the real world, but also suggests gaps or discontinuities in that reality. Expressing a recognition of these discontinuities through laughter—which itself is also a response—is thus an assertion of selfhood and presence. When this laughter comes from below, as was so often the case with those who espoused the comic sensibility, it has the power to sustain and strengthen social bonds: to establish intimacy, to use Cohen's term.

For example, one might consider "Ingratitude of Rosenfeld," a short story by Bruno Lessing published in William Randolph Hearst's *Cosmopolitan* magazine in 1906 and illustrated by William Glackens. The unnamed narrator is having drinks in a café in New York City with his aggrieved friend Zalinsky, who soon launches into his tale of woe: clocked in the gut with a brick when mistaken for the miserly rich man Rosenfeld by one of Rosenfeld's enemies, Zalinsky is outraged when Rosenfeld fails to compensate him for the injury he has suffered on Rosenfeld's behalf. Zalinsky declares that Rosenfeld is simply "stingy! Stingy iss no name for it!" Yet Zalinsky reveals himself to be just as grasping, vowing to be "revenged" when Rosenfeld repeatedly ignores Zalinsky's hints that he deserves a reward. Finally, Rosenfeld writes Zalinsky a blank check that he might make out for any amount he chooses. However, he must, of course, write the check for no more than the amount that the account actually holds—and Rosenfeld refuses to tell Zalinsky how much that is.[39]

The ethical conundrum Zalinsky faces—that he must name a price for having saved Rosenfeld's life—is quickly eclipsed by his desire to maximize his profit on the check. He eventually pays the dry goods man Sammis, a "smart feller," $10 for coming up with a scheme for doing so. Sammis's plan works perfectly, but in the end, Zalinsky discovers to his utter chagrin that Rosenfeld has only deposited $5 into the account. We imagine him shaking his fist as he tells the bank clerk, through clenched teeth, "Ven you see Mr. Rosenfeld again, you tell him mit my compliments dot he iss a loafer vot vould cheat a sick dog. Unt if you ever see a man vot iss going to hit him mit a brick, you take my adwice unt get der man anudder brick." The shocked clerk reminds Zalinsky that he did, after all, get $5. "I gave him a nasty look," Zalinsky tells the narrator. "'Five dollars? V'y,' I said, 'I gafe Sammis ten dollars for der idea!'"[40]

The laughter produced by the joke that ends "Ingratitude of Rosenfeld" is heightened by Lessing's rendering of Zalinsky's outrage, filled with misspellings, malapropisms, Yiddish idiom made comical through translation, and American slang filtered through Yiddish dialect. Glackens's illustrations for the story also cue the reader for comedy, even though Lessing's narrator claims that Zalinsky's story will echo the "tearful andante doloroso which wails through all the long list of Magyar woes" (see figure 5). Rosenfeld's hand—drawn splayed over his checkbook against the white tablecloth and against the dark backdrop of Rosenfeld's dark, shapeless coat, unkempt facial hair, and tall, black Shabbat hat—conveys in a few quick strokes the greedy, secretive nature at the heart of Rosenfeld's character, while Zalinsky's longing for Rosenfeld's riches is conveyed through his lean physiognomy and the doleful gaze he casts at Rosenfeld's checkbook.

The story and its accompanying illustrations engage the reader on an almost tactile level. Glackens's blunt, sketchy marks and the use of high contrast convey a strong sense of activity despite the emptiness of the café and the static poses of the characters, while the informal composition of the scene conveys a sense of immediacy, a scene directly observed from life. The placement of an empty chair in the foreground of the composition practically invites the reader to have a seat at the table and listen to the story. Lessing's narration, which begins in third person but quickly shifts to Zalinsky's first-person narrative, begs to be read aloud—or even performed. This is an utterly "sensible" story, viscerally engaging both ear and eye.

Though it belongs to the genre of fiction, "Ingratitude of Rosenfeld" embodies the style of the New Journalism, what Hearst himself described as "the journalism that acts." Filled with outrage, sensation, and controversy, the newspapers and magazines published by Hearst, Pulitzer, and Samuel McClure appealed to an enormous middle- and working-class audience by exposing the corruption and greed at the top of the socioeconomic scale and elevating the concerns and struggles of the middling masses to the level of high drama. "60 Instantly Killed"! "Fears Her Rejected Lover"! "$10,000 for a Woman's Eye"![41] Scandalous divorces, natural and industrial disasters, petty criminals and corporate kingpins brought to justice—the headlines alone depicted the tumult of a society experiencing rapid transformation. The yellow-press publishers took advantage of newly developed printing technologies to incorporate photographic halftones, sketches produced on the scene, and especially, color images in order to further dramatize their offerings. Transforming news into

"'ZALINSKI, I VANT TO SHOW YOU DOT I CAN BE GRATEFUL'"

Figure 5. William Glackens, headpiece for "Ingratitude of Rosenfeld" by Bruno Lessing, *Cosmopolitan Magazine*, August 1906: 387.

entertainment, the publications associated with the New Journalism created a print version of popular spectacles such as vaudeville, the circus, the amusement park, and the department store, offering consumers constant variety, constant amusement, constant stimulation.

Rudolph Block, who wrote "Ingratitude of Rosenfeld" under the pseudonym Bruno Lessing, was a longtime editor for Hearst's *New York Journal* and was instrumental in bringing talented artists and writers together on the feature pages, the sports section, and the new comic supplement. Glackens, the story's illustrator, had not only studied painting at the Philadelphia Academy of Art, but he had also learned to sketch as a news illustrator for the *Philadelphia Press* and as a cartoonist and illustrator for Joseph Pulitzer's *New York World*. Both

Block and Glackens were conversant with the verbal and visual rhetoric and style of the New Journalism and the New Humor; in fact, they came of age within it. And the story appeared in *Cosmopolitan Magazine*—a mass-market magazine recently purchased by Hearst and infused during this period with much of the same energy and hard-edged humor as his newspapers.

Historian Albert McLean described the New Humor as being "more excited, more aggressive, and less sympathetic than that to which the middle classes of the nineteenth century had been accustomed"; it was not only aggressive, but could be downright "sadistic" in its methods, featuring both physical violence and vulgar language."[42] A typical late nineteenth-century variety duo was described in Douglas Gilbert's 1940 volume *American Vaudeville: Its Life and Times:* "Basco and Roberts did a very rough, almost brutal, burlesque trapeze act. They worked in black face, full black tights, large feet like apes, and frowzy wigs. They jumped on each other's stomachs, kicked each other merrily in the face, fell from the traps with awful thuds that would mean a hospital case for persons less tough and calloused."[43] The New Humor was strongly identified with the new immigrants from eastern and southern Europe, and provided the comic foundation for the vaudeville stage, the weekly humor magazines, and the new comic supplements. Edward "Ned" Harrigan, part of the renowned 1870s musical and comic duo Harrigan and Hart, commented in the first years of the twentieth century that "there's been a great change in the sense of humor.... The great influx of Latins and Slavs—who always want to laugh not with you but at you—has brought about a different kind of humor. It isn't native, it isn't New York. It's Paris, or Vienna, or someplace."[44] Fast-paced, topical, and filled with slang, dialect, slapstick pratfalls, and double entendre, it was exemplified by comic strips such as *The Katzenjammer Kids*, as well as vaudeville acts such as that of the "Dutch" duo Mike and Meyer (Joe Weber and Lew Fields) and burlesque troupes such as the High Rollers Extravaganza Company and the Rose Hill English Folly Company.[45] Even more than the comic strips, vaudeville and especially burlesque tapped into the vulgar, bodily humor that Mark Twain's Royal Nonesuch deemed unfit for "Ladies and Children." Weber and Fields's Pool Room Sketch, for example, featured exchanges like the following:

> MEYER: Once more, ain't I told you? Drop dot ball! (MEYER manhandles MIKE and the game resumes. MEYER shoots, misses and drives the white cue ball into a corner pocket. Both jump up and down exultantly.)
> MIKE: Hooray! A scratch!
> MEYER: Sure! A scratch! Dot gifs me four balls. Only best players can dodge all der other balls und get in der hole. I surprise meinself.[46]

The sketch plays on the characters' conception of pool as being about nothing but using "sticks" to get balls, and to get balls in "holes," resulting in an opportunity to engage in broad sexual innuendo; though Mike exults in Meyer's "scratch," Meyer claims that he still retains "four balls" while also showing his ability to "dodge all der other balls und get in der hole."

Vaudeville "blue performer" Johnny Forbes was known for his performances of "Such a Delicate Duck," a song based on a similar premise:

> I once knew a girl so modest I swow,
> (I can't remember her name just now),
> She wouldn't touch a flower pot, oh no, dod rot 'em,
> For the nasty things had holes in their bottoms.
>
> *Chorus:*
> Such a delicate duck
> I never did see.
> She was too damned particular,
> She never suited me.
>
> I took her out one night for a walk,
> We indulged in all sorts of pleasantry and talk.
> We came to a potato patch, she wouldn't go across,
> The potatoes had eyes and she didn't wear drawers.[47]

While acts like Mike and Meyer and Johnny Forbes were disparaged as nothing more than low, vulgar comedy, their sheer energy could not be gainsaid. Italian futurist F. T. Marinetti, for one, praised variety theater "because it proposes to distract and amuse the public with comic effects, erotic stimulation, or imaginative astonishment."[48]

The comic sensibility got cheap laughs by giving its audience cheap thrills, but it could also engage ethical questions. To return to Lessing's "Ingratitude of Rosenfeld," the story is carefully crafted to make a point. The reader who passes over the details of the story too quickly may believe, like the bank clerk, that Zalinsky should be thankful to have received $5, which, after all, was not an inconsequential sum in the early years of the twentieth century (approximately $140 in 2018 dollars). Moreover, since Zalinsky comes out on the short end of the deal, Lessing implies that he is being punished, through some form of cosmic justice, for attempting to capitalize on what Rosenfeld himself points out was an "accident" rather than an intentional act of self-sacrifice. Zalinsky simply found himself in the path of the brick intended for Rosenfeld, and took it; he had no choice in the matter. So we laugh at Zalinsky's ill-conceived greed while also learning a lesson.

But the joke may finally be on the reader. Zalinsky claims Rosenfeld is the rich one, "so rich he can't sleep," with "twenty tenement-houses in his vife's name." He contrasts Rosenfeld's wealth with his own poverty; "A t'ousand dollars in der bank I had," he says, "—not a cent more—not a cent more."[49] But a thousand dollars in the early twentieth century would have been worth over $25,000 today. Even though Lessing's story traffics in stereotypes of Jews as materialistic and greedy, it also pushes back against perceptions of Jewish immigrants as impoverished, starving laborers, blankly and silently accepting their fate. Zalinsky's sheer volubility, a stark contrast to the silent stares of Riis's Bohemian cigarmakers, is also evidence against this last point.

Caricature and dialect could simultaneously elicit reactions of alienation and identification; they could even produce identification *with* alienation. While many readers of "Ingratitude of Rosenfeld" or members of Weber and Fields's audience might laugh at the characters' and actors' misguided notions of morality or of billiards, they might also recognize their own bewilderment at a moral system that rewarded material acquisition, or their confusion at the complexities of the game of pool. They might laugh at Zalinsky and Mike for their inability to speak "correct" English, but they might also laugh out of a recognition of their own difficulties speaking the language. And finally, they might identify with—and laugh because—the stereotypes existed at all: a laughter tinged with sadness at the apparent need to see others as aliens.

While the comic sensibility produced laughter, it was a laughter that expressed a recognition of the truth. Ernest Gombrich described caricature in 1937 as an art that sought not "the perfect form but the perfect deformity, thus penetrating through the mere outward appearance to the inner being in all its littleness or ugliness." Examining the work of European caricaturists from the sixteenth to the eighteenth centuries, he shows how artists move, step by step, from a depiction of their subject's form in their entirety to the selection and grotesque exaggeration of a single detail: a hooked nose, a bulbous head. When effectively accomplished, the resulting depiction "produces a comic sensation . . . but also it is a likeness more true than mere imitation could be. And caricature, showing more of the essential, is truer than reality itself."[50] More recently, Henry Wonham writes that both caricature and realism "claim a unique capacity to lay bare the 'essence' of the human subject," while each also "operates on the phrenological and physiognomic premise that the essence of identity can be gleaned through observation and interpretation of the exterior form."[51] Dialect, too, grew out of a desire to depict the real, the true; emerging with the fields of anthropology and ethnography in the mid- to late nineteenth century, it was a way of categorizing and transcribing languages and linguistic variants. Realists such as Mark Twain, William Dean Howells, and Sarah Orne Jewett used dialect to convey the linguistic nuances of different regions and populations. Gavin Jones writes that even as it became a stock feature of popular forms of entertainment such as vaudeville, dialect was still seen as a form of "utter realism."[52]

The cultural valence of dialect as a marker of verisimilitude, or at least the intent to convey it, explains the now jarring intrusions of dialect in realist works such as Howells's *A Hazard of New Fortunes*. Lindau's earnest declamations against "pusiness motifes," "monobolies," "drusts and gompines"—and above all, "gabidal"—are intended to provide a strong ethnic presence in the novel and also provide the moral backdrop against which Fulkerson's opportunism and the Marches' glib, middle-class propriety become sharply apparent. But the characters, and even the narrator, find Lindau's "nople gonduct" laughable, a subject of mockery.[53] At Fulkerson's dinner, Basil March listens to Lindau's indignant exchange with Dryfoos, who brags about quashing his workers' attempts to unionize; at the height of Lindau's rage—"He's an infamous traitor!" Lindau finally declares to March, in German—Howells writes that "something in it all affected him comically; he could not help laughing."[54] Howells, at least, displays an uncomfortable recognition that his use of dialect, by its very presence, undercuts the possibility of serious consideration.

At the same time, both caricature and dialect could be subversive. Jones maintains that "dialect could encode the possibility of resistance, not just by undermining the integrity of a dominant standard, but by recording the subversive voices in which alternative versions of reality were engendered."[55] Likewise, Gombrich argues, caricature privileged the expressive power of the artist regardless of his or her subject: "The strokes of his pen show a sublime freedom. . . . The abbreviated style gains its own significance, as if the artist were to say to us: 'See, this great man is nothing but a lot of lines; I can grasp his personality in a few strokes.'"[56] Many practitioners of the comic sensibility examined in *How the Other Half Laughs* identified with or were members of marginalized populations. All of them espoused the power of the comic sensibility to level the social playing field, from above as well as from below.

While the comic sensibility retained the essentially sympathetic orientation of subjective humor, it expressed that sympathy in a very different way. Rejecting the genteel manner, rejecting anything that smacked of sentimentality, the comic sensibility expressed common wisdom by cracking wise. Eliciting laughter through displays of violence and through exploiting the grotesque and deformed, it both appealed to and at times inverted the Aristotelian and Hobbesian characterization of the "superiority" or "deformity" theory of laughter. Laughter resulted not just from feelings of superiority, but from the recognition of common deformity, the recognition of the ironies of difference itself in a nation that claimed to make out of many, one.

Howard Jay Patterson, who founded the vaudeville act the Flying Karamazov Brothers, put it this way:

> To me it seems like a kind of group therapy that the country went through. Suddenly, the nation wasn't all white, Anglo-Saxon Protestant anymore. To us the humor of the time seems racist, bigoted and sexist, but I think what really was happening is that they were processing it. "This is my new neighbor, and he talks kind of like this . . ." So instead of one powerful group laughing at one particular other group, it was all of us laughing at how different we all were.[57]

■ ■ ■

The following chapters are organized roughly chronologically, beginning with the emergence of a particularly grotesque form of the comic sensibility in the works of George Luks in the closing years of the nineteenth century. Luks, born to well-educated parents and raised in the coal-mining region of central Pennsylvania, received artistic training in the US and Europe, and also performed in vaudeville, as part of a blackface duo with his brother Will. These incongruous impulses came together in 1896, when Luks was called on to take over his friend R. F. Outcault's phenomenally popular *Hogan's Alley* comic strip, featuring the character the Yellow Kid, at Pulitzer's *New York World* after Outcault was lured away to the rival *New York Journal*. Luks soon made the Yellow Kid his own. Taking his cue from the "twinning" of the Yellow Kid, who now appeared simultaneously in both the *World* and the *Journal*, Luks capitalized on the grotesque potential of twinning, doubling, and replication to question the social order from below. Doubling, tripling, and quadrupling "kids" in his strips, he laid bare—and then savagely mocked—fears of the rapidly growing immigrant and ethnic populations in the United States. In subsequent strips, including *The Little Nippers* and *Mose's Incubator*, his representations of polyglot America become positively fantastical, even monstrous, reflecting the interchangeability and reproducibility of ethnic identity that formed the logical basis of the "melting pot."

Chapter 2 turns from the expressive mode of the comic grotesque to the actual form of the comic strip, showing how the early comic strip was developed and then came to influence comic fiction in the early twentieth century. Rudolph Block, longtime editor of the Hearst papers' comic supplement, oversaw a motley crew of artists, including Outcault and Dirks. As their editor, Block regularized their use of panels, repetitive storylines, and caricature—formal characteristics adapted from the vaudeville "gag" as well as the cartoon weeklies—which greatly facilitated the translation of the comic strip into multilingual editions as well as easy syndication, and thus resulted in the consistent, multi-panel format that became standard in the comic strip genre. While Block is occasionally remembered as a loyal and long-lived employee in the Hearst organization, his active role in the development of the comic strip has gone largely unrecognized. At the same time, it is as a prolific writer of so-called "ghetto fiction" that Block has been almost completely forgotten. Between 1905 and 1920, Block, under the pseudonym Bruno Lessing, published nearly a hundred stories, almost all set in New York's Lower East Side, in Hearst's *Cosmopolitan Magazine*. Lessing applied the notion of translation to his fiction as well, albeit in very different ways, translating the multiethnic culture of the Lower East Side for a mainstream, English-speaking audience. Unlike Jacob Riis, however, Block recognized the power of caricature and dialect, not only in their power to mark people as ethnic or alien, but also as sites of negotiation and play; opportunities to display identity in multiple and shifting forms.

Lessing's stories were identified with a genre of fiction, ghetto fiction, which achieved immense popularity in the early twentieth century. This genre was a staple of the mass-market, heavily illustrated periodicals that emerged during this time, including *Cosmopolitan*, *McClure's*, and the *Saturday Evening Post*. These stories appealed both to the curiosity of suburban and rural readers while also expressing the smart, urbane, and topical tone of the New Humor that infused these periodicals. Many of the artists who illustrated the work of Bruno Lessing and other writers of ghetto fiction, however, struggled to reconcile the distortions of caricature with illusionistic modes of representation. Chapter 3 focuses on William Glackens, one of the artists who succeeded. A friend and associate of George Luks, Glackens combined a close attention to narrative with a style of sketch-drawing that neither promised absolute fidelity to reality nor resorted to caricature. A careful use of perspective and composition almost literally pulled readers toward the story and characters on the page. This chapter focuses especially on Glackens's illustrations for the "Denny the Jew" stories of Edward Lipsett that appeared in *Everybody's Magazine*, which like *McClure's* and *Cosmopolitan*, appealed to a middle-class audience. Lipsett's "Denny the Jew" stories depict a young Irish immigrant to New York who observes the economic success of his Jewish neighbors and decides to pass as Jewish himself. Through masterful, improvisational deployment of dialect, Lipsett heightens rather than erases individual identity in his depiction of Denny and other residents of the Lower East Side; on the visual side, Glackens's images rely on a sketched-from-life technique that contrasted with caricature by reflecting close observation of individuals rather than portrayals of types.

These stories exemplify the ways that textual and visual strategies worked together to convey the comic sensibility in illustrated magazine fiction.

African Americans, by and large, were largely excluded from the empowering forms of the comic sensibility. The final chapter examines whether or not the comic sensibility extended to blacks in any way at all. Comics historians go so far as to claim that the "black comic," as such, did not exist until black artists began creating comic strips for black newspapers beginning in the 1920s. I suggest, however, that several strips appearing in several of Hearst's newspapers, by George Herriman and James "Jimmy" Swinnerton, display a distinctly black comic sensibility that drew on visual and literary conventions originating in the minstrel tradition and further developed and replicated in burlesque and vaudeville. Multiplying irony through a sensitive awareness and exploitation of Du Boisian double consciousness, Swinnerton's *Sam and His Laugh* (1905–1906) and various cartoons Herriman created for both the Sunday supplements and the sports pages made their readers laugh even as they deftly undercut white supremacist attitudes. Herriman, a mixed-race Creole who passed as white throughout his career, would create a transcendent form of the black comic sensibility in *Krazy Kat* (1913–44); this strip, in turn, influenced modernist writers and artists including Willem de Kooning, E. E. Cummings, Langston Hughes, and Ralph Ellison. I argue that one need not be black to understand black humor, and need not be black to create black comics. In fact, we can see a form of Du Boisian double consciousness in George Luks's comic twins, who are the focus of this book's initial chapter. They literalize and visualize the sense of twoness—"two souls, two thoughts, two unreconciled strivings"—that Du Bois described as foundational to the black experience. What Toni Morrison identified as an abiding "Africanist presence" throughout American culture, then, is part of the comic sensibility as well.

Whether one speaks of the comic grotesquery of George Luks or the grotesque comedy of double consciousness, the comic sensibility in all its forms ultimately concerns the idea of otherness itself: the uncanny shadow of the self that is both revealed and suppressed. The Other Half is recognized as being *like* us, or others' conception *of* us, but fundamentally not the same *as* us. This recognition of difference, this disruption of a shared reality assumed by realism, functions as an intrusion of the "real real"—actual reality—which in fact offered no coherent narrative, and whose rough, sometimes shocking edges realism itself attempted to smooth over.

CHAPTER ONE

The Comic Grotesque

> Technique, did you say? . . . Guts! Guts! Life! Life! That's *my* technique!
> —George Luks[1]

By the early 1890s, Mark Twain had been recognized for decades as the foremost of "American humorists."[2] Yet in his golden years, he seemed to have lost his way; he certainly wasn't funny, at least to most people most of the time. Scholars have noted Twain's "turn to darkness," reflected in the increasing bitterness of his social commentary, veering toward invective, especially regarding the United States' ventures in Hawaii, the Philippines, and Cuba. He seemed to have lost his footing in the American comic landscape as well. In "How to Tell a Story," he lambasted the teller of what he described as the "comic story," who tells his joke "with eager delight" and "is the first person to laugh when he gets through." The punch line? "He shouts it at you—every time." For Twain, the problem with the joke—a staple of the New Humor of the 1890s—was that it demanded no subtlety or nuance. No sleight of hand was needed to tell a joke; a "machine could tell" it. In short, he lamented, "It is a pathetic thing to see."[3] Daniel Wickberg writes that Twain's objections to the joke reflected a shift in the perception of humor, a shift away from the personality or skill of the teller and onto the content of the joke itself. If the punch line could be shouted, delivered by a machine, it could be delivered by anyone.[4] Indeed, during this time, jokes became a cultural commodity, produced by the hundreds—even thousands—by professional joke writers, whose products were sold to the popular humor weeklies such as *Puck*,

Judge, and *Life* and printed and reprinted, without byline or attribution, in magazines and newspapers all over the country.[5]

If a joke could be told by anyone, even a machine, then had not humorists become reduced to machines themselves? Susan Gillman notes that Twain's writing during this period revolved around questions of his identity as an author;[6] in an environment where authors had become celebrities, "personalities," paid by the word or by the inch for their poetry, stories, and novels, were authors autonomous creators of art? Or were they, like the professional joke-tellers, interchangeable and faceless producers of cultural matter, mere manufacturers of entertainment?[7]

At the same time that Twain felt himself erased as an author, he also found himself more and more alienated from his fellow citizens, people whom he felt distinctly *un*like, yet was called upon to include in his vision of the American nation. Twain's writings on Siamese twins, culminating in the twin narratives *The Tragedy of Pudd'nhead Wilson* and *The Comedy of Those Extraordinary Twins* (1894), explore the possibility of "a unitary, responsible self" in an American society that seemed increasingly chaotic or even anarchic in its makeup. On the one hand, individuals seemed nothing more than machines, identical and endlessly reproducible; on the other, the polyglot society of the late nineteenth-century United States seemed unmendably fractured. Gillman writes that in works like *Pudd'nhead Wilson*, Twain appealed to legal and scientific definitions of personhood in order to determine who was real and who was not, to determine "whether one can tell people apart, differentiate among them." For, "without such differentiation, social order, predicated as it is on division—of class, race, gender—is threatened."[8]

In both *Pudd'nhead Wilson* and *Those Extraordinary Twins*, Twain calls upon what Leonard Cassuto has termed the racial grotesque in his exploration of identity, classification, and differentiation. Tom Driscoll, born Valet de Chambre, believes he is white and unthinkingly assumes all of the privileges his presumed whiteness affords him; the real Tom Driscoll, switched for Valet de Chambre by his desperate mother, Roxy (who is only one-sixteenth black and could pass for white herself), believes he is "all black." As a result, Chambers, as he is known, adopts the "manners of the slave": he becomes subhuman, if not almost absent of human characteristics altogether. When their "real" identities are revealed, Tom and Chambers are unable to embody them. Of Chambers (the real Tom), Twain writes: "The poor fellow could not endure the terrors of the white man's parlour, and felt at home and at peace nowhere but in the kitchen. The family pew was a misery to him, yet he could nevermore enter into the solacing refuge of the 'nigger gallery'—that was closed to him for good and all."[9] Chambers becomes, in Cassuto's words, "the anomalous embodiment of cultural anxiety," the racial grotesque, which "is born of the violation of basic categories. It occurs when an image cannot be easily classified even on the most fundamental level: when it is both one thing and another, and thus neither one."[10] *Those Extraordinary Twins*, Twain's supposedly comic story of the Siamese twins Luigi and Angelo Capello, also ends in a grotesque tableau, albeit one based on their identity as "freaks" (or as a single freak), rather than their racial difference. The twins are judged as separate individuals, one innocent, one guilty. However, when Luigi is hung for the crime he has committed, Angelo must die along with him; in the end, they comprise a single biological entity, a single body.

As his depiction of the Capello twins implies, Twain's notion of the grotesque applies not just to race and ethnicity, but also to the essential composition of the human body. In *Playing the Races*, Henry Wonham performs an extended reading of Twain's late work "Three Thousand Years Among the Microbes," where Twain imagines a cholera microbe (oddly given two names, Bkshp and Huck) coursing through the body of a recent Hungarian immigrant named Blitzkowski. While Blitzkowski is easily identified as the quintessential, stereotypical Eastern European immigrant ("wonderfully ragged, incredibly dirty"), Bkshp/Huck discovers that Blitzkowski's body "contains swarming nations of all the different kinds of germ-vermin that have been invented for the contentment of man."[11] Wonham writes of this anecdote that "the joke might be summarized as follows: what appears to be one turns out to be many"; what appears to be "a knowable, unitary type" is revealed to be "a complex of different entities and energies."[12] This is, of course, exactly how the author/humorist Twain wished to view himself, as a complex individual rather than a unitary "type." At the same time, Blitzkowski is no different from anyone else: we are all simply collections of molecules, not to mention microbes. Yet certainly Bkshp/Huck—much less Twain—clearly is repulsed by him; he wishes to be differentiated from him.

The grotesque, as it emerges in Twain's work, is a twin realization that things that appear to be different are actually equivalent, and also, that what appears to be a single entity is in fact full of difference. Hungarian immigrants and native-born Americans (not to mention blacks and whites and Siamese twins) have differentiating characteristics, yet they are all members of the same species, *Homo sapiens*, and also, ostensibly, the same nation, the United States. At the same time, no one, least of all Twain, could deny that the *unum* that comprised the American nation was also the *pluribus*, whether that plurality was made up of different ethnicities or simply human individuals. Cassuto writes that the racial grotesque reflects a "*desire* for order" but also is an acknowledgment of actual *dis*order; if the categories and classifications by which one builds societies are shown to be permeable and fluid, then society itself is shown to be nothing more than a willful act of the imagination.[13]

Regardless of whether difference is rooted in race, ethnicity, or biology, few thought any of it was funny. Twain himself seemed far more disturbed than amused by the grotesque form of American society at the end of the nineteenth century. In the "Final Remarks" he wrote at the conclusion of the combined edition of *Pudd'nhead Wilson* and *Those Extraordinary Twins*, Twain apologized for having subjected his readers to such "an extravagant sort of tale," one that "had no purpose but to exhibit that monstrous 'freak' in all sorts of grotesque lights."[14] He explains that having begun the story of Tom, Roxy, and Chambers, it "began to take a tragic aspect," while the characters comprising the "twin-monster," the Capello twins, "were merely in the way." Unlike Siamese twins, he decided, his stories had "no connection between them, no interdependence, no kinship." And so he split the story into two, in what he described as a "literary caesarean operation."[15] Critics have found *Pudd'nhead Wilson* a puzzling if not wholly inferior work within Twain's oeuvre, even while acknowledging the general unevenness of Twain's work as a whole. Malcolm Bradbury, for one, succinctly described it as "a bad book with a good book inside it struggling to get out."[16] Bradbury yearns for the "good" Twain, the affable, genial, funny Twain, to "get out"—but all the "bad" societal stuff gets in the way.

Gillman, for her part, finds it strange that Twain was unable to recognize the impossibility of separating the pseudo-tragic narrative of *Pudd'nhead Wilson* from the pseudo-comic one of the Capello twins, especially considering his deep understanding of societal contingency and his doubts about individual agency.[17] The illustrators for *Pudd'nhead Wilson* also seemed to be unable to reconcile Twain's turn to the grotesque with their expectations of the comic, humorous Twain. Louis Loeb drew the illustrations for the initial serialization of the novel in the genteel *Century* magazine, while E. W. Kemble, who had earlier illustrated *The Adventures of Huckleberry Finn* and was generally known for his comical drawings of "pickanninnies" and "plantation types," drew the illustrations that appeared in the 1899 edition published by Twain's own American Publishing Company. Both appear literally unable to draw Roxy, choosing to depict her, when she is depicted at all, in the shadows or behind other characters, her features, especially her hair, obscured by her clothing (see figure 1.1). Both Twain and his illustrators display their desire to maintain the fixed differences and racialized distinctions that comedy heretofore had depended on—and their inability to do so.

Gillman relates how Twain described, in his notebooks, a dream in which he is invited to share a pie with a black woman, an act that "disgusts" him yet also elicits fantasies of sexual union and the sharing and mixing together of bodily

Figure 1.1. Roxy's head, obscured by a headscarf, peeks out from the shadows behind three of the other Driscoll servants. E. W. Kemble, *Roxy Harvesting Among the Kitchens, Pudd'nhead Wilson and Those Extraordinary Twins*, vol. 14 of the Authorized Works of Mark Twain (American Publishing Company, 1908), frontispiece. This illustration also appeared in the 1899 Harper and Brothers edition, and was used as the frontispiece for the 1922 "Authorized Edition" published by *Collier's*.

fluids.[18] Perhaps Roxy is the fictional analogue of Twain's dream mistress-wife, the literary manifestation of Twain's latent fascination with racial mixing and his anxieties about his own unified subjectivity. Twain was not alone in his anxious fascination with the grotesque; James Goodwin notes that "in the early decades of nineteenth-century American literature the grotesque is commonly invoked through the presence of strange, misshapen, or intimidating forms, and these in turn often reflect anxiety over an encounter with 'foreign' or 'alien' elements." These "elements," he writes, ranged from "Native Americans, black slaves, Italians, the Dutch, and Turks to untracked nature, mysterious strangers, Catholic icons, masquerade disguises, and political spies."[19]

Elsewhere, however, many found opportunities for amusement in the conundrum of identity and differentiation. In *Techniques of the Observer*, Jonathan Crary describes children's games and optical toys that engaged the playful possibilities of twinning, doubling, and attempts at differentiation. The thaumatrope, for example, presented two different images: a bird and a cage, for instance—or a man's face and a lion's body. Each image would be applied to one side of a paper disk; strings attached on either side, when twisted and then pulled taut, would spin the disk, whirling two images together into one. (Alternately, the disk could be mounted on a vertical stick, which could be spun by quickly rubbing it between the hands.) The stereoscope, in contrast, presented two similar photographs, usually of the same scene but taken from slightly different vantage points. The two photographs would be placed in a viewer that would allow each eye to see one, but not both, of the images. Through the process of binocular vision, the viewer's eyes would combine the two separate images into a single, seemingly three-dimensional one. The fascination with the stereoscope, Crary writes, comes from the viewer's simultaneous knowledge that he or she "perceives with each eye a different image," yet is seeing it "as single or unitary"; one becomes increasingly conscious of the imaginative and even muscular effort required, moreover, the closer one gets to the perceived object(s).[20] (The phenomenon of binocular vision continues to amuse, in the form of the View-Master as well as in 3-D projection). These optical toys illustrated the merger between the crisis of vision and national perception in the United States at the end of the nineteenth century. Jennifer Greenhill describes a children's game called Sliced Nations, where players were challenged to reassemble national types from their sliced-up bodies—and names—suggesting simultaneously that people of different nationalities and ethnicities could be made whole and also endlessly combined (see figure 1.2).[21]

The popular press, too, played with notions of duality, replication, and identity. A hallmark of the *New York World*'s feature pages and Sunday magazine, for example, was the article informing readers of ways to identify criminals, the

Figure 1.2. Game pieces and box top for the Sliced Nations children's game. Courtesy of The Strong, Rochester, New York.

insane, or, in contrast, the rich or the intelligent, often by presenting illustrations that elicited side-by-side comparisons. These illustrations, unsurprisingly, drew heavily on phrenology and other pseudoscientific theories relating physiognomy to psychology and behavior, but they also incorporated visual games based on relationships of symmetry and the detection of differences between seemingly similar images. In the new comic supplements, first appearing in the *World* in 1895, then followed in early 1896 by William Randolph Hearst's upstart newspaper, the *New York Journal*, artists not only depicted codified ethnic types but also combined, doubled, and transformed these types to produce grotesquely comic effects (see figure 1.3). The idea of mixing ethnicities, races, nations, and physiognomies that disgusted yet fascinated Twain also elicited childish delight.

The immensely talented and largely self-taught painter George Luks, who would become a member of Robert Henri's The Eight and exhibit in the 1913 Armory Show, emerged within this environment, first as a regular contributor to the humor weekly *Truth*, then as an artist-reporter and illustrator for Philadelphia and New York newspapers including the *New York World*. Luks, like Twain, recognized the disturbing, even disgusting, aspects of the grotesque that challenged the cherished illusion of societal order and autonomous selfhood. However, he also reveled in the grotesque's inherently dynamic, unstable nature.[22] In doing so, he revealed humorous and restorative aspects of the grotesque that demonstrated an abiding confidence in the powers of the imagination to encompass and even accommodate the often startling, and sometimes frightening, features of an American landscape undergoing rapid, radical transformation.

Enter George Luks

When Luks arrived in New York City in 1896, he witnessed a city in a state of constant change. Immigrants poured into the city through Ellis Island by the tens of thousands, skyscrapers erupted out of the ground at an almost unearthly pace, miles of city streets were paved each year. New York during this time was a city of "merciless multiplication,"[23] Henry James wrote; novelist Stephen Millhauser later vividly described "a city with trains in the air and trains under the ground, a fierce and magical city of moving iron, while along the trembling avenues there rose, in the clashing air, higher and higher, still buildings."[24] The restless, chaotic energy of the city would animate Luks's art throughout his career.

Although he had been in New York before, this time Luks was here to stay. Through a series of lucky circumstances, he had just been hired at the *New York World*, then the epitome of sensational journalism. Earlier that year, he had been sent as a special correspondent for the *Philadelphia Evening Bulletin* to cover the Cuban insurrection against the Spanish colonial authority, and he had sent back a number of gruesome illustrations that had proved popular with readers.[25] The paper, however, fired him after only a few months due to his excessive drinking. Luks did not contest his termination; he had in fact engaged in very little actual reportage while in Cuba. He based his images on stories from soldiers and correspondents whom he encountered at the hotel

Figure 1.3. Frank H. Ladendorf, "Turn About Is Fair Play." Billy Ireland Cartoon Library & Museum, SFS55-8-1, p. 6.

bar in Havana, and then embellished them with his own imagination. While Luks's employers fired him for shirking his responsibilities, Luks may have abandoned them because he was so horrified by the scenes he witnessed. In a letter to Everett Shinn, he depicted a reporter for the *Evening Bulletin* "gathering news" by ransacking the dead bodies of mutilated, even beheaded, Spanish insurgents, unperturbed by bombs exploding all around him.[26] In later years, Luks sneered at the foolhardiness of war correspondents who saw their time in Cuba as nothing more than an exhilarating adventure. In an anecdote he was fond of retelling, he claimed to have met Stephen Crane and Richard Harding Davis in Cuba (Crane and Davis, in fact, were correspondents in Cuba during 1898, not 1896, so the anecdote was almost certainly a fabrication); when a battle breaks out nearby, Luks tells them to go ahead without him while he takes cover, for, he said, "*I* have a future."[27]

Even if he did not witness battles with his own eyes, Luks nevertheless produced drawings that grabbed the attention of readers. Robert Gambone, who has published the only extensive analysis of Luks's early newspaper work to date, notes that the impact of Luks's illustrations and cartoons came from their dynamic composition, Luks's use of "schematic," suggestive sketching rather than close observation, and his creation of composite images rather than depicting "scenes of life." While they may strike even the present-day viewer as being realistic, they are not photographic. Instead, following on the tradition of pictorial news established by Winslow Homer and other artists during the Civil War, Luks produced images that helped readers to *imagine* what was happening, rather than depicting what he had actually witnessed "on the spot," as was often claimed in the captions accompanying newspaper illustrations. In one particularly noticeable instance, Luks submitted an illustration of a man lifted from his horse by the impact of a bullet in his chest—an image that would have been impossible to actually sketch from life.[28] For Luks, as with many of the artist-reporters dating back to the Civil War, factual accuracy was of "less concern ... than 'authenticity.'"[29]

On the boat returning him to the States, Luks met Arthur Brisbane, who had just been hired by Pulitzer to edit the *World*'s feature section after William Randolph Hearst had hired away the Pulitzer's star editor, Morris Goddard. Brisbane, no doubt impressed by Luks's forceful personality as much as his artistic ability, encouraged the brash young artist to look him up in New York. Luks followed through on the suggestion immediately upon his return to the mainland.[30] In what was most likely his first cartoon for the *World*, Luks depicted a variety of Spanish atrocities committed in Cuba, including a mass burial, a "peaceful workman" being dragged to his death by a Spaniard on horseback, and soldiers slaughtering women and children (see figure 1.4). These scenes, in full view of the reader, are screened from the bugged-out eyes of President Grover Cleveland by the unnaturally elongated, claw-like fingers of Spain. "Look Between the Fingers of That Concealing Hand, Mr. Cleveland!" reads the caption. The text appearing below the cartoon is nearly as sensational as Luks's illustrations:

> There is a realism in a picture that no arrangement of words can equal. And these picture-stories of Spanish cruelty were made by the Sunday World's special artist, who has just come back from Cuba. He saw with his own eyes. He has been in the Spanish camps and on the field where insurgents have died for their country. He has seen non-combatants, unresisting and unarmed, shot down by Spanish soldiers. And those who have been incredulous about what was going on in Cuba cannot fail to be convinced by these terrible pictures.
>
> It will be well for Mr. Cleveland to look upon these pictures. They stir the blood. They bring the fearful struggle now going on in Cuba vividly before the mind. They speak more loudly than polite, explanatory phrases from Spanish diplomats. They throw the X-ray upon the Spanish accounts of "the fight against bandits and marauders." And you see not a war against lawless elements, but the bloodthirsty Spanish Government trying to murder the spirit of freedom and love of country.
>
> Do not let Spain blindfold you, Mr. Cleveland, to what is really going on at our very doors.[31]

While Luks's "terrible pictures" could not fail to stir the blood, to bring the events in Cuba "vividly before the mind," they were not particularly realistic. The figures of Cleveland and Spain are bizarrely proportioned, while the smaller figures within the cartoon are awkwardly foreshortened, violate the rules of perspective, and are themselves unnaturally proportioned (one might note, in particular, the women in the bottom right corner of the frame, whose feminine innocence is accentuated by their balloon-like bosoms and wasp-like waists). The exaggeration of various details and lack of verisimilitude might make Luks's cartoon subject to criticism as a work of art. However, the crudeness of his drawing emphasized the human presence of the artist at the scenes of the crimes, as well as the anguish experienced by the artist in facing and depicting the horrors that Cleveland was only too willing to have hidden from view. The drawings are not particularly realistic, but the impression they produce, in large part due to their grotesque elements, is visceral and disturbing. Another illustration, Luks's *The Garrote for Cuban Patriots*, shows a hooded Cuban about to be executed by a garrote, a device that gradually chokes its victim to death by twisting a rope around his neck. This illustration was clearly so successful at

Figure 1.4. George Luks, "Look Between the Fingers of That Concealing Hand, Mr. Cleveland!" *New York World*, March 15, 1896: 21.

horrifying its audience—and generating sales—that it was printed twice, in the March 29, 1896, *Sunday World* and again the following Wednesday.

Even though Luks may not have been an ideal reporter, in these illustrations he demonstrates the lessons he had learned working at the *Evening Bulletin* and at the *Philadelphia Press*.[32] Photographic reproduction on a mass scale had been used in magazines such as *Harper's Monthly* since 1889, but limitations in technology prevented daily newspapers from availing themselves of these images. Instead, artists either created engravings from photographs, or were sent to events to sketch what they saw and then to convert those sketches into pen-and-ink drawings from which plates could be made.[33] In this environment, where speed, clarity, and impact were paramount, the artist's ability to highlight salient details through effective composition, strength of line, and use of contrast and selective exaggeration enabled him (or her, in a few cases) to provide readers an image that purported to depict reality, like a photograph, but could also convey an emotional impression more directly and intentionally than was then possible using a photograph. Although *Frank Leslie's Illustrated Newspaper* and *Harper's Weekly* had employed artist-reporters since the Civil War, the *World* was the first daily newspaper to use artist-reporters in this fashion, in 1884; they quickly became a stock feature of all of the great daily newspapers.[34] The heyday of the artist-reporter, however, was short-lived. With the rapid improvement in printing technology that was driven by the circulation wars between Pulitzer and Hearst in the mid-1890s, mass reproduction of photographic halftones became possible, and quickly de rigueur, by the close of the century, rendering the artist-reporter obsolete.[35]

Luks, however, joined the *World* when the vogue of the artist-reporter was at its height. Within the first few weeks of his employment, the newspaper published several of his images from the Cuban theater and also assigned him stories to illustrate for the Sunday magazine. While the *World*'s Sunday magazine contained a women's section, games for children, and profiles of popular actresses and politicians—features that remain in Sunday newspaper magazines to this day—in Pulitzer's *World*, it was dominated by fare unlikely to win approval as edifying "Sunday reading." In a single issue from March 1896, the front page featured the *World*'s stunt journalist Kate Swan's latest escapade, spending the night as a sort of "living corpse" in a moratorium; a regular feature of "Eight Queer Facts," including stories about a "monster blackfish" discovered in Cape Cod, the six-foot-long fingernails of a visiting Chinese dignitary, and the Venezuelan Yak-a-mik, an "ornithological freak"; a quarter-page X-ray image of a rat's body inside a boa constrictor (the X-ray had only been discovered the year before, and so was a sensation in and of itself); and a story about a talking cat. For his part, Luks contributed illustrations for "Two Sketches of Human Driftwood," a side-by-side comparison of a man "born a criminal" and a woman "born incompetent," as well as illustrations depicting self-flagellation and a reenactment of the crucifixion performed by the Penitentes religious sect in Taos, New Mexico during the Easter season (see figures 1.5a-b). The illustrations of the half-naked, masked, and bleeding Penitente "celebrants" are particularly shocking, especially when contrasted

Figure 1.5a-b "Fashion's Display in the Easter Parade" (illustrations by Bessie Moser Gordon) and "Tragic Rites of the Penitentes" (illustrations by George Luks), *New York World Sunday Magazine*, March 22, 1896: 18–19.

with the story on the other side of the spread, which displayed an array of Easter dresses that would be worn by New York's leading society ladies in the upcoming holiday parade down Broadway. The juxtaposition of Easter fashions with the bloody Penitentes must have elicited a gasp of horrified laughter, if not outright censure, from Pulitzer's readers.[36]

Luks seemed to find this sort of artistic production more to his taste than eyewitness reportage. Although he had been raised in a comfortable, middle-class

German/Bavarian family in the coal-producing regions of Pennsylvania, he had shown an affinity for the grotesque—and its attendant celebration of transformation and boundary-crossing—early on. In his teens, he and his brother Will formed a blackface minstrel duo: as "Buzzy" and "Anstock," the stocky, manic George and the lanky, sad-faced Will toured throughout Pennsylvania and the northeast (see figure 1.6). Here, they discovered a veritable olio of liquor, sex, comedy, and violence, where "Welsh and Cornish miners in the coal and iron warrens of Pennsylvania fought bare-knuckle bouts in the rear of the halls" and "$15-a-week comics were harassed by a brawl a night."[37] Throughout his life, Luks was known—and castigated by his friends—for picking fights with strangers in the saloons and dives he loved to frequent in New York City; he was discovered dead outside one of these saloons at the age of sixty-six, possibly as the result of one of these altercations. In lighter moods, however, he entertained his friends with comic impressions, and was able to re-enact entire scenes or plays, taking on all the parts by himself. Luks's roommate for several years, the painter Everett Shinn, recalled that Luks always seemed to be performing, even in the privacy of their rooms.[38] In 1905, the *World* described a recent night at the uptown Café Francis, featuring a cartoon of Luks dancing on top of a table and surrounded by a group of well-known newspapermen, artists, cartoonists, and men about town (see figure 1.7). After extolling the talents of the group assembled, the article declares, "But anyone can sing a song or tell a story. All these fellows do it well. What is a song and story, when George Luks can imitate an entire comic opera, orchestra and all?"[39]

Luks's interest in theater developed simultaneously with and was ultimately trumped by his love of art. In the late 1880s or early 1890s, when he was still a teenager, he left touring as Buzzy to enroll at the Pennsylvania Academy of Fine Arts in Philadelphia, but left after a month; a few years later, he abandoned minstrelsy again in order to study painting at the Stäatliche Kunstakademie in Düsseldorf, Germany. In Europe, he immersed himself in the Bohemian nightlife of Paris and London as well as the controversial new paintings by Manet, Renoir, and Velásquez. These experiences may have caused him to lose patience with the meticulous technique of the Düsseldorf academicians and their fidelity to the history-painting tradition; again, he left art school after a single month. His lack of training, however, did not prevent him from getting work as an illustrator. In the early 1890s, before his stint at the *Philadelphia Evening Press*, he published hundreds of illustrations and cartoons in the weekly humor magazine *Truth*, which had just begun publication as an upstart competitor to *Puck*. Here, he specialized in ethnic caricature, merging his experience in the variety theater with his skill as a visual artist.

At *Truth*, he also made the acquaintance of a fellow "specialist" of ethnic types, Richard F. Outcault.[40] Outcault had been trained as a commercial artist in Ohio, and was discovered, after a fashion, by Thomas Edison, who brought him to his new laboratories in Orange, New Jersey, as a technical illustrator in the late 1880s. By 1893, Outcault had abandoned technical illustration for humor. At *Truth*, he and Luks drew illustrations for jokes, primarily ones that centered on urban and ethnic themes. Comics historian Bill Blackbeard argues that *Truth* hired Outcault to compete with the humorously sentimental and immensely

Figure 1.6. Will (left) and George (right) Luks as Anstock and Buzzy, n.d. Luks Family Collection, reprinted in *George Luks: An American Artist* exhibition catalog, Sordoni Art Gallery, Wilkes College, 1987: 11.

Figure 1.7. C. de Fornaro, "At a 'Select and Special' with Artists, Actors and Newspapermen at a Popular Uptown Café," *New York World*, February 26, 1905 (Archives of American Art, film 95, frame 119).

popular cartoons of street urchins by Michael Angelo Woolf, which were then appearing in *Life*. While Outcault specialized in depictions of children, Luks's cartoons, for the most part, featured their adult counterparts.[41] According to Blackbeard, Luks and Outcault were "rising stars" who helped *Truth*'s circulation to rise "in fits and gasps" during the early 1890s.[42]

Luks, Outcault, and Their Twins

Even though Luks had begun drawing for *Truth* two years earlier than Outcault, it was Outcault who got his break first in the highly remunerative and widely distributed pages of Pulitzer's *World*. Pulitzer had established the first color comic supplement section, a kind of tabloid, newsprint version of the comic weeklies, in May 1893. Initially, the comic supplement comprised an amalgamation of cartoons, jokes, and humorous anecdotes that were for the most part reprinted from other publications, including *Truth*.[43] Outcault continued drawing for both *Truth* and the *World* until 1896, but it was for the *World* that he developed his first recurring-character comic strip, *Hogan's Alley*. Featuring the wisecracking, baldheaded street urchin Mickey Dugan—better known as "the Yellow Kid"—*Hogan's Alley* became so popular that many historians attribute the skyrocketing circulation of the *World* in the mid-1890s directly to this strip. By the time Luks had joined the *World*'s staff of artists, *Hogan's Alley* had spawned an entire industry of toys, games, chewing gum, and other collectibles, and had also inspired a Broadway show, spurring Outcault to copyright the character in September 1896.[44]

Hogan's Alley elbowed its way into the world of New York print culture, embodying in form what it conveyed in content: a rabble-rousing crowd of street kids wreaking havoc in the tenement districts. In the course of its development the cartoon gradually grew more and more complex, and took up more and more space on the page; from the single-panel cartoons published in *Truth*, which illustrated a single, succinct joke provided in a typeset caption appearing under the image, Outcault's vision widened to a half-page cartoon that communicated multiple jokes without a caption, and finally expanded into a full-page panorama of the entire alley containing a variety of simultaneously occurring vignettes, including some rather horrific repeating gags (such as a boy falling from a fire escape each week).[45] In some of the full-page cartoons, Outcault's image literally squeezes the printed matter (jokes, anecdotes) into a corner of the page. Sometimes, he even breaks up the columns altogether (see figure 1.8).

By the time Luks joined the *World*'s staff in the spring of 1896, *Hogan's Alley* dictated the visual style of the *World*'s comic supplement section. Luks's

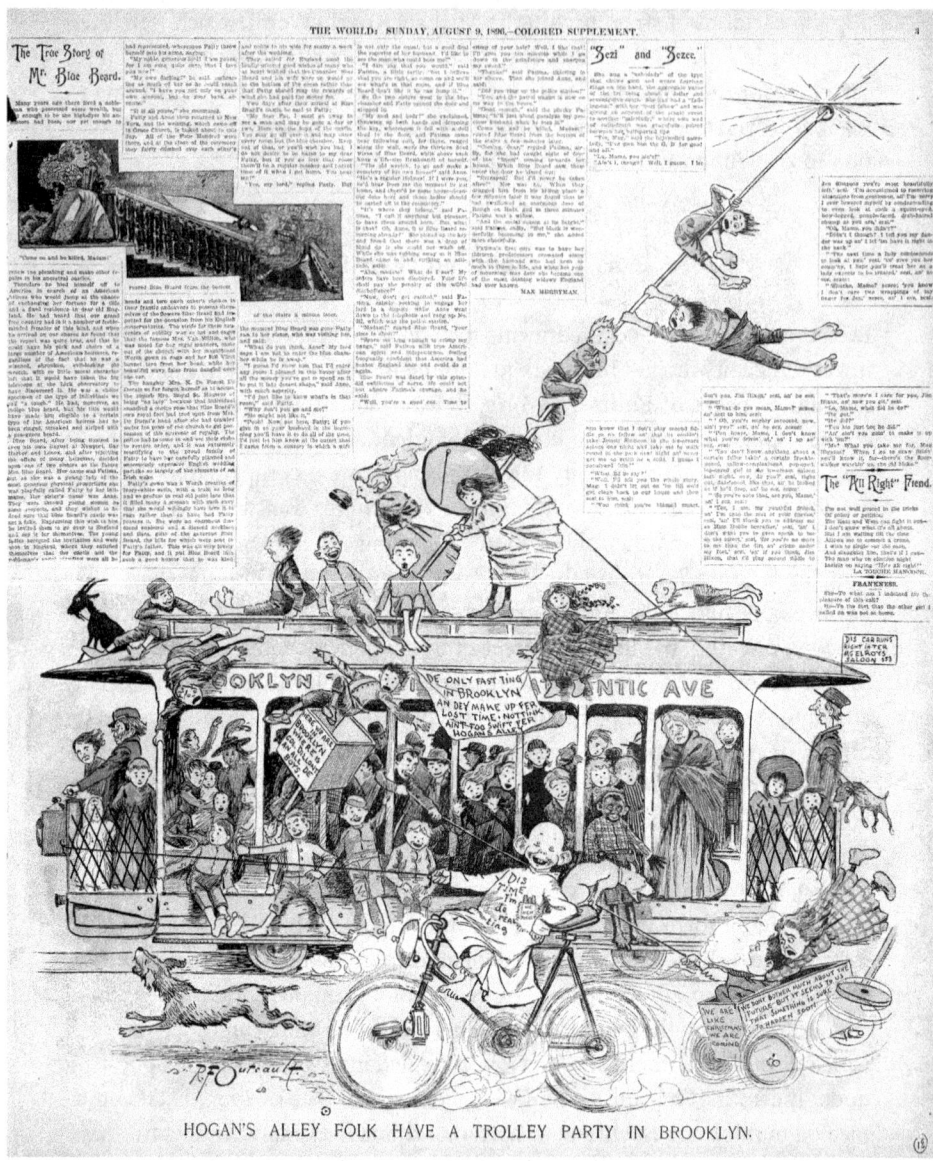

Figure 1.8. Richard F. Outcault, "Hogan's Alley Folk Have a Trolley Party in Brooklyn," *New York World* comic supplement, August 9, 1896.

drawings for the *World*'s Sunday magazine, in turn, effectively complemented the comic supplement. Luks provided illustrations for the sensational trial of serial killer Henry Howard Holmes as well as stories including "New York's Queer Claw-Finger Colony" (August 23, 1896); "The Crazy Sultan—Europe's Disgrace" (September 20, 1896); and "Outrages in the Congo Free State" (September 27, 1896).[46] While his drawings accompanied stories that were not intended to be humorous, they are certainly entertaining; like tabloids today such as the *National Enquirer* or the *Weekly World News*, they are so outlandish, so outrageous, that they provoke laughter by challenging the boundaries of believability.

No assignment seemed too freakish, gory, or violent for Luks's pen. (Everett Shinn describes one drawing, probably "lost to the world," that featured a cannibalistic leper colony that was so revolting that it "whirled one's sensibilities into a dizziness that heaved one in gulps of nausea from its presence."[47]) Perhaps for this reason, he was chosen to take Outcault's place when Outcault left the *World* for a much higher salary at Hearst's *New York Journal* in October 1896. Hearst, who had purchased the *New York Journal* in late 1895, engaged in a veritable marauding campaign in his efforts to increase circulation: within the first year of his New York gambit, he hired away Pulitzer's best editors, writers, and artists, copied Pulitzer's features and visual style, and competed with Pulitzer for scoops and scandals. While an editor or writer could be replaced, certainly a strip like *Hogan's Alley*, so distinctive in subject matter and style, could not. But the higher-ups at the *World* decided not to simply cede their "property" to Hearst. Instead, they responded with cool audacity: the *World* would simply continue the strip as though nothing had happened. Luks was chosen to continue drawing *Hogan's Alley*, while Outcault, now installed at the *Journal*, established a new strip called *McFadden's Row of Flats*, set in a new but equally decrepit tenement neighborhood and featuring the same characters he had drawn at the *World*. The original strip, then, remained at the *World*, though drawn by a different hand; meanwhile the "new" strip, the apparent impostor, was drawn by *Hogan's Alley*'s original creator.

The twinning of the strip immediately raised questions of authenticity. Which was the "real" Yellow Kid, and who, in the end, owned him? Was it Outcault, who actually drew the strip? Or was it Pulitzer, at whose behest the strip was drawn, and who printed and disseminated it?[48] Or, one could throw out the idea of ownership altogether; after all, the print culture of the United States, as Meredith McGill has argued, had been a "reprint culture" since the mid-nineteenth century, enabled by the lack of international copyright law, characterized by the widespread piracy of literary works, and epitomized in the 1890s by the commodification of the joke and the emergence of syndicate publication and wire services.[49] In this case, one could argue that originality itself was unimportant. Who *cared* whose strip it was? Wasn't it a gas that now there were, in fact, two of them appearing every Sunday?

Luks seemed to thoroughly enjoy the bizarre—one might say, grotesque—situation in which he'd been placed. He copied Outcault's style and characters but made no attempt to conceal his identity. He even called attention to the fact that he was not Outcault through a variety of verbal and visual puns (see figure 1.9). For example, in one of his first *Hogan's Alley* strips, he depicts the denizens of the alley practicing for the big football game against the Hoboken Pretzel Club (which he himself had invented in a parody of Outcault published in the *World* on May 31).[50] The depiction of the newly popular sport, played at northeastern colleges including Yale, the University of Pennsylvania, Harvard, and Princeton, calls to mind the changing of sides, the passing of the ball, and violent conflict—poking fun at the competition between Outcault and Luks that was about to commence in the next installment of Hearst and Pulitzer's circulation war. Meanwhile, Mickey, the Yellow Kid, incongruously announces that he is holding his "mudder's switch," referring to hair extensions popular in the late nineteenth century, which gave women the appearance of fuller, longer locks—a pun, obviously, on the switching of Luks for Outcault, but also acknowledging Luks as a false extension of *Hogan's Alley*'s creator. Next to the Kid is a small goat that announces himself as "de new kid," alluding to Outcault's frequent incorporation of a satyrical goat in his version of *Hogan's Alley*. The caption on the Kid's shirt declares that this Kid "ain't gun to raise no kollij hare," implying that he has no desire to compete at the college level—a dig, one presumes, at Outcault's elevated status as celebrity cartoonist of the *Journal* and his newly augmented salary.

In the bottom right corner, a set of actual twins, themselves bald and outfitted with nightshirts like the Yellow Kid himself, exchange fisticuffs in front of a sign that reads, "We're trainin too." These twins, the apparent but unnatural progeny of the Kid, would become a mainstay of Luks's *Hogan's Alley* strip, and would later become the central characters in a spinoff strip, *The Little Nippers*. Often depicted copying whatever the Kid is doing, here they emphasize the idea of practice, of training; they are a self-deprecating representation of Luks as an understudy or apprentice to Outcault's mastery. As Luks's tenure at the helm of *Hogan's Alley* continued, the twins themselves became more like each other, usually drawn in identical poses, but named "Alex" and "George" and given slightly different (though equally disconcerting) smiles. They create an additional level of replication and mimicry in Luks's strip that becomes almost surreal. They also become a site of aberrant behavior, mocking the actions of

The Comic Grotesque 51

Figure 1.9. George Luks, "Training for the Football Championship Game in Hogan's Alley," *New York World* comic supplement, October 11, 1896.

the already aberrant Yellow Kid, and engaging in cross-dressing, suggestive dancing, and even feigning sexual acts.

In "A Seeley Dinner in Hogan's Alley" (see figure 1.10), Luks used Alex and George to attack the sham propriety of the rich, while also lampooning readers' voyeuristic interest in public scandal. The bachelor party of New York socialite Herbert Seeley had been raided by New York City police when they got wind that the famous belly dancer "Little Egypt," a.k.a. Ashea Wabe (a.k.a. Catherine Devine), had been hired to perform nude—"in the all-together," as she reportedly testified later. In Luks's strip, Little Egypt appears, but only as a dark, tiny figure in the corner near his signature. Alex and George are shown dancing on stage instead, wearing the kind of revealing costumes that prevailed in the dance halls and variety theater.[51] Taking on Little Egypt's role, they declare that they "can do the all together too." Clearly, this cartoon was not intended for children! Yet the Yellow Kid makes explicit the prurient interest the Seeley dinner scandal would have generated among children and adults alike, declaring on his shirt-caption that he had told his girlfriend Liz "to skoot but she wuz fascunated!" Sure enough, Liz is still present, visible on the right side of the image, held rapt by the dancing twins. So are Alex and George's girlfriends, Jen and Em; their hats are captioned with their horrified public exclamations, but they can't help but gaze at the stage. It's not clear if the girls are "fascunated" by the prospect of male nudity or if they are expressing nascent lesbian desire.

Blackbeard acknowledges that Luks's version of *Hogan's Alley* demonstrated "a new, savage and vigorous graphic competence" and praises Luks's "active and restless pen." However, he ultimately dismisses Luks's version of the strip because it lacked "elaboration of background detail" and was "unfocused" in its depiction of action.[52] Gambone, however, more accurately interprets Luks's apparent lack of focus as a resistance to "notions of proper bourgeois manners" and an embrace of "alternate modes of being," including open sexuality, sexual promiscuity, and even anarchy.[53] While Outcault's strip brought "tenement types" to the pages of the *World*, his treatment of them remained largely picturesque and was frequently tinged with sentimentality. Like Jay Hambidge's composite view of Bone Alley (figure 3 of introduction), Outcault's alleys and flats are carefully mediated; they are meticulously constructed and colored to provide the utmost variety to the viewer, aligning with William Gilpin's notion of the picturesque—albeit applied to an urban, rather than rural, environment. Like a crazy quilt, or a pastoral landscape, the individual elements combine in colorful, unsymmetrical, yet nevertheless harmonious ways; the image is irregular, even "rough," but conveys pleasure by sparking curiosity and interest.[54] Luks's images, in contrast, are an assault—a disorganized jumble of images. His kids aren't cute; they're often misshapen and crudely drawn.

Figure 1.10. George Luks, "A Seeley Dinner in Hogan's Alley," *New York World* comic supplement, January 24, 1897. The caption on Jen's hat reads: "It's shocking Alex I'll never speak to you again! I'm sorry I came"; Em's reads: "Why did you bring me into a place like this? Isn't George awful! My! My!"

Outcault's strips are dominated by text written on objects—signs, boxes, fences, the Yellow Kid's shirt—rather than being spoken by the characters themselves. The words, then, act as labels, applied by Outcault, the mediating consciousness. In contrast, the kids in Luks's strips do much of their own talking. Their speech bubbles are squeezed into the spaces between figures, sometimes at severe, awkward angles; sometimes their words are simply written next to the character, not contained within bubbles at all. One can't help but be carried away by the gleeful chaos of Luks's street kids; they thumb their noses at boundaries, whether they are imposed by the rules of artistic composition or by society itself; Outcault's comics appear almost refined in comparison. Luks's images transform the mildly transgressive urban picturesque of Outcault into full-out comic grotesque.

The Comic Grotesque and the "Double-Faced Fullness of Life"

While Luks's strips are clearly intended to be humorous, the humor they possess is hard-edged and aggressive. It's often difficult to see how they would appeal to children. In "The Bad Boys' Santa Claus," for example, a positively satanic Santa, red-faced, with glassy blue eyes and green fingernails, is shown squeezing a screaming boy between his fleshy thumb and finger, and actively chewing on two other boys with discolored, unnaturally large teeth (see figure 1.11). The comic grotesque, like the New Humor, relied on "low," even vulgar, forms of comedy, including slapstick, double entendre, and dialect. What made it grotesque was how it challenged acceptable standards of behavior and the social order itself. In his overview of theories of the grotesque, Robert Evans assigns the following characteristics to the grotesque: a "typically incongruous 'mingling of the fantastic and the ideal, the sordid and the real, the comic and the horrific'"; "suddenness, surprise, and estrangement"; "violent juxtapositions of laughter and disgust."[55] As early as 1827, novelist Sir Walter Scott claimed that the purpose of the grotesque is to provoke feelings of shock and dislocation in the reader (or viewer), as well as to demonstrate the imaginative power of the artist. Luks loved to shock his audience; at the same time, he loved to display his imaginative fecundity. The grotesque, then, suited him well.

In *Rabelais and His World*, Mikhail Bakhtin locates a deeper purpose to the grotesque, and especially, its comic forms. In its juxtaposition of opposites, its use of paradox, its unlikely combinations and multiplicity of forms, the grotesque, he writes, conveys the "contradictory and double-faced fullness of life."[56] And this, too, was consistent with Luks's view of the world. Although he was, in fact, a gifted painter, he scoffed at those who valued technique

Figure 1.11. George Luks, "The Bad Boys' Santa Claus," *New York World* children's pages, December 13, 1896. San Francisco Academy of Comic Art Collection, Ohio State University, Billy Ireland Cartoon Library & Museum.

above all else: "Technique, did you say? My slats! ... It's in you or it isn't! Who taught Shakespeare technique? Or Rembrandt? Guts! Guts! Life! Life! That's *my* technique!" His roommate Shinn confirmed that life, in a sense, *was* in fact his technique; he saw everything, did everything—often to excess—and appeared to sketch or paint everything, during the day or at night, at the polo grounds on Long Island or the seamiest dance hall in the Tenderloin, even using beer to dissolve his watercolors if water was unavailable. "He was a glutton for life," Shinn wrote. "Depend on it, that if it was life, Luks was living it in person or following it with his notebook."[57]

Luks's grotesques achieved an apotheosis of a sort in *Mose's Incubator*, which ran in the *World* between January and May 1898.[58] The strip featured a trained chicken who has invented an incubator that can hatch eggs of any type. While eggs had been artificially hatched using various methods since ancient times, the first commercial egg incubator was developed in the early 1880s; Gambone writes that "egg incubators brought the wonders of science directly to the American heartland as farmers now witnessed applied technology revolutionizing agriculture."[59] Mose's incubator is especially wondrous because it can hatch more than just eggs: it can hatch any object at all. From week to week, Mose would put chocolate drops, feather dusters, sausages, and the like into his machine and see what would emerge.

The strip was announced on January 16, 1898, with the help of the twins Alex and George (see figure 1.12). "Try your hand at our little shell game," reads a sign above the magical machine. The incubator contains two chicks; behind it is a "China Egg In-que-bator," with a pair of (newly hatched, one assumes) "little Chinamen" inside. The strip engages, from the outset, the questions of similarity, difference, and reproduction that Twain attempted to resolve in *Pudd'nhead Wilson* and *Those Extraordinary Twins*. The fact that the incubator hatches twins seems inspired by the twins Alex and George, who themselves were spawned by the Yellow Kid (or at least, the Yellow Kid's twinned creator, George Luks). The chicks, "Chinamen," and Alex and George bear a relationship with one another through their yellow clothes and feathers (and/or skin), even though they differ from one another by species or by race. They form, in effect, a society where "twinness" is a normative, rather than anomalous, state. The world of *Mose's Incubator* is idealized in other ways as well; the chicks declare, "We shall have no work to do except to eat," while the little Chinamen, it appears, will not be subject to deportation through the Kearney Exclusion Act, which since 1882 had barred the immigration of Chinese to the United States. The twins will be both nurtured and protected. For this, the chicks declare their allegiance to their erstwhile "mother," Mose: "We will always respect the hen that laid our eggs," a sign next to them reads, "but Mose is our

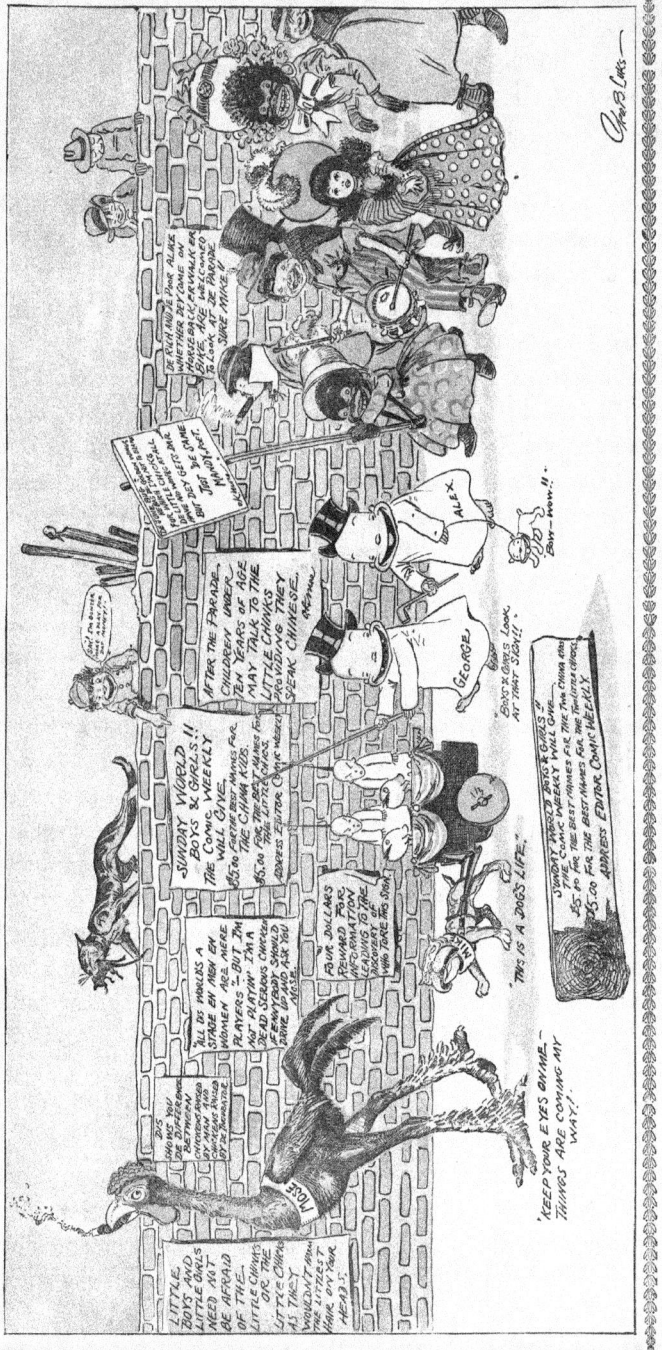

Figure 1.12. George Luks, "A Street Parade to Advertise Mose's Incubator Show," *New York World* comic supplement, January 16, 1898. San Francisco Academy of Comic Art Collection, Ohio State University, Billy Ireland Cartoon Library & Museum.

mother because he hatched us." The sign alludes to the fact that egg incubators were also called "foster mothers" in advertising copy of the time, but also emphasizes the social (not to mention mechanical), rather than biological, ties between Mose and his "flock."

It is, to be sure, a bizarre conceit, one rendered even more bizarre because the incubator is presented as a sideshow attraction, a machine that produces freak twins to be displayed for the public. As the strip continued, it became increasingly freakish, as the incubator did not just cultivate chickens and Chinamen, but also produced a pair of monkeys from a pair of fur muffs, two Indians from a pair of feather dusters, and two dachshunds from a pair of frankfurters. These productive pairings were not wholly random, but rather based on verbal and visual metaphors: Chinamen, per stereotype, are not only yellow like the chicks; "Chinks" are also verbal echoes and orthographic derivatives of "chicks." The dachshunds echo the shape of frankfurters, recall the slangy term "hot dog," and also allude to the sausages' German origin (see figure 1.13). The names that readers submitted for the twins carried the metaphors and puns even further; young Carter Laughlin of Columbus, Ohio, for example, named the Chinamen "Wah-Shing-Tun" and "Muk-in-lee," punning on their new identities as Chinese Americans.[60]

Naming, of course, is a form of labeling. It also gestures toward possession, if not exactly inclusion. The names of the Chinese twins, for example, appropriate key signifiers of American identity and apply them to the newborns. At the same time, the names give these quintessentially "Muk-in" words a distinctly exotic, if not altogether alien, accent by mimicking Chinese transliteration conventions. A number of the "twinsets" produced by the incubator produced opportunities for Luks to engage in ethnic and racial typing, often in ways that are difficult to see as being anything but crude and dehumanizing. The feather dusters that produce the Indians play on stereotypical indigenous dress, while the names they receive—"Tommy" and "Hawk"—evoke an obvious symbol of Indian bloodlust. And the "coons," born of chocolate drop candies, are not given proper names at all; "Jet" and "Jot" fix their identities as being black and nothing more: at most, a stone or a spot of ink.

Like Israel Zangwill's 1908 play *The Melting Pot*, Luks's *Mose's Incubator* strip presents a metaphor of the contemporary state of American society. But in Luks's conception, the ingredients don't melt. They are not atomized individuals. Each has a twin, and all are connected to each other, first through the fact that they have been produced by an incubator rather than sexual reproductive processes, and second, through their identity as twins. At the same time, they are not all the same. In fact, many of the strips show the twins squabbling, competing, and fighting one another, just as all children do. Yet they do not

Figure 1.13. George Luks, "More Twins Born But There Are Others to Come," *New York World* comic supplement, March 6, 1898.

engage in mortal combat. "No biting or scratching. All fighting must be fun," Mose instructs his charges in one strip (February 27, 1898). In *Mose's Incubator*, Luks puts on display, in parades, in circuses, in picnics in the park, a spectacle of multiethnic, cross-species society that even included cannons and flying machines as its members. This society is led by the benevolent, maternal ringmaster Mose, who is depicted with a blue head, a white mask around his eyes, and a red comb and wattle. Mose frequently refers to his spurs, a characteristic identified only with roosters; however, he behaves more like a mother hen, feeding his flock, making sure they don't get lost, and teaching them life lessons. In contrast to the twins, who represent single zygotes split in two, Mose is both parents combined into one, embodying both the masculine figure of Uncle Sam and the maternal one of Lady Liberty. "It's a wise child that knows its parents," he says (March 6, 1898).

The rollicking if sometimes hard-edged fun of *Mose's Incubator* was a prescient prelude to the eruption of jingoistic fervor that resulted when the USS *Maine* exploded in Havana harbor on March 16, 1898. During the Spanish-American War, the United States exercised its imperial muscles on the world stage. After vanquishing Spain in the Battle of Manila Bay in May 1898, the United States annexed Hawai'i the following month, and public sentiment strongly favored the colonization of the Philippines. The US, in effect, could be an "incubator" of new peoples, who would be raised under the permissive but caring eyes of a parental government. President McKinley's proclamation of December 21, 1898, echoed the sentiments implied in Luks strip when he insisted that "the mission of the United States" in the Philippines "is one of BENEVOLENT ASSIMILATION substituting the mild sway of justice and right for arbitrary rule."[61] Initially, Luks gleefully participated in the media circus surrounding this "splendid little war." He dubbed one strip "Mose's In-Cuba-tor," where he depicted Mose in a general's uniform and had his twins march in a military parade; the incubator, meanwhile, produced a pair of Spanish dons (named Torpe and Pedro), warships, and cannons.

Yet Luks discontinued *Mose's Incubator* within a few months of the *Maine* disaster.[62] While he continued to produce cartoons lambasting the Spanish, he appeared ambivalent at best about the prospect that the United States would expand its boundaries to include Cuba, Hawai'i, and the Philippines. Luks was never what one would describe as a systematic thinker, but later strips done for the *World* and then, for the weekly magazine *The Verdict*, demonstrate his strong populist, anti-imperial bent. He routinely attacked McKinley, the trusts, and big-business interests, while championing the working classes and the urban poor. As early as May 1898, he attacked American militaristic braggadocio in cartoons including "Modern Heroes" (May 8, 1898) and "Will the Military Spirit Have This Effect on Our Future?" (May 22, 1898); in "Charity Begins at Home" (May 15, 1898), he demonstrates concerns that the United States' growing interests on other continents will become a drain on resources already in short supply (see figure 1.14).

Figure 1.14. George Luks, "Charity Begins at Home," *New York World* comic supplement, May 15, 1898.

It may very well be that Luks was only able to accept a multiethnic, multicultural America so long as it remained imaginary; he may have been unable to accept the actuality of expanding American boundaries, societal as well as geographical, to include Hawai'ians, Cubans, and Filipinos. (Throughout his life, Luks demonstrated marked ambivalence toward blacks, Jews, and Asians, for starters.) The comic grotesque may only have remained comic as long as it remained a fantasy. Yet the fact that he saw the comic potential in such a world contrasts with people like Twain, who could only imagine a multiethnic America in the form of a nightmare. Luks chose to see the fun and the fantastic in the weird and potentially horrifying.

Luks as Painter

Within a year, Luks had abandoned cartooning altogether. For years, the friends he had made while working at the *Philadelphia Press*—Everett Shinn and

William Glackens, who both briefly joined Luks at the *World* before focusing on magazine illustration and painting; John Sloan, another artist-reporter who also had turned to painting; and Robert Henri, the painter who had taught Shinn, Glackens, Sloan, and briefly, Luks himself—had encouraged Luks to take up the brush.[63] His move to *The Verdict* in early 1899 may have been motivated by the opportunity to do finer, more intricate work in color; the magazine, unlike the newspaper, was printed on coated paper rather than newsprint, and used color lithography rather than line cuts. His cartoons, especially the numerous centerfold cartoons that he published during his tenure at the magazine, show an artist using line and color with a sure, deft hand (see figure 1.15). Of this work, Shinn wrote, "One drawing, a double page, was proof of his power.... His pen made laughs, hoarse, belly laughs that drove political swine into a smothering huddle to hide their guilty, spoil-stained deeds."[64] Yet Luks did not stay at *The Verdict* for even a year; it's not clear whether he left the magazine of his own volition or if he was replaced.

In any case, in 1899 he completed his first mature painting, *The Amateurs*, a starkly humorous portrait of two young vaudeville performers. By 1904, he was exhibiting with Henri and other members of The Eight at various galleries around New York City. He quickly became better known as a painter than a comics artist, to the extent that a 1905 feature in the *World* had to ask, "Sure you have heard of him? He used to draw for the colored comic Sunday Supplements, but he has reformed."[65] Reviewers found his paintings forceful, vigorous, and assertive, sometimes shockingly so. But they also praised Luks for his sympathetic portrayal of the underclass. "Luks is their interpreter," wrote *New York Sun* art critic James Huneker in 1906; "Luks is a hand and an eye."[66]

In paintings like *Woman and Macaw* (1905) and *Allen Street* (1905), one can see how Luks has reduced his subjects to their most basic elements: shape, line, and color. He uses color to highlight and unite areas of a painting, just as the yellows of *Mose's Incubator* united his disparate twins. It's not clear whether Luks learned to use color from his newspaper and magazine work, or if he applied a nascent painter's eye for color to his cartoons. He never discussed his work for the newspapers at any length. However, he never expressed any regrets about this period of his life. He once said: "I have utterly no patience with the fellows whose style is 'ruined' if they must make drawings for newspapers or advertisements, whose 'art is prostituted' if they must use it to get daily bread. Any style that can be hurt, any art that can be smirched by such experiences is not worth keeping clean. Making commercial drawings, and especially doing newspaper work, gives an artist unlimited experience, teaches him life, brings him out. If it doesn't, there was nothing in him to bring out, that's all."[67]

The Comic Grotesque 63

Figure 1.15. George Luks, *The Great American Simoleon Sextette* (centerfold illustration), *The Verdict*, February 13, 1899: 8–9.

While there's no evidence that Luks ever met Mark Twain, Shinn did. In 1900, Shinn had received a commission from *The Critic* to do a full-length portrait of Twain. Unable to find any full-length photographs of the famous author, Shinn extrapolated Twain's bodily proportions based on his stature as an author: "The structure that must carry that head, I assumed in following my idolatry of genius, must be so gigantic that no sheet of cardboard would be available to hold" it. Perlman wrote in his chronicle of The Eight that the resulting drawing depicted "a fully seven-foot-tall literary giant."

When the publication appeared, Shinn learned that he had created a "ghastly caricature" of Twain and fled to Europe. Nearly a year later, he returned to New York to find that Twain had moved to a house just a few blocks from his apartment. The editor of *The Critic* suggested he "go and apologize for making that drawing." Twain graciously received Shinn, and brought out his copy of the magazine. When Shinn apologized for drawing him so inaccurately, Twain commented that even writers who "drew" accurately, like Charles Dickens, attained their accuracy through "gigantic exaggeration." To make his point, he took up Shinn's portrait:

> Placing it flat on the desk, he folded it up from the bottom, turning back enough of the elongated legs to bring the feet up to the knees. 'That's more normal, but less inspiring. My parents would have liked me like that." His gentle eyes sparkled as his delicate hands folded the paper again and again, always keeping the feet in view. With each fold he made some amusing comment. At last the feet were directly under his chin and stuck out like the ends of a bow tie. "Now, that's final," Twain stated triumphantly. "That's the way my wife sees me."[68]

Twain, whose career had been so dependent on newspapers and periodical culture of an earlier time, seemed to acknowledge in this act of self-effacement that there was nothing left in him to "bring out" in the contemporary moment. William Dean Howells had declared him "the most popular humorist who ever lived" in 1882, appealing to a sense of humor that was "not of a class for a class," but rather aimed at "the intelligence bred of like experience."[69] Tracy Wuster writes that this characterization of Twain as a genial humorist, an "old sage" appealing to a homogeneous, folksy, everyman audience, became the accepted view, even though—or perhaps because—it glossed over the ways that Twain disrupted the conventional "distinctions between class-appropriate leisure and burgeoning forms of mass entertainment, between uplifting humor and debased laughter, and between the literature of high culture and the passing whim of the merely popular." It was also a valuation of humor that became irrelevant in the heterogenous 1890s, when Twain's works were virtually ignored by the popular press.[70] It would not be until the 1960s that Twain as a humorist would again be fully unfolded.

CHAPTER TWO

Rising from the Gutter

> I'm a journeyman cartoonist, and the editor's in charge. What the editor wants I have to give him.
> —Al Jaffee[1]

In the first two decades of the twentieth century, Rudolph Block published, under the pseudonym Bruno Lessing, nearly one hundred stories that were set in the New York Jewish "ghetto." Featuring characters including sweatshop workers, *schadchens*, *schlemiels*, Jewish widows on the make, and gypsy musicians, Lessing's stories conveyed the syncopated linguistic rhythms of the streets, cafés, and tenements of the Lower East Side. Lessing's works were not published in obscure immigrant newspapers, or in tiny editions produced by fly-by-night avant-garde publishers. Rather, they appeared in some of the most widely read magazines of the day, including *Cosmopolitan* and *McClure's*.

Beginning in 1897, Block, under his own name, also edited the Sunday comics section of William Randolph Hearst's *New York Journal*, a post he would occupy for nearly thirty years. As editor, he reviewed the thousands of submissions of jokes, poems, and cartoons that appeared in the supplement in its early years, cultivated the newspaper's young stable of artists, and oversaw the standardization of what we now know as the "funny pages": the eight-page color section made up of half-page and full-page comic strips divided into multiple panels, drawn in a cartoonish style, and featuring regular characters and repeating storylines. It was certainly not Hearst but Block who had day-to-day responsibility over the comics section and who marshaled the chaotic energies of the early comic strip into the unified, cohesive format that made Hearst's comics supplement distinctive and would ultimately define the comic strip itself.

Despite his prolific output as a writer and his prominence as an editor, Block has been mostly forgotten. He hardly even appears in the footnotes of biographical and historical treatments of Hearst and his publishing empire. Comics historians sometimes give him credit for "discovering" Rudolph Dirks, the artist who created the *Katzenjammer Kids*, established in 1897 and continuously distributed well into the twenty-first century. But no one has examined his role as an editor, except to note that many of the artists at the *Journal* chafed under his authority—unsurprising, given the process of standardization he imposed on the *Journal*'s comics section.[2] Bruno Lessing, meanwhile, is omitted from nearly all of the major (and minor, for that matter) anthologies and histories of Jewish American literature. The few that include him focus almost exclusively on *Children of Men* (1903), his first collection of stories, ignoring the dozens of stories he published in the subsequent decades.[3]

Why have Bruno Lessing and Rudolph Block been forgotten? Block certainly made some bad choices if a literary legacy was on his mind. Magazine fiction and comic strips were not until recently (if even now) considered to be literary. Certainly, the work of editors, too, has remained largely invisible in literary studies; if comic strips have been dismissed as a serious subject of scholarship, an *editor* of comic strips would receive even less notice. That said, the reasons that Block was forgotten show us as much about literary historiography as they do about Block's work itself. For one thing, it is not clear that Block in fact was Jewish.[4] Even if he was, he was of German rather than Eastern European extraction. And in response to anti-German sentiment following World Wars I and II, Jewish American literary historians have deemphasized the contributions of German American Jews in the formation of Jewish American literary history.[5] Block was reticent about his religious background, and his adoption of a pseudonym—not a particularly Jewish-sounding one, it should be noted—could just as well have been a move to hide his identity as Hearst's comics editor rather than to signal "Jewishness."[6] The fact remains, however, that regardless of whether or not Block personally identified as a Jew, Bruno Lessing certainly wrote about them. And to borrow language from Benjamin Schreiber, the point of studying Jewish American literature is not "to read a Jewish author for his ... texts' 'Jewishness,'" but rather to develop a "literary critical concept of Jewish identity," which includes the range of different identities perceived, imagined, and appropriated by Jews of various stripes, as well as non-Jews.[7] Simon J. Bronner echoes this sentiment when he says that by expanding our study of Jewish literature to include the

Jewish *subject* rather than simply studying Jewish *writers*, we can then examine Jewishness itself as an "image and identity."[8]

The uncertainty surrounding Block's Jewishness underscores the liminal position he occupied between the "Jewish" and the "American," one that enabled him to function as a cultural translator of a distinctly comic sort. As Rudolph Block, he translated Hearst's English-language *New York Journal* and specifically, its comics section, for a multiethnic and multilingual working class audience. As Bruno Lessing, he translated the polyglot culture of the Lower East Side, filtering it through his own perspective as a secularized, possibly Jewish German American for a mainstream, English-speaking audience. In contrast to Luks, whose comic grotesque elicited physiological responses of laughter, disgust, and shock through visual means, Block's performed the comic sensibility through speech and language. In both his stories and his comics pages, he demonstrates the power of the comic sensibility, and especially, caricature and dialect, not only in their ability to mark people as ethnic or alien, but also as sites of negotiation and play—opportunities to display identity in multiple and shifting forms. In doing so, Block provided points of access for immigrant consumers of mass-market magazines and newspapers and turned them into readers and subscribers. His depictions of linguistic and cultural incompetence may have elicited the laughter of the scornful multitude. Yet he also created solidarity among immigrant readers by making the difficulties of linguistic and cultural translation and assimilation occasions for self-deprecating and communal laughter.

Rudolph Block and the *New York Journal*

Rudolph Block was born in New York City in 1870. His parents—who originated in Bohemia, Czechoslovakia, or Austria, according to different sources—immigrated to the United States more than a decade before Eastern European immigration began in earnest. Educated, secular in outlook, and believers in the American experiment, German Americans of the mid-nineteenth century, whether they were Protestant, Jewish, or Catholic, generally maintained a strong sense of ethnic identity while also assimilating relatively easily to American society. By the 1850s, Germans had established themselves on the Lower East Side in Kleindeutschland, "Little Germany," which became home to a vibrant German-language print culture and socialist labor movements decades before the great migration of Eastern European Jews to the United States that began in the 1880s.[9]

The Blocks appeared to be typical of their generation. George Block worked in the skilled trades and wrote for the socialist *New Yorker Volkszeitung* for many years.[10] His work as a journalist may have paved the way for his son's career as a writer and an editor; while a student at the City College of New York, Rudolph worked as a reporter for the *New York Sun* and an editor for the *New York Recorder* and Joseph Pulitzer's *New York World*. Despite his father's affiliation with the socialist press, Block claimed that he did not become "interested" in the world of the Lower East Side until he was assigned to cover the cloak-makers' strikes and labor unrest in the garment industry for the *Sun* in the late 1880s and early 1890s. It was then, he said, that he gained an appreciation for "the terrible earnestness of the East Side Jews, their poverty and frightful sufferings, and finally their picturesqueness."[11]

When he was the editor of the astoundingly popular Sunday magazine section at Joseph Pulitzer's *New York World*, Block attracted the interest of William Randolph Hearst, who hired him along with Pulitzer's Sunday editor Arthur Brisbane and news editor Charles Russell in a series of raids on Pulitzer's staff in the summer and fall of 1897. Block's familiarity with the German community and his ability to speak German may have made him particularly attractive to Hearst, who had purchased the *New York Journal* and its German-language counterpart, the *Morgen Journal*, in late 1895. According to Peter Conolly-Smith, Hearst believed that retaining the *Morgen Journal* in his portfolio would enable him to tap into New York's large German-speaking population, so rather than cutting loose the unprofitable German-language edition, he expended additional resources on it, translating "most everything" from the English-language *Journal* into German until the *Morgen Journal* closed up shop in 1918.[12] The comics section—or at least parts of it—were translated for the *Morgen Journal* along with everything else; although no copies of the *Morgen Journal* before 1911 are extant, other German-language newspapers referred to the translated strips that appeared in the *Morgen Journal* and subjected them to "much angry debate."[13]

Initially, the comics supplement section was simply a shorter, newsprint version of weekly humor magazines: a humor miscellany with a full-page cartoon on the front, and on the inside, a mishmash of single-panel cartoons, comic strips running horizontally, vertically, and scattered across the columns of the page, anecdotes, songs, and jokes (see figure 2.1). Editing the comic supplement itself was a daunting task; it's difficult to imagine how it could possibly be translated into a German-language version week after week without requiring at least a few dedicated translators. By 1905, however, the section had undergone a startling transformation. All of the purely textual matter had vanished; the strips all ran horizontally and nearly all were divided into panels; all of the words were contained within these panels, either within dialogue "bubbles" or as sound effects; and the visual style of the various strips had become much more unified (see figure 2.2). These changes did not occur all at once. The text-based features (stories, poems, jokes) disappeared by about 1900, the horizontal format was largely adopted by 1901, and multiple-panel strips with recurring characters were the norm by 1903. All of these transformations worked together to streamline and regularize the content of the supplement section.

Histories of the newspaper industry often focus on the (mostly) men at the top and the groundbreaking innovations they introduced, rather than tracing incremental change or detailing the processes by which the actual newspaper was created. Likewise, histories of the comics tend to stress individual creators of strips rather than the editorial practices that shaped their form and enabled their production. It's difficult to pinpoint exactly who was responsible for changes and innovations or even whether the decisions that resulted in the creation of the American newspaper comic strip were made consciously.[14] Nevertheless, we know that editors played a key role in determining each issue's content, organization, and appearance. We also know that Block was one of the few constants at Hearst's *Journal* during the formative years of the comic strip's development. Even if he was not the singular genius behind it, he was a crucial and central collaborator in this process. Ray McCardell, a cartoonist at the *World* at the time, must have been describing Block when he wrote, "Every Sunday comic colored supplement is edited by a special man, highly paid, and responsible in proportion to his pay. He and his immediate assistants are constantly planning, weighing, eliminating. To them suggestions are made ... If they please the public, they are carried on until the people weary of them; if they fall flat, they are dropped at once, like a hot potato."[15]

During these years, Hearst and Pulitzer shared many of the same comic strip artists, including R. F. Outcault, who created the Yellow Kid; George Herriman, creator of *Krazy Kat*; Frederick Opper (*Happy Hooligan*); and Gene Carr (*Lady Bountiful*). Yet Pulitzer was surprisingly slow to adopt the changes that appeared in Hearst's *Journal*. For Hearst, the advantages seem obvious but have gone unrecognized. Simply reducing the quantity of text made the work of creating both an English-language and German-language comics section much, much easier. Regularizing the visual style and simplifying the page layout also visually aligned the English-language and German-language versions of the newspaper as sister publications; doing so also would distinguish the Hearst publications from Pulitzer's *World* as well as the weekly humor magazines that inspired the creation of the comic supplement in the first place. The standardization of size and form enabled Hearst to syndicate his comic strips to other newspapers around the country, which led other newspapers

Figure 2.1. *New York Journal* Sunday comic supplement, August 22, 1897: 12. This page from near the beginning of Block's tenure as comic supplement editor contains a miscellany of text and visual matter. San Francisco Academy of Comic Art Collection, Ohio State University, Billy Ireland Cartoon Library & Museum.

Figure 2.2. *Chicago American* Sunday comic supplement, March 5, 1905: 2. By 1905, a representative page shows the regularized strip format, absence of textual matter, and use of speech balloons for dialogue that would become conventions of the comic strip form. San Francisco Academy of Comic Art Collection, Ohio State University, Billy Ireland Cartoon Library & Museum.

(including Pulitzer's, at last) to follow suit.[16] What Block helped create, in other words, was an identifiably new kind of publication: the comics section, or the funny papers. This publication, in turn, was based on a new genre of creative expression that emerged in the 1890s in the pages of the *Journal* and other American newspapers, the comic strip: a multi-paneled, narrative-based work incorporating both text and image, confined to the width of a single newspaper page, usually humorous in nature, and often incorporating repeating characters and repetitive story-lines.[17] And the comic strip became one of the most important vehicles for the comic sensibility itself.

Cultural Translation, Ethnic Identification, and Comic Alienation

The newspaper comics section was just one of many instances—and a very successful one—of cultural translation. Conolly-Smith uses the term in a very specific sense, to describe an active process of negotiation between the German American community and mainstream American society in the late nineteenth and early twentieth centuries, a process in which the *Journal/Morgen Journal* played an important part. The Germans, he argues, did not passively assimilate; they were not simply "incorporated," in Alan Trachtenberg's well-known formulation. Instead, they engaged in a "reciprocal exchange between their own and American values that at least initially merged the two into a transitional, hybrid culture drawing equally on both traditions and fusing them in temporary negotiation of old and new." In addition to the comic strip, Conolly-Smith describes other examples of cultural translation such as the Bronxer Literaten Club's outing to see the 1914 film *Damon and Pythias*, an adaptation of Friedrich Schiller's poem "Die Bürgschaft," or entertainments that featured combinations of tawdry vaudeville sketches with arias from German operas or *lieder*.[18] And it was in the German beer gardens of the Bowery where the variety theater, which evolved into that other key outlet of the comic sensibility, vaudeville, took root.[19] In *Maggie: Girl of the Streets*, written in the early 1890s, Stephen Crane depicted such a scene, where a singer of "brazen soprano tones" follows up with a strip-tease parody of dances featured in "theatres up-town"; she is succeeded by a ventriloquist, a sister-act, and a female blackface minstrel, capped with a heartfelt rendition of "The Star-Spangled Banner" which is taken up with "a great cheer ... from the throats of the assemblage of the masses." These masses include Maggie, the prostitute-in-formation, as well as her Bowery b'hoy suitor, Pete; but they also include, notably, "quiet Germans, with maybe their wives and two or three children," who "sat listening to the music, with the expression of happy cows."[20]

The comic strip as it developed at the turn of the century in the United States was, in fact, a direct descendant of German illustrated stories popularized by Rodolphe Töpffer and Wilhelm Busch. Busch's *Max und Moritz* books were immensely popular in Germany and among German-speaking Americans in the years following the Civil War; he was an inspiration for the Vienna-born Joseph Kessler, founder of *Puck*, and it was *Max und Moritz* specifically that Block asked artist Rudolph Dirks (himself a US-born German American) to adapt for Hearst's *Journal*. Beginning with these Germanic roots, the comic supplement incorporated writers and artists from a variety of ethnic and religious backgrounds, who brought together different forms of ethnic caricature and dialect in frenetic, at times almost anarchic, combinations. While Dirks lampooned German Americans in *The Katzenjammer Kids*, Frederick Opper drew cartoons featuring the Irish tramp Happy Hooligan and the effete Frenchmen Alphonse and Gaston; and Outcault depicted a wide range of urban types, epitomized by his ethnically indeterminate Yellow Kid. Racially indeterminate himself, George Herriman, the creator of *Krazy Kat*, was called "the Greek" by his colleagues, and drew cartoons featuring characters of different races, as well as characters like Musical Mose, a black man who attempted (and predictably failed) to adopt different ethnic personae (see chapter 4). The *Journal*'s artists parodied one another's styles, included each other's characters into their own strips, and subbed in for one another when they were ill or went on vacation (see figure 2.3). The comics, then, constituted a site of cultural representation, variation, exchange, and translation.

Conolly-Smith describes a specific instance of cultural translation concerning the English-language strip *Bringing Up Father*, by George McManus, which ran in both the English-language *Journal* and the German-language *Morgen Journal* beginning in 1913. The strip featured the hapless Irish immigrant Jiggs, who is incapable of being "brought up" to the nouveau-riche lifestyle he blunders into by winning the lottery. In the *Morgen Journal*, the strip's title was translated as *Die gesellschaftliche Erziehung des Herrn Gradmichel* (*The Societal Education of Mr. Gradmichel*), *Gradmichel* indicating an upstanding, proper sort of person (the name combines a contraction of the word *gerade*, meaning straight or just, with a reference to Deutscher Michel, a figure akin to Uncle Sam in representing German national identity).[21] Conolly-Smith argues that by translating the strip's title as well as Jiggs's ethnic identity, the strip "provided German-language readers with strategies of accommodation to American life, usually by way of negative example: what *not* to do if one wished to be accepted."[22] In the first *Bringing Up Father* strip from 1913, for example, Jiggs is castigated for his "extremely vulga'" speech and for appearing *en deshabille* in company (see figure 2.4). Middle- and upper-class readers might interpret

Figure 2.3. Rudolph Dirks, "Yellow Kid? Ach, No! It's Only the Katzenjammer Kid—(and His Brudder)," *New York Journal*, March 27, 1898. In this strip, Dirks took over R. F. Outcault's sensationally successful strip *Hogan's Alley*, spoofing a number of Outcault's regular characters and transforming the Irish neighborhood of Outcault's strip into a German—ish—one. SFACA Collection SFS61-4-4, Billy Ireland Comics Library & Museum.

this strip as an example of the "unassimilable alien," but German-language readers would learn from this strip not to appear in public in stocking feet, to discuss one's corns in front of guests, or to complain even in private about dressing in a shirt and tie.

This *Bringing Up Father* strip also displays two of the most salient features of early comic strips, which also became the loci of controversy and critique: their use of caricature, and their use of "vulga'" speech, dialect in particular. One of the puzzling ironies of the early comic strips is that they appealed to working-class and ethnic readers despite their reliance on denigrating, even vicious, stereotypes of ethnic and racial minorities. Their popularity with ethnic and immigrant readers indicates that these audiences did not read caricature simply as a method of "ensuring that ethnic identities remain fixed and discernible in the bewildering flux of a multiethnic society,"[23] nor did they read dialect only as "a highbrow convention which employed exaggerated, humorous speech to camouflage a patronizing sentimentality and satire," [24] as critics have stated. In the comics, caricature and dialect took advantage of the taut line between differentiation and identification and highlighted cultural translation itself as an act performed not just by the comics artist, but by comics readers as well.

Scott McCloud argues that caricature does not just "fix" ethnicity into discernible, alien types, but also enables identification between the image and the reader. In *Understanding Comics: The Invisible Art* (1992), he presents an array of human faces, gradually lessening in level of detail from a photograph of a man's face on one end, to a simple circle with two dots for eyes and a line for a mouth, on the other. The photographic image, McCloud argues, is seen as someone else, "not-me," while the figure on the extreme right could be anyone.[25] This "universification" of the image is a paradoxical effect of the caricature: it is at once recognized as not representing an actual human being, while being accepted as a representation of many humans—an ethnic group, a nation, or even the entire human race.

McCloud writes that our impulse is to identify rather than to other; when confronted with an enclosed shape with a dot in the middle, we invariably see a face. He writes, "The cartoon is a vacuum into which our identity and awareness are pulled[,] . . . an empty shell that we inhabit which enables us to travel in another realm. We don't just *observe* the cartoon, we *become* it." For McCloud, our imaginative identification with the cartoon becomes one of actual transmutation, where we replace the drawing with our very selves. In the case of ethnic caricature, this sense of identification was of course less total. Jared Gardner writes that working-class, immigrant characters like Happy Hooligan invite the "imaginative *embrace* . . . of the untouchable American, the 'other' in our midst," a gesture of inclusion and perhaps even sympathy, but not total identification.[26]

Figure 2.4. George McManus, *Bringing Up Father*, New York Journal, January 2, 1913.

In the case of *Bringing Up Father*, Jiggs's character created multiple forms of identification and was translated in multiple directions. English-speaking readers identified with Jiggs's difficulties negotiating the minefield of expectations and obligations of the nouveau-riche lifestyle. At the same time, they laughed at the incongruity between his coarse, stereotypically Irish features and the "hard-boiled shirt" and bow tie he was expected to wear as markers of his newfound economic status. Conolly-Smith reports that German-speaking readers, in contrast, did not "read" the character as Irish but German, even though he was depicted using the same illustrations used in the English-language version. However, German readers wryly smiled at his failure to adapt successfully to the lifestyle to which he'd risen—in part, because his failure could be interpreted as a harbinger of their own fate. Readers conversant in both languages (or simply aware of both versions of the strip) could have understood the character as representing all immigrants, or perhaps the working class, seeing the translation of the character into two different ethnic contexts as a fundamental aspect of George McManus's treatment of cultural assimilation in a general sense, across different ethnicities.[27]

Dialect, the verbal corollary to caricature, directly engages questions of translation and identification. A speech rendered in dialect is marked, through orthographical means, as simultaneously belonging to a particular language and being alien to it. Gavin Jones describes a "cult of the vernacular" that dominated American letters and entertainment at the end of the nineteenth century; the accents and idioms of various races, ethnic groups, and geographical regions permeated literature, theater, and popular discourse.[28] The comic supplements might be seen as one of the period's most unfettered outlets for vernacular expression. As in caricature, points of difference are visually exaggerated and distorted; "the," "why," and "with" look very little like "der," "vy," or "wid." The speaker's language is rendered alien—that is, fundamentally different from the "standard dialect"—through changes in orthography. At the same time, dialect was developed as a way to depict the actual sounds of speech, to distinguish between different regional (but still "American") speech patterns. When read, one identifies the depicted *sound* of the dialect as representative of a particular group—maybe even one's own ethnic group—while also rejecting it as a representation of what we think of as "language" in its standard written form.

The enjoyment of both caricature and dialect results from the play, in both senses of the word, between differentiation and identification, between alienation and recognition. In this way, dialect writing functioned as a verbal manifestation of the racial and comic grotesque, as discussed in the previous chapter. As such, it too expressed the tension between ethnic groups (much depends on who is actually performing the dialect or drawing the caricature, and for whom), or simply, anxiety about the boundaries that distinguished different groups and the ease or difficulty with which it was possible to pass between them. Jones writes that the writing of dialect could reflect a "political dynamic of subordination *and* resistance that defined linguistic conflict at the end of the nineteenth century." He continues:

> Dialect writing was not always a proof of hegemonic command. It could also register an anxious, constantly collapsing attempt to control the fragmentation and change that characterize any national tongue. And dialect could encode the possibility of resistance, not just by undermining the integrity of a dominant standard, but by recording the subversive voices in which alternative versions of reality were engendered.[29]

The process of subordination and resistance that we see in caricature and dialect drives the narrative—or is the basis of the gag—of many of the early comic strips. In both Dirks's *The Katzenjammer Kids* and Opper's *Happy Hooligan*, we can see this very clearly in the spankings suffered by Hans and Fritz at the end of each episode, or by Happy, inevitably, landing in the clink despite his best intentions (see figure 2.2). On the basic level of story, one sees rebellion quashed, over and over again; one sees German scamps, Irish hobos, and other racial and ethnic "others" disciplined, reprimanded, put in their proper place.[30]

Yet it should be noted that while ethnic identity remains fixed and discernible in many ways, what might be even more rigid and unchanging in these strips are authority figures and the institutions that they represent. The Captain in *The Katzenjammer Kids* is always shocked at the Kids' perfidies—"Vot iss?" he exclaims in nearly every strip; Mama is always disappointed at the behavior of her "little anchels"; the whiskered policeman is always at the ready to take Happy Hooligan to jail. The early strips were not just about suppressing the downtrodden, but also about fixity itself. Gardner argues that the reader enjoyed the early comic strips precisely *because* of their repetitive nature. Noting that stories about social fragmentation, technological innovation, and the seemingly continuous acceleration of urban life—the "shock of modernity"—dominated the newspaper's other pages, the comics "celebrated the modern body's *resilience* in the face of these same forces, its ability to bounce back, to recover, and to find humor and humanity in the midst of these inhuman conditions." Thus the stability of types served a restorative function: the characters in the strips, like the largely working-class readers of Hearst's *New York Journal*, could laugh in the face of repeated defeats, and thus endure.[31]

The comic supplement mirrored other popular sites of ethnic representation, impersonation, and repetition. Vaudeville, in particular, emerged from the nineteenth-century variety theater and minstrel show, and like the comic strip, relied on ethnic humor to appeal to a broad, middlebrow audience. While ethnic stereotyping was certainly used in vaudeville in dehumanizing and denigrating ways (just as it was in the comic strip), Jones writes that its appeal also "depended on new types of comic dialect that had the power to mediate difference by sustaining multiple interpretations and staging ethnic hybrids," revealing "a sociolinguistics of ethnic contact and cultural struggle remarkable for its diversity and complexity."[32] In one sketch performed by the "Dutch" comedians Mike and Meyer (Joe Weber and Lew Fields), the characters engage in rapid-fire wordplay performed in dialect, demonstrating their virtuostic ability to manipulate language while also underscoring the difficulty of pinning down meaning:

> MIKE: In two days I vill be a murdered man.
> MEYER: A vot?
> MIKE: I mean a married man.
> MEYER: I hope you vill always look back upon der presendt moment as der habbiest moment uff your life. . . . [U]nd furdermore, upon dis suspicious occasion, I also vish to express to you—charges collect—my uppermost depreciation of der dishonor you haf informed upon me in making me your bridesmaid.
> MIKE: Der insuldt is all mein.
> MEYER: As you standt before me now, soo young, soo innocent, soo obnoxious, there is only one void dat can express mein pleasure, mein dissatisfaction——
> MIKE: Yes, yes?
> MEYER: Und I can't tink of der void.[33]

While audiences might laugh at Meyer's malapropisms, they also admired Lew Fields, the actor who portrayed him and incorporated knowledgeable manipulations of antonym and pun to reverse Meyer's intention to impress Mike with his linguistic fluency. Henry Jenkins writes that an essential aspect of the "vaudeville aesthetic" was its ability to elicit spontaneous responses through fragmentation, heterogeneity, and infinite variety, both in the combinations of different kinds of acts and through the combinations of different linguistic registers and dialects; "In the end, what vaudeville communicated was the pleasure of infinite diversity in infinite combinations."[34]

At the same time, audiences also could identify with Meyer's inability to "tink of der void," as well as the possibility that one's words could be in fact void of meaning. The early historian of vaudeville Albert McLean wrote of the cathartic value of vaudeville, describing it as an expression of "pertinence

Figure 2.5. *New York Journal* comic supplement page showing a combination of sequential, film-like action, a single-panel cartoon, and a sequence of narrative vignettes. *New York Journal*, January 16, 1896: 6.

and explosiveness" that, in scandalizing the tastes of the cultured elite, could constitute "an effective gesture of retaliation against an environment which promised much and yet never yielded quite enough."[35] While Meyer demonstrates an ability to mimic the linguistic conventions of the cultured classes, Fields's performance also exposes Meyer's language as mimicry rather than expression. The act emphasizes the frequently perceptible void between "voids" and meanings, a void that uneducated and immigrant audiences must have felt all too keenly in a bewildering world full of advertising, a chaotic print culture, and seemingly constant technological innovation.

In the comic strip, the gap between expression and meaning upon which both caricature and dialect depended became literalized in one of its most distinctive features, its division into panels and its incorporation of the gutter. This space, an apparent void, in fact points to meaning, calling to be filled in or bridged by an engaged and active reader. Film theorists have described the way viewers knit together a series of still images—twenty-four frames per second—as "persistence of vision": that is, a desire to see these images as connected rather than as individual stills.[36] Many early comic strips replicated segments of film, depicting a single, continuous action separated into a progression of images (see figure 2.5). As the comic strip form developed, each panel came to represent isolated moments within a narrative sequence rather than steps in a single action. Connecting these moments requires not just persistence of vision but also the *imposition* of vision, of imagination, which effects what McCloud calls "closure"—the relating together of images in a logical sequence. The chronological division of time implied by the regular grid of images, Thierry Smolderen writes, echoes the photographic sequences of images used by Eadweard Muybridge beginning in the 1870s in his attempts to depict motion through photographs. When adopted by comic strip artists, "Muybridge's regular grid, strictly identical framings, and precisely timed intervals gave temporal, dynamic meaning to the gaps between successive images."[37]

We can see the complex interactions between caricature, dialect, and the gutter by examining a single half-page *Katzenjammer Kids* strip from 1903 (see figure 2.6). If one looks only at the images without reading the dialogue, one sees the depiction of a series of scenes: Hans and Fritz put on dresses, they meet the Captain and Mama Katzenjammer having tea and doughnuts; suddenly, Hans is on the floor, his striped pants showing; then Hans is getting spanked while Fritz runs away. Many of the causal triggers or motivations for the action, including their desire for doughnuts as well as the cause of Hans's calamitous fall, must be inferred through context. Contemporary commentators scoffed that comic strips could only have been "designed for the exclusive refreshment of the feeble-minded,"[38] but the actual process by which one can understand

Figure 2.6. "Delia and Maggie—Katzenjammer Kids." *Richmond Times-Dispatch* Sunday comic supplement, March 1, 1903: 11.

the basic events of a strip involves a complex knitting together of image and text. The gutter stands in for all that is *not* depicted but also becomes a point of entry for the reader's imagination and creativity.[39]

We can see a similar invitation for readers to play with meaning in Dirks's use of language. The two boys try on a series of alternate identities, both ones they choose and ones that are imposed on them by others. They are "goils"; they are "ladies"; they are "misses," even "peaches"; and of course they are also Hans and Fritz, Delia and Maggie. As "goils," they present themselves as girls with an accent, rather than *frauleins* translated into plain American "girls." By taking on the names Maggie and Delia, they even adopt a different ethnic identity, as these names were strongly identified, at the time, with Irish Americans. Mama refers to them as "ladies," a perception Hans and Fritz confirm by declaring themselves to be representatives of moral authority, the church. The Captain, however sees them as unmarried, available "misses" (succulent peaches, with "such fine little shapes, dod gast em"!). Once the skirts come off, however, they are revealed to be just two little boys, or perhaps, "bunglers." The mixture of different linguistic registers in the strip, as well as the mixing of gender, class, and nationalities, give rise to the experience of the comic sensibility, with its merging of the physiological deformations of dialect and caricature, collective yet self-deprecating laughter, and appeal to the violent ruptures of modern experience. As such it is an exercise (albeit a rather crude one) in acculturation—both for immigrants learning American customs and social hierarchies, and for more "cultured" readers interested in contemporary slang and dialect—and, like vaudeville, an opportunity for ethnic (not to mention gendered) impersonation and masquerade.

The early comic strips' ability to unleash the reader's imagination through acts of identification, translation, and interpretation demonstrates the power of the comic sensibility. Many of Block's contemporaries as well as later cultural critics recognized this power but have dismissed it, perhaps out of contempt for popular mass culture, perhaps out of a latent fear of the mass itself. Block, however, defended the comic supplement as being on par with the best that Europe could offer. When told that continental visitors were "aghast" and "completely puzzled" by American comics, he responded,

> I have for many years—and with painful regularity, I must add—followed *Punch, Judy, Pick-Me-Up, Ally Sloper, Comic Cuts, Le Journal Amusant, Le Petit Journal Pour Rire, Fliegende Blätter, Meggendorfer Blätter, Kikeriki, Simplicissimus, Jugend,* and the humorous periodicals of Russia, Spain, Hungary and Norway. . . . Making allowance for national characteristics which are as

clearly marked in humor as they are in literature, in art, or even in food, you will find that what is truly humorous in these publications is alike in each.[40]

By comparing Hearst's rough-and-tumble Sunday comic supplement pages to the best-known English, French, and German humor journals, Block aligned them with a cosmopolitan, freewheeling ethos that would characterize the humorous absurdity of the Dadaists and other early modernists.

Rudolph Block as Bruno Lessing

It's difficult to believe that Block had time to write fiction while editing the comic supplement for the *Journal*. The early years of his tenure as editor, however, were some of his most productive as a writer. In 1903, he published his first collection of stories, *Children of Men*, which received highly complimentary reviews. In the January 1904 issue of *The Bookman*, he was singled out with Richard Harding Davis, Jack London, Joseph Conrad, and Owen Wister as having produced work of "undoubted importance" in the previous year.[41] When Hearst purchased the moribund *Cosmopolitan Magazine* in 1905, he quickly engaged Block to write a series of "funny yarns" for the magazine under Lessing's name that would be modeled on one of *Children of Men*'s few humorous tales, "A Swallow-Tailer for Two."[42] Block delivered on his contract, and then some. Three stories by Bruno Lessing appeared in September, November, and December of that year, five more in 1906, twelve in 1907—one for each monthly issue—and at least a half dozen per year for some years after that, ultimately, totaling seventy stories in less than ten years: an astounding publication record by almost any standard.[43] Quantity, of course, is not equivalent to quality. But there is a marked difference between the stories Lessing published in *Children of Men* and those he began publishing in *Cosmopolitan*. It is difficult to call most of the stories in *Children of Men* actual stories; many are little more than sketches, impressionistic and diffuse in effect. The *Cosmopolitan* stories, in contrast, are tightly plotted and fully developed. They also replace the tragic and at times brutal naturalism of the earlier stories with ebullient, often raucous humor.

In making the comic turn in his fiction, Block applied the lessons he learned editing the comic strips and the comic supplement. Deftly wielding the double-edged weapons of caricature and dialect, he displayed a facility with language—and languages—and demonstrated the varied uses to which dialect could be put, translating the alien and often incomprehensible speech of the Lower East Side for the English-speaking audience of *Cosmopolitan*. At the same time, his stories demonstrate a keen awareness of the limitations of dialect and caricature as expressive modes; while they could be used to assert alternative and original forms of expression, they also reduced individuals to types, and risked reducing subjectivity to ethnicity.

Many of Lessing's stories are translations, in a sense, of conventional plots from Jewish folk tales: the story of the clever son-in-law, the smart man fooled, stories of the *schnorrer*, the *shadchen*, the *schlemiel*.[44] While many of Lessing's plots are repetitive and predictable, like those of the comic strips he edited, Lessing introduced variety and interest through his incorporation of wordplay and by mixing different registers of speech for humorous effect. As with the comic strips, the point of Lessing's stories was not so much the actual story, but how the story was told; the fun and the funny came from the play of dialect, as well as the identification with and rejection of caricature. In "The Big Tree" (*Cosmopolitan*, September 1906), for example, Lessing effortlessly combines standard English, the syntax and idiom of Yiddish, Talmudic incantation, street insults, the trite expressions of story-paper melodrama, and American slang. His character Simkovitz has resolved to commit suicide, and in a fit of pique spurred by indigestion, writes the following letter to one of his customers:

> When you see this word I shall be gone to my fathers with a bullet, but Barraboth, who was my partner, will be alive and you can go for him. *He is a cheater*. He cheated me and he cheated you, because I know it and helped him. Life is too miserable when your best friends go behind your back; but I am independent. I say Bah! to the world. Do you remember the big box of furs that were full of moth-holes? We said they were O.K. when you bought them. . . . *It was a lie*. Barraboth . . . says to me old Lazarus is easy to fool because he doesn't know nothing about furs or nothing else except the synagogue. . . . Send him to the prison. You can do nothing with me because I am dead.[45]

Here, Lessing incorporates phrases ostensibly from the Yiddish ("I shall be gone to my fathers"), American slang ("O.K."), English-language grammatical errors ("he doesn't know nothing"), and expletives ("I say Bah! To the world"). Simkovitz's letter also combines written genres: the poison pen letter and the suicide note. Lessing's transgression of boundaries between languages, genres, and linguistic communities provokes laughter, but, like Weber and Fields's "Dutch" act, it also demonstrates his mastery of the different linguistic codes and registers of New Yorkese, "a language of absolute cultural otherness that remained virtually inarticulate to the 'proper' speaker."[46] Like Simkovitz, Lessing is unapologetically "independent" in his use of language and exudes a spirit of improvisation and creativity that paralleled the comic antics of Dirks's *Katzenjammer Kids* and Outcault's *Hogan's Alley*.[47]

In his stories, Lessing engages in what translation theorist and translator Lawrence Venuti calls "minoritizing translation," which signals, rather than effaces, the "linguistic and cultural differences of the text." In highlighting these differences, this kind of translation emphasizes the inherent heterogeneity of any language, "exposing the contradictory conditions of the standard dialect, the literary canon, the dominant culture, the major language"; it "indicates where the major language is foreign to itself."[48] In doing so, however, Lessing's incorporated foreign elements in ways that did not render his stories unintelligible to readers. Rather, each story was "a real, throbbing chapter of a life," the editor's headnote to "A Trifle Light as Air" (1911) declared, an opportunity for readers to identify with rather than feel alienated from this segment of society.[49] The fact that Lessing's stories convey a realistic view of life, or were perceived to be doing so, underscores Wonham's observation that caricature and realism, so often seen as antithetical, in fact shared the same goal: to "lay bare the 'essence' of the human subject."[50]

In taking the Lower East Side as his subject, Lessing appears to have taken his cue from his now better-known contemporary, Abraham Cahan, who also impressed readers with his realism and whose work was also infused with dialect and humor. Although it is unclear whether or not the two writers and editors knew each other in either a personal or professional capacity, Block had undoubtedly seen William Dean Howells's effusive review of Cahan's *Yekl* (1896), which appeared in the Sunday *World* in July 1896 and declared Cahan a "New Star of Realism." Block also likely read the stories Cahan subsequently published in major magazines, including *Scribner's* and *Century*. Cahan and Lessing published in some of the same magazines, though years apart; Cahan's "Dumitru and Sigrid" appeared in *Cosmopolitan* in 1901, four years before Lessing began publishing there, while *The Rise of David Levinsky* was serialized in *McClure's* in 1913, ten years after the magazine published Lessing's first short story, "The End of the Task" (1903). Block also undoubtedly would have known of Cahan's editorial work at the helm of the Yiddish-language daily *Forverts*.[51] However, while their stories bore many similarities in characterization, subject, and theme, the two writers differed fundamentally in both tone and outlook.

They also used dialect to different ends. In *Yekl*, Cahan uses dialect to delineate his characters' attempts to speak English, while translating their native Yiddish into standard English. Their use of dialect thus demonstrates their *inability* to speak rather than their fluency. Hana Wirth-Nesher notes that Cahan's dialect renders his characters unintelligible; from the moment Jake (née Yekl) announces himself as "Dzake," the "Americanized" name is not just "unpronounceable," it is "destabilizing, nearly unreadable."[52] Jake shows himself to be most alien when he tries hardest to show how American he is. Jones writes that in *Yekl* and elsewhere, Cahan depicted the "ambivalent linguistic psychologies" that characterized the immigrant experience. "The immigrant simultaneously occupies two cultural worlds," he writes, "neither of which is strictly either American or foreign, and simultaneously speaks two different languages, neither of which corresponds fully to American English or to European Yiddish."[53]

As a result, Cahan's characters are more often than not reduced to silence. At the end of *Yekl*, Jake seems to have gained everything he wanted, yet vaguely feels himself "the victim of an ignominious defeat." In the carriage on his way to City Hall, where he is to marry the Americanized Polish Jew Mamie, he wishes the journey to be never-ending, that each "pause" taken by the hack "could be prolonged indefinitely."[54] Characters in Cahan's subsequent collection, *The Imported Bridegroom and Other Stories* (1898), are also silenced: Rouvke, at the end of "A Providential Match," is left "staring as if he were at a loss to realize the situation," while the Russian intellectual Boris ends "Circumstances" in rooms filled with "dead emptiness."[55] This silence or emptiness represents these characters' inability to successfully negotiate American culture and the linguistic terrain, an environment, Jones writes, where all language, "the vernacular and the genteel, the immigrant and the American, were mutually contaminated";[56] as a result, they are voided, effaced. In Cahan's later works, including the journalistic pieces he wrote for the *Commercial Advertiser* between 1897 and 1902 as well as his 1917 novel *The Rise of David Levinsky*, he largely abandoned the use of orthographically marked dialect, translating his characters' Yiddish using standard English words and spellings, but retaining some characteristically Yiddish syntax and idioms.[57] For Cahan, it was most important to portray immigrant Americans as engaged, intelligent, and articulate, and his decision to purify ethnic American language of its aural and grammatical "contaminations" conveys his desire to communicate the realism of his subjects' thoughts and ideas, which Cahan presented as quintessentially American in contrast to the "alien" sound of their speech.

Lessing, in contrast, did not see dialect as an opportunity to stigmatize but rather an invitation to improvise. In "The Big Tree" as well as in dialect-dominated stories such as "Ingratitude of Mister Rosenfeld" (August 1906) and "Monahan's Musical Education" (February 1907), dialect conveys the bohemian cosmopolitanism of the Lower East Side. It's no surprise that so many of Lessing's stories are set in cafés. He describes one of them in "Monahan's Musical Education"; here, linguistic, musical, social, and even culinary boundaries are crossed and mixed in an environment of synesthetic stimulation:

> Arponyi's café was the literary, artistic, musical, and social center of the Hungarian colony. . . . All sorts and conditions of men came there, from the

Magyar habitués who sat each day at the same hour, at the same table, and hungry or thirsty passers-by who were attracted by the bright lights and the music, to Bohemians from all parts of the city who loved to hear the gypsy music of Bela's band, and society folk on sight-seeing tours who felt that they were "slumming." And I can assure you that it was a delight to spend an evening in that crowded café, surrounded by the murmur of foreign voices that suggested picturesqueness of all kinds, listening to the intoxicating strains of wild Romany airs, watching the various types of faces, tasting the queer-looking beverages that you had never heard of before, and, eke, eating a plate of *gulyas*.[58]

The story centers on the burly Irishman Monahan, who offers to help the Hungarian café owner, Arponyi, rein in his rebellious "bant" of "gypsy" musicians. Although the musicians bring crowds to the café, they refuse to play what is requested by the customers and take breaks whenever they wish. As Arponyi relates:

I say to Bela, "Play der Hungarian Rhapsodie," unt he say he iss too tired. He play ragtime. I say, "Vould it not be better if you rest only ten minutes between der playing?" But he say, "Ve rest until ve feel rested." I say to him he should not make der sweet eyes on der ladies because maype der escorts don't like it, unt he say, "Bah! Vot do I care?"[59]

In the end, they "do chust vot they please": no more, no less. When Arponyi admits that he is unable to "boss 'em" or to "give it to 'em, fierce"—as Monahan suggests—Monahan offers to get them in line. He succeeds for a time, but is eventually trumped by the crafty band leader, Bela. The story ends with Arponyi obsequiously fawning over Bela, asking when he might "haf der pleasure of hearing der next selegtion uf der music." With a "sweet smile," Bela responds, simply, "When I get ready."[60] Bela, we are told, is "proud of his English," and is the only character in the story—besides the narrator—who speaks in standard dialect. As a group, the gypsy band is able to speak in Hungarian-inflected dialect, in Romani, and in fluent English, reflecting an adaptability they attained by virtue of the nomadic way of life that systematic discrimination has imposed upon them. While Lessing's depiction of the Romani—not to mention the Hungarians and the Irish—reinforces negative stereotypes, the resolution of this story demonstrates a recognition of the ways that oppression could cultivate strength.

Although Lessing stressed the virtuostic performance of dialect in many of his stories, he also displays, no less than Cahan, a nuanced understanding of its limitations. In "The Parrot of Uncle Hurwitz" (1906), Lessing explores the "linguistic bind" facing many Jewish Americans, like Cahan's Yekl/Dzake, who find themselves unable to express themselves fluently in any language. The story centers on two brothers, Sammy and Isidore, and their wealthy Uncle Hurwitz, who cares only for his vicious pet parrot. Isidore is disowned by Uncle Hurwitz when he defiantly marries an Irish girl; Sammy, in contrast to Isidore, decides to curry his uncle's favor by teaching the parrot to say, as though he has heard Sammy say it many a time, "Dear, dear uncle! His happiness is der only t'ing in der vorld vot interests me!" This phrase, spoken in dialect, not only serves to stroke his uncle's ego, but also caters to the fact that his uncle "loved to display his familiarity with English." However, the parrot resists Sammy's lesson, responding insistently in Hebrew, "*Shema' Yisroel!*" which Lessing translates as "'Hear, O Israel!'—the opening words of the Jews' daily prayer." The parrot "would fly into a fury and scream '*Shema' Yisroel!*' a dozen times, very rapidly," every time Sammy attempts to coax him into speaking the desired phrase.⁶¹

Happily, Sammy discovers that he can get the parrot to say the magical phrase if he whacks it over the head with his walking stick. Upon hearing the bird produce the words Sammy has taught it, Uncle Hurwitz is thrilled to discover this evidence of his nephew's devotion, and Sammy appears headed to inherit his uncle's fortune. But Uncle Hurwitz, on his deathbed, asks Sammy to get the parrot to speak, discovers Sammy beating the bird, and throws him out of the house. Uncle Hurwitz reverses his will, bestowing his fortune on Isidore. However, he does not forget Sammy. Lessing writes of Uncle Hurwitz that "no one had ever accused him of being a fool," and in keeping with this characterization, he leaves a small legacy—twenty dollars a week—to Sammy. "It was less than [Sammy] expected," Lessing writes, "But it was something—yes, he would not have to work." Sammy discovers, however, that he has also been left the parrot, who must remain alive under his care in order for him to continue receiving his weekly income. "Vot iss it?" the lawyer asks when Sammy comes to this realization at the conclusion of the story. "Are you sick?"⁶²

The story, in many ways, is a parable about language. Sammy, desperate to inherit his uncle's fortune, panders to Uncle Hurwitz's preference for English by speaking only in that language, which he is only able to do through tortured dialect. The phrase he teaches the parrot, then, is only a deformed approximation of the phrase he actually *wishes* he could say, and as a result, his saying it only emphasizes his lack of sincerity. The parrot, meanwhile, has no actual language, but simply parrots back what it is taught—or forced—to say. The fact that it only knows one phrase prior to the advent of Sammy's walking stick—the Hebrew phrase "*Shema' Yisroel!*"—is a jab at the many Jews who could recite Hebrew prayers but did not actually understand the language. Thus, for the parrot, the Hebrew phrase is as meaningless as the expression of love and devotion Sammy "teaches" it to say. The parrot, tied to Sammy's fate at last, functions as a metaphor for Sammy's own linguistic dilemma: they are both unable to speak or understand either Hebrew or English, and thus remain alienated both from Jewish and American culture. If anything, Sammy ends up in an even worse position than the parrot, since he ends up wholly dependent on the parrot's fortunes for his own.

Rudolph Block, as an editor and as the short-story writer Bruno Lessing, demonstrates the range of expression available to multiethnic American writers during the early twentieth century. In shaping the form of the "funny pages," Block was instrumental in the development of the comic strip, a hybrid genre of literature that responded to the needs of an important new readership that emerged in the late nineteenth century: immigrants, particularly those from Eastern Europe, Ireland, and Italy. The comic strip conveyed meaning through simplified images and minimal amounts of text, and through rigid, repetitive narratives structured on the vaudeville sketch and the joke. While Block, no less than the comic strip artists he edited, depended on caricature, stereotype, and dialect to assert an ethnic presence in Lessing's fiction, he also recognized their limitations. As an editor and as a writer, Block stands as a bridge figure: between the world of New York Jewry and the mainstream/Gentile publishing industry; between the tragic and comic treatments of the Jewish "ghetto"; and between the fiction and visual culture of the early twentieth century.

CHAPTER THREE

Illustration and the Narrative Quality of Appeal

A drawing is not a copy but an invention.
—Robert Henri[1]

Bruno Lessing was just one of many writers of so-called "ghetto fiction." Montague Glass was perhaps the most successful; his Potash and Perlmutter stories initially appeared in the *New York Evening Post* before being collected in book form and adapted for Broadway (1913) and film (1923). Other prolific producers of stories featuring immigrants in the tenement districts included Myra Kelly, I. K. (Isaac Kahn) Friedman, and Edward Raphael Lipsett. The genre's popularity reflected a general diversification of literature that resulted as writers became increasingly interested in depicting different segments of American society at the end of the nineteenth century, and as these segments of society—rural, urban, working-class, ethnic—began to produce writers in their own right. Realism's most vocal proponent, William Dean Howells, described the turn toward pluralism in the years following the end of the Civil War: "As soon as the country began to feel life in every limb with the coming of peace, it began to speak in the varying accents of all the sections."[2]

Strongly identified with the urban immigrant working class and functioning as a fictional counterpart to the comic genres of newspaper comic strip and vaudeville, ghetto fiction almost demanded to be illustrated. Yet the adamantly unsentimental aspects of the genre proved challenging for art editors and illustrators, who generally tried to be "sensitive and expressive" in their depictions of the urban poor.[3] This tendency toward sympathy and pathos is marked in the illustrative treatment of Lessing's stories. While they were initially assigned to comic artists including Rudolph Dirks (see figure 3.1), Arthur Dove, Rose Cecil O'Neill, and William Glackens, as they continued to be published in *Cosmopolitan* and elsewhere, they were taken up by realistic artists who strangely treated Lessing's buffoonish characters with grave, artistic seriousness (see figure 3.2).

Some ghetto fiction did receive comic visual treatment. In "smart magazines" such as the *Saturday Evening Post* and *Collier's*, artists specializing in comic treatments of urban life found an open field. Yet just as its fictional counterpart has been overlooked by literary historians, "ghetto illustration" has been overlooked by historians of art and illustration. In part this is because of the dominance of the lush, painterly illustrations of the artists associated with Howard Pyle, which figured prominently in the frontispieces and color plates of the most important national illustrated magazines—*Century, Harper's*, and *Scribner's*. Yet it is also because of the devaluing of the comic generally in histories of American culture.

In this genre of illustrated ghetto fiction, a group of artists identified with emerging forms of American artistic modernism—including Arthur Dove, John Sloan, and especially for our purposes here, William Glackens—established their careers. And they engaged the urban environment through the comic sensibility, turning to sketch, caricature, and cartoon, and employing the iconography, visual syntax, and physical gestures of vaudeville, the comic strip, and advertising to depict urban environments with both sympathy and humor. Michele H. Bogart writes that "in the U.S., as in Europe, the development of modern art in all of its aspects was inextricably bound up in the same social frameworks that produced mass-market periodicals."[4] Even though modernism as an aesthetic eschewed so-called commercialism and mass culture, the hardening of the divisions between highbrow and lowbrow, elite and mass was, Bogart argues, a response to perceived permeability, a sense that the ramparts of Art were under siege from base elements.

Certainly, many artists and writers alike embraced, or at least found appeal in, mass and commercial culture. These cultural workers often straddled the divide between crass commercialism and artistic refinement. Walt Kuhn, for example, drew comic strips for the *New York Herald* but also organized the 1913 Armory Show, and Robert Henri was a member of the National Academy of Design but also encouraged his students to pursue careers in illustration and the decorative arts. Writers continued to seek out the enduring forms of deckle-edged author's editions and placement of their works in highly esteemed publications such as the *Atlantic* and *Century*. But even Henry James published

WITH AN EXPRESSION OF MOURNFUL RESENTMENT, HE TURNED AND LEFT THE ROOM

Figure 3.1. Rudolph Dirks, *With an expression of mournful resentment, he turned and left the room*, illustration for "Jablinowsky" by Bruno Lessing, *Cosmopolitan* 39.5 (September 1905): 530.

in the newsy, advertising-filled *Collier's*, while other writers, including Willa Cather and Stephen Crane, actively sought to place their work in mass-market periodicals and in newspapers through the syndicates.

William Glackens was one artist who immersed himself in illustrating urban fiction in the magazines. The hybrid sketch-cartoon style he developed, his sensitivity to the interplay between image and text, and his sheer love of drawing made his illustrations a crucial aspect of the text's meaning and the way the text is experienced, and it seems clear that many writers of ghetto fiction, including Lessing, depended on their illustrations and conceived their stories with illustration in mind. One might even consider "illustrated ghetto fiction" a distinct genre, a discrete manifestation of the comic sensibility that infused the linguistic, visual, narrative, and physiological appeals of the comic strip and stage comedy into the more traditional forms of magazines and books. This comic, textual-visual genre, as much as the realism of illustrators associated with the "Golden Age of Illustration," drove the sales of magazines such as the *Saturday Evening Post, McClure's, Collier's*, and *Cosmopolitan*, and played an important part in cultivating a broad, national readership.

William Glackens, Visual Comedian

William Glackens has been remembered neither as a jokester nor a wit. Art historians consistently characterize him as the most serene, the least excitable,

GIMPLOVITZ BROUGHT HIS FIST DOWN UPON THE TABLE WITH A CRASH

Figure 3.2. William Oberhardt, *Gimplovitz brought his fist down on the table with a crash*, illustration for "Under His Nose," by Bruno Lessing. *Cosmopolitan* 46.6 (May 1909): 663.

and the least demonstrative member of the so-called Ashcan group. His son Ira remarked in his biography of his father that Glackens was "a man of few words," making the writing of his life's story difficult. Luckily, Ira Glackens's mother, Edith Dimock, was "a voluble *raconteuse*," and he relied on her written and spoken recollections, as well as those of the "delightful and colorful group" of friends and associates who surrounded his father, to recreate his life.[5] William Glackens also seemed removed from the social milieu of those generally associated with the comic sensibility. Raised in a solidly middle-class Philadelphia family, his financial situation was to a great extent stabilized by his 1904 marriage to Dimock, who brought an inheritance to the union; and because his painting turned to apparently politically disengaged—and some would argue, more "sensual," epicurean, even hedonistic—themes, including domestic scenes, landscapes, and still-lifes in bright, luminous colors, he has been written off by art historians as a mere "painter of the bourgeois experience."[6]

Nevertheless, Glackens was a central figure in the art world of the early twentieth century United States. He was a key participant in the revolutionary exhibition of The Eight at Macbeth Gallery organized by Robert Henri, and later helped to organize the Society of Independent Artists' 1910 exhibition, which took the radical position of offering no prizes and requiring no jury for selection. He later served as the SIA's first president. He also was the head of the American selection committee for the Armory Show; and in the 1910s, he advised collector Albert C. Barnes in selecting fine examples of modernist French art, which would form the basis of the renowned Barnes Collection. Most pertinent to this chapter, Glackens was a founding member of the Society of Illustrators, established in 1901;[7] his illustration work appeared in the leading national illustrated magazines including the *Saturday Evening Post*, *McClure's*, *Century*, and *Scribner's*.[8] With one foot firmly planted at the leading edge of the art world, and the other equally planted in the worlds of commercial art, popular entertainment, and fashion, Glackens was able to bridge the base, grotesque underpinnings of the comic sensibility and the slick glibness of commercial and mass media.

Glackens's comic sense appeared most forcefully in his illustrations, which show that he not only drew humor, but drew *off* of the humor of everyday life and contemporary literature. As in the comic strip, Glackens's illustrations draw strong connections between viewer and reader, artist and subject, image and narrative. Also like the comic strip, Glackens's illustrations were quickly drawn, though carefully planned; the visceral appeal of the drawn image enhances the emotional connections between himself, the viewer, the story, and its subject—which, in many of the illustrations for which he is best known, is far removed from the reader's experience. He specialized not just in depictions of the "urban crowd,"[9] but in cross-ethnic comedy, works that feature ethnic impersonators, ethnic and racial mixing, and ethnic ventriloquism. In addition to Bruno Lessing, who depicted a wide range of Eastern European ethnicities, he illustrated works by a number of other writers who addressed similar themes. Among them were I. K. Friedman, a German Jew from Chicago writing in the voice of an Irish American street hustler in *The Autobiography of a Beggar* (1902–1903); Myra Kelly, an Irish American whose stories depicted the Jewish community of the Lower East Side; and the Irish-Jewish writer Edward Lipsett, whose "Denny the Jew" stories featured a New York Irish immigrant who decides to pass as Jewish in New York City. In fiction, as on the comics page and the vaudeville stage, ethnicity was staged, framed, and performed, and Glackens's illustrations played a crucial part in the act.

Glackens's illustration work, as is true of most of the illustration work undertaken by painters, has been largely dismissed as work simply done to pay the bills. Avis Berman even suggests that the reason why Glackens did not include many city scenes in his painting after the 1908 The Eight exhibition was because "the miseries of the Lower East Side and other poorer neighborhoods were part of and reminded him of illustrating, which he undertook as employment."[10] In reality, while he may have publicly denigrated the practice of illustration generally for being governed by "gross commercialism," he never dissociated himself from his illustration work.[11] He continued to take commissions for illustrations long after making the marriage that supposedly saved him from having to do so, and his work continued to develop in its sophistication. He admired English and French illustrators including Charles Keene and Honoré Daumier and made no bones of saying so; his papers include two expensively produced volumes produced by one of the era's best-known commercial illustrators, Harrison Fisher.[12]

Illustration work may have appealed to Glackens because it enabled him to engage with narrative in ways that were difficult in easel painting. His work suggests that he agreed with a contemporary critic who declared, "in the field of illustration, more truly than in that of painting, has contemporary life been reflected. Turn the pages of any of our leading magazines and one will see familiar tableaux from all stations in life.... Are not all these in a measure significant of American ideals?"[13] In one of his only extended statements on art, Glackens explained his goals as an artist by laying out his selection criteria as chair of the American Committee for the International Exhibition (better known as the Armory Show). American art, he said, demonstrated an impressive degree of technical skill, but "is not the kind of painting in which one feels that the artist is actually enjoying himself." It "is arid and bloodless," he continued. "It is nothing so much as dry bones."[14] He lamented the lack of "the

Figure 3.3. A photograph of Glackens from the 1890s shows him performing in one of the "theatricals" he and others concocted during their social gatherings at Robert Henri's studio at 806 Walnut Street, Philadelphia. Reproduced in *William Glackens and the Ashcan School*, by Ira Glackens: 7.

much-lauded American energy" which appeared "everywhere but in our art"; yet he argued that if one could only "inoculate the energy shown elsewhere into our art and I should not be surprised if we led the world" (162).

Glackens believed that the strict rules and guidelines for artistic depiction set out by the art academies had reduced art to "bloodless" formulas rather than "actual values" (160). Art had to break free from these rules in order to be truly vital. But artists were "afraid to be impulsive, afraid to forget restraint, afraid above everything to appear ridiculous" (160). Despite his apparent reserve, Glackens himself was not afraid to appear ridiculous. A photograph of Glackens from the 1890s shows him performing in one of the "theatricals" he and others concocted during their social gatherings at Robert Henri's studio at 806 Walnut Street, Philadelphia (see figure 3.3). In a child's dress with an enormous bow, his knock knees are visible below the hem; a preposterously tiny hat is perched on his head as he dances and sings in an "entr'acte divertissement."

More importantly, however, he was not afraid to portray ridiculousness in his art. Albert Barnes, who was a classmate of Glackens at Central High School in Philadelphia, recalled that rather than write notes on what his teachers said, Glackens took down incisive, witty drawings of the teachers themselves. These drawings represented "what the teacher was in reality, never what the teacher would have us believe that he was." Barnes wrote that these drawings "made it impossible for the rest of the class to study," but Glackens escaped punishment. "Nothing could have saved him from expulsion except his obviously great intellectual endowment, a personality universally loved and respected and a sense of humor so contagious that it disarmed the justifiable wrath of his teachers."[15] A few years later, Glackens successfully courted the independent-minded artist Edith Dimock by depicting her with her Sherwood Building roommates, May Wilson and Louise Seym, as chorus girls, showing plenty of leg—in a drawing he later used as the basis of an illustration depicting the fictional "Sherwood Sisters" vaudeville act.[16]

Like his friend George Luks, Glackens started his career as a professional artist in the newsroom. At the *Philadelphia Press*, he became known for his ability to quickly—and accurately—sketch complex scenes, including fires, parades, and street scenes.[17] After a few years, however, he, with Luks, was drawn to New York City. There, perhaps with the help of Luks, as well as the influence of his older brother Louis, who had been cartooning for *Puck* for over a decade, he was briefly employed as a comic strip artist by the *New York World*. Glackens's initial foray into the commercial world of comic art was brief: his strip *The Merry-Go-Rounders*, which appeared in two installments in early 1898, paired a fantastical drawing with a humorous poem by R. K. Munkittrick, an editor at *Puck* (see figure 3.4).[18] The strip takes full advantage of the four-color printing presses that distinguished Joseph Pulitzer's comic supplement from his competitors, and also displays Glackens's skill at depicting both movement and strong perspective.

Yet his career as a comics artist ended almost before it began. On the strength of his earlier newspaper illustration work, he was sent by editors at *McClure's* to accompany staff correspondent Stephen Bonsal to cover the conflict in Cuba after the explosion of the USS *Maine* in Havana Harbor. These illustrations appeared with one of Bonsal's reports as well as two others by Stephen Crane, who had also covered the war as a celebrity correspondent following the success of his novel *The Red Badge of Courage* (1895).[19] These illustrations provided Glackens with an entrée into magazine illustration, where he quickly became associated with regional humor, romantic comedy, and pieces set in colorful urban locales, including the theater and the tenement districts. Particularly in his urban work, he developed visual strategies of invitation and inclusion that contributed to the urban picturesque's familiarizing tone; at the same time, his careful delineation of individual character and communal

Figure 3.4. William Glackens, *The Merry-Go-Rounders*, *New York World* Sunday comic supplement, January 16, 1898. Billy Ireland Cartoon Library & Museum.

differences underscored the nation's rich diversity. Though Glackens was not known as much of a reader, perusal of his work shows that he read the works he was assigned to illustrate carefully and intelligently. His use of composition and representational strategies enhanced characterization and theme, and above all, actively engaged readers in the narrative.

Critic Regina Armstrong praised him early in his career, in 1900, as a "typist," likely based on illustrations he created for *Scribner's Magazine* in 1899 for pieces on the theater as well as the story "Rabbi Eliezer's Christmas," by Abraham Cahan (see figures 3.5a-c and 3.6). In her six-part series on "The New Leaders of American Illustration," she wrote, "Mr. Glackens seeks for the representation of an idea, for the depiction of life in all its teeming naturalness, and the treatment of his subject is not considered."[20]

This early assessment of Glackens's illustrations fails to recognize characteristics of his work that became more apparent as it evolved. In fact, his mature illustration style could be more accurately characterized through her description of the "storyteller," the subject of an earlier installment in the series:

> The pictorial story-teller has the easiest of tasks; he has the hardest of tasks. If he succeeds in expressing that touch of human nature which truly makes the whole world kin, then his task may be accounted an easy one; for the most irresistible human interest, in the purely mental pleasures, is awakened through the recognition of familiar traits of character by the narrative quality of appeal. If, however, the artist cannot educe this human touch, then his task has proven impossible, regardless of the artistic qualities that may prettily conspire to hide the essential defect. His result stands as nothing more than dummy pose and studio trumpery. Thus, character interpretation too often becomes caricature, lacking in the legitimate portrayal of the emotion it attempts to reveal; and this is because its expression undoubtedly requires more resources in its interpreter than are needed in any other feature of illustration—judgment, taste, humour, discrimination, refinement, poetic sympathy and dramatic sensibility and vigor.[21]

Many comic illustrators, needless to say, reduced character to caricature. Glackens, in contrast, caused readers to recognize "familiar traits of character by the narrative quality of appeal." Making viewer/readers participants in the visual narratives he created, he invited them to create connections between illustration and story across the gutter of white space on the page, and between image and text itself.

Critics have recognized the narrative appeal in Glackens's large-scale comic panoramas of New York City published in *Collier's* as cover illustrations and as full-page, stand-alone interior cartoons in the early 1910s (see figure 3.7). Zurier

Figure 3.5. William Glackens, illustrations for "The Vaudeville Theater" (*Scribner's*, October 1899): a) *Singing Soubrettes*; b) *Irish Comedians*; c) *German Dialect Comedians*. Helen Farr Sloan Library & Archives, Delaware Art Museum.

writes that Glackens, modeling his "cartoonist's" style on the quick, confident strokes of *Punch* artists Harry Furniss and Charles Keene, was able to capture what Randolph Bourne described as the "strange power of this mass-life" that attracted millions to the cities in at the turn of the century; Glackens, she writes, drew crowds not as "a unified entity; a sea in which one could lose oneself," but rather as "a series of individual portraits that put faces on the threatening herd and gave viewers something to look at"—a visual and social spectacle.[22]

"Why should you be afraid to tell us how much?"—Page 664.

RABBI ELIEZER'S CHRISTMAS

By A. Cahan

ILLUSTRATIONS BY W. J. GLACKENS

Figure 3.6. William Glackens, headpiece for "Rabbi Eliezer's Christmas," by Abraham Cahan, *Scribner's* (December 1899): 661. William Glackens Illustration Collection, Helen Farr Sloan Library & Archives, Delaware Art Museum.

As Carrie Tirado Bramen noted of the urban picturesque, written and visual narratives like these helped to domesticate the alien by characterizing "the heterogeneity of the city as 'charming' and 'quaint' rather than exclusively deleterious."[23] Zurier writes of Glackens in particular, "The aggregate suggests infinite variety while inviting further scrutiny. The effect is to take subjects that many of Glackens's contemporaries found disturbing—the crowded conditions of urban life and the violent play of unsupervised children—and teach viewers to look at them for pleasure."[24]

Heather Coyle Campbell echoes Zurier when she writes that Glackens "gave viewers a magisterial view of a confusing landscape, while his figures—playing children, strolling women, and courting couples—encouraged

Illustration and the Narrative Quality of Appeal 105

Far from the Fresh Air Farm

The crowded city street, with its dangers and temptations, is a pitiful makeshift playground for the children

Figure 3.7. William Glackens, *Far from the Fresh Air Farm* (*Collier's*, July 8, 1911): 6.

Collier's readers to recognize the ordinary human element of city life in every neighborhood."[25] She also emphasizes the deft characterization of Glackens's mini-portraits, describing them as "a conglomeration of individual figures and stories" presented in an active, yet structured composition that replicated the "rhythm" of contemporary city life.[26] The implicit narrative (or interweaved narratives) contained within these full-page cover illustrations echo the paintings of Pieter Brueghel the Elder, an artist Glackens admired; they also recall, and may have been intended to recall, the full-page comics of Richard F. Outcault (see chapter 1), Dan McCarthy, and others. They are also a culmination of narrative strategies that Glackens had developed over the previous decade.

Creating Appeal

In several of his earliest illustration commissions, Glackens brought readers into the world of the story by depicting its characters in close proximity to the reader and on the same plane. In contrast to the later *Collier's* cartoons, which presented city scenes viewed from above, illustrations Glackens created for stories such as "Rabbi Eliezer's Christmas" (see figure 3.5) and "A Tune in Court" (*McClure's*, June 1900; see figure 3.8) included the reader as part of the action. In "Rabbi Eliezer's Christmas," the reader is depicted standing almost immediately behind Rabbi Eliezer, feeling the press of his customers crowding up to the counter. In "A Tune in Court," meanwhile, the reader is figured as part of the jury—or the judge, facing the courtroom crowd, and thus mirroring their own transfixion by the strains of the violin music being played by the young Italian boy Tinto during the story's climactic scene. The progression of postures along the line of men correlates with the gradual enchantment of the courtroom by the boy's music-making, as they gradually straighten from left to right, culminating in the alert, upright young doctor. The reader, like the courtroom and Tinto himself, is gradually transported to "fairyland itself upon the bridge-like, golden, vibrating notes of Schumann's 'Traumerei,' the dream song of dream songs."[27] What makes the illustration especially effective is Glackens's inspired decision to depict, at the climactic moment of the story, the audience's reaction to Tinto's playing. Rather than stress the pathos of a young immigrant boy facing a jury of disapproving elders, as one would guess would be most illustrators' initial impulse, Glackens illustrates the effect of the music on his listeners. He then imagines the reader into the story, by placing him in the jury box—in the place of judgment—and requiring him to imagine the boy playing, since Tinto is left out of the picture.

Figure 3.8. William Glackens, *A young doctor...*, illustration for "A Tune in Court," by Marion Hill, *McClure's*, June 1900: 174.

Glackens clearly paid close attention to details in the text and used them to provide visual entry points to its meaning. Other strategies engaged the reader much more viscerally, through dramatic foreshortening that made the characters seem to leap off the page, or by having the image intrude into the text columns (see figure 3.9). These images, like those placing the reader on the same perspectival plane, physically connect the reader to the image. Even more, they create a multidimensional "space" that includes the text and image on the page, the reader in her chair, and the events in narrative being constructed in her head. The reader becomes an active participant not just in the construction of the narrative, but also in the experience of reading itself, negotiating the gutter between the image and text, on the plane of the page, and the "gutter" of space between her own body and the page she is reading.[28]

Although Glackens's sketchy style implies that his illustration work was effortlessly and casually executed, extant drawings in the William Glackens collection at Nova Southeastern Art Museum show that Glackens worked deliberately and carefully to achieve these effects. We have already seen how Glackens used the seemingly improvised quality of the sketch to invite the reader into the opening scene of "Ingratitude of Rosenfeld" (introduction,

—DOUBLING HIS PACE, FLEW DOWN THE ALLEY

Figure 3.9. William Glackens, *Doubling His Pace, Flew Down Alley*, illustration for I. K. Friedman, "The Autobiography of a Beggar," *Saturday Evening Post* (December 27, 1902). William Glackens Illustration Collection, Helen Farr Sloan Library & Archives, Delaware Art Museum.

figure 4). A closer look at the drawing Glackens provided to *McClure's* shows the care with which he makes the empty chair the unexpected focal point of the illustration (figure 3.10): while the drawing almost exclusively uses charcoal, the seat of the chair is highlighted with strokes of white gouache, bringing the chair, already in the foreground, into sharp focus.[29]

Glackens also experimented with perspective and point of view to enhance the reader's affective response. In a scene from Myra Kelly's "The Wiles of the Wooer," the "scholar and salesman"[30] Isaac Blumberg is described jealously watching the object of his affections, Esther, fit a pair of gloves on a plump, self-satisfied truck driver. An exploratory sketch places the reader behind Esther, obscuring the view of her face while able to witness both the fawning smile of the driver as he tries on a glove, and Isaac glowering behind

Figure 3.10. Detail of William Glackens, drawing for "Ingratitude of Rosenfeld," with visible use of white gouache on chair seat. NSU Art Museum, Fort Lauderdale.

him in the background (see figure 3.11). In the drawing that was published with the story, the reader now occupies a vantage point that parallels that of Isaac, who is in fact the central consciousness of this scene (see figure 3.12). Taking rules of perspective into consideration, both the reader and Isaac are essentially equidistant from Esther and the driver, though the reader ostensibly has an even more revealing view. Though Isaac himself is less central to what is literally "happening" in this scene, the reader is directly invited to experience his feelings, which are at the center of Kelly's story, by taking on a similar perspective. One shares Isaac's mental image: "His poet's vision showed him the store full of men, Esther at the service of men, Esther smiling upon men; himself fitting rubbers to the feet of men, and Esther looking upon him in that position. It was more than he could endure" (540). Kelly's humorous exaggeration of Isaac's feelings is further exaggerated by the contrast between Isaac's pinched expression and the brewery driver's florid cheeks in Glackens's drawing.

While depicting faces was not one of Glackens's strengths, he took great pains to individuate his characters, again paying close attention to the textual descriptions offered by the author he was illustrating. Kelly notes on the first page of "The Wiles of the Wooer" that Esther Mogilewsky, the heroine, is a blonde, resting her "golden head" atop a pile of clothing (537). Glackens makes this image the center of the first illustration in the story.[31] In other stories by Myra Kelly,

Figure 3.11. William Glackens, rejected sketch for "Wiles of the Wooer" by Myra Kelly, NSU Art Museum, Fort Lauderdale; gift of the Sansom Foundation.

illustrators avoid individuation of character, either relying on the exaggerated physiognomy of ethnic caricature to indicate their characters' Jewish identity, or subsuming all of the characters under a general representational type—children, for example. Glackens's friend and fellow illustrator Florence Scovel Shinn took exactly the latter approach in two stories by Myra Kelly that she illustrated, "Love Among the Blackboards" (*McClure's*, March 1903; see figure 3.13) and "The Gifts of the Philosophers" (*Ladies' Home Journal*, Dec. 1904), where the characters are more definable by Shinn's personal style (one recognizable to many as a result of the fact that she had illustrated Alice Hegan Rice's bestselling 1901 novel *Mrs. Wiggs of the Cabbage Patch*) than by any characteristics Kelly gives them in her story—despite the fact that Kelly's characters are strongly differentiated and repeatedly appeared in the dozens of stories Kelly published in *McClure's* and elsewhere during the first two decades of the twentieth century.

The care Glackens took in differentiating his characters, and his resistance to caricature, was appreciated by his authors. Isaac Kahn Friedman, whose *The Beggar's Club* and *The Autobiography of a Beggar* were serialized in the *Saturday*

"With a brewery-driver's huge hand between her two slender ones"

Figure 3.12. William Glackens, *With a brewer-driver's huge hand between her two slender ones*, McClure's 29.5 (September 1907): 541.

Evening Post in 1902–1903 and later published in book form with Glackens's illustrations, thanked Glackens on the acknowledgments page "for his sympathetic pencil portraits and illustrations, without which the touching appeal of its members to the public for charity and forbearance might have been made in vain."[32] While it stops short of recognizing Glackens's ability to depict gesture and motion, Friedman's description of Glackens's illustrations as "pencil portraits" emphasizes strong characterization and depiction of individual identity.

Glackens's approach made him particularly suited to the works of an author whose ethnic code-switching and depictions of ethnic impersonation exceeded Lessing, Kelly, and Friedman: Edward Raphael Lipsett (1868–1931), author of a series of stories about "Denny the Jew from Ballintemple," which appeared in *Everybody's Magazine* between 1912–15. Like the fictional Leopold Bloom of James Joyce's *Ulysses*, Lipsett was Irish, Jewish, and peripatetic. Beginning in 1905, he began writing under the pseudonym "Halitvack" for the London-based *Jewish Chronicle*, telling stories of pious Russian Jews and describing bygone

Figure 3.13. Florence Scovel Shinn, headpiece for "Love Among the Blackboards" by Myra Kelly, *McClure's* (1903): 485.

Jewish traditions and religious practices in columns with titles such as "Yom Kippur as I Knew It" (October 6, 1905) and "Succoth as I Knew It" (October 13, 1905). As a Jew in Ireland, he felt misunderstood and out of place; in 1906, he wrote that "the term 'Irish Jew' seems to have a contradictory ring upon the native ear; the idea is wholly inconceivable to the native mind."[33] But he also found the Jewish community in Ireland "a stray, loose quantity, held together by nobody, caring for nothing"; he lamented the fact that his hometown of Cork was incapable of supporting even a single synagogue, despite being home to some seventy Jewish families.[34]

Seeking a more cohesive, vibrant Jewish community, he immigrated to the United States in 1907, drawn by the idea of joining the "greatest and mightiest Jewish city that probably ever was." But what he found was still lacking. "New York Ghetto Judaism is a Sham and a Lie," he wrote less than a year after arriving on American shores. He was appalled by the control that an uneducated and unscrupulous "Rabbonim" class maintained over the Jewish population, comparing them to "bosses" who profit by their self-proclaimed "Rav" status; "all they know is to work it for all it is worth in dollars and cents," he claimed.[35]

He also was appalled by the state of Jewish American letters. In "The Jewish Press in America," written soon after he arrived in the United States in July 1907, he averred that "American Jewry does not boast of a single *littérateur* of conspicuous merit" despite having some "eighty or ninety" newspapers appearing each week.³⁶ The Lower East Side was "practically bubbling over with humour and pathos at every step," but no Jewish writer had "come forward to scoop from it material for the magazines."

Perhaps referring obliquely to both Lessing and to Abraham Cahan, who had published fiction in magazines including the *Atlantic Monthly, Century, Scribner's,* and *Cosmopolitan,* Lipsett scoffed that the "one or two" Jewish writers of fiction in the United States were "only sickly, stupid specimens; they are the merest tyros, writing only so far as their limited, very limited, vigour goes; they are wholly unable to penetrate below the commonplace surface; they do not feel." He recognized only one writer who presented anything like "transcripts" of Jewish American life. "It begins and ends with Miss Myra Kelly, a lady of Irish descent," he wrote with thinly veiled disgust. Though he described her stories as "exceedingly pretty," he continued: "Her themes never are Jewish, and cannot be. The dialogue employed by her is neither the bad English such as is spoken in the Ghetto, nor the idiomatic Yiddish; it is all her own concoction, wholly unjustifiable and impossible, and that passes as Jewish work."

No wonder Lipsett took up the pen himself. While continuing to write his columns for the *Jewish Chronicle* as well as the American *Jewish Advocate,* which was published in Chicago, he developed a distinctive fictional style. In stories like "Baer's Last Rosh Hashana" (*Jewish Chronicle,* September 1, 1907) and "Mayer the Sinner" (*Jewish Chronicle,* April 24, 1908), he combined English, Hebrew (initially using Hebrew characters but eventually transliterated), Yiddish, and a smattering of other Eastern European languages in telling stories of the faithful, often returning to past times and European locales. These stories functioned as elegies to a lost—or forgotten—Jewish past, overshadowed by oppressive governments but bound together through an unwavering faith and strong communal ties. And they were written for a distinctly Jewish audience, including vocabulary, references to Jewish religious traditions, and cultural practices without gloss or explanation:

> It was neither Pesach, nor Succos, nor any other such season set aside for Israel only; but it was the season of judgment. The *Yom Hadin* was approaching, when all creatures, men of all beliefs and all races, were to be judged. *Steitz!* Was it not a morning for the entire world to arise in fear and trembling and hasten before God to crave His mercy? Baer felt it incumbent upon him to warn the Goyim, as well as the Yidden, to come to *Selichoth,* and if the Goyim did not come, Baer could not help it; he was sincerely sorry for them.³⁷

Lipsett's stories began appearing under the name "Halitvack" in Jewish American publications, including the *American Hebrew and Jewish Messenger* ("When Yenkel Was King," April 24, 1908) and the *Reform Advocate* of Chicago (the short novel *Two Pair of Misfits: A Romance of Old Pavonda*, July 9, 1910). But as "The Jewish Press in America" implied, he aimed higher, or at least, wider—for the national audience reached by writers like "Miss Myra Kelly."

To reach this audience, he made two strategic decisions: first, he adopted the ingenious conceit of "Denny the Jew from Ballintemple," a young Irish immigrant who decides to pass as Jewish; and second, he transformed the lament, elegy, and critique of his *Jewish Chronicle* pieces into comedy. In "Denny the Jew," Lipsett's narrator demonstrates an easy familiarity with the locale, the people, and the lingo of the Lower East Side, which he distinguishes as welcoming, accommodating, and assimilating rather than as impenetrably alien. Shifting easily between standard American English and Irish and Yiddish idiom, he portrays himself as literally conversant with the polyglot character of the area, though he does not clearly identify himself as the member of a particular ethnic or national community. Denny, his protagonist, is similarly intimate with but not part of the community. Though the title of the story declares Denny to be a Jew—not only *a* Jew, but "Denny *the* Jew"—at the outset of the story itself, Lipsett makes clear that Denny is, in fact, "not a Jew," having been born in Ireland and baptized Catholic, to boot.[38] Yet Denny's family, having come to the United States and having established a grocery on Monroe (locally known as "Manrole") Street, are easily accepted into the community, even though Denny's father Patrick Joseph declared that he "had nothing to do with thim frankfurters and pratie salad other fittle-fattles that thim furrin div'ls were making a business of in New York" (46). Associating processed food with the patent medicines that he ascribed to "furrin" swindlers, on his storefront sign he declares that his store provides "ALL PURE GROCERIES AND NO PILLS" (46).

Though he cannot "guarantee" the salt herrings that his customers demand, being a food he personally is unfamiliar with in either its character or its sourcing, he will supply them, and by pairing an accommodation of his customers' needs with the promise of wholesome, pure merchandise, the family establishes itself in the middle of the Jewish "ghetto." The meeting of the Nolan family and the Jewish members of the Lower East Side on a basis of common standing is depicted by Glackens in a street scene much like his *Far from the Fresh Air Farm*, but at street level rather than an elevated perspective (see figure 3.14). The viewer, too, seems to be on the street, not perceiving "Manrole" Street as a colorful spectacle so much as a participant. The people on the street are oblivious to the viewer, marking her either as unseen or unnoteworthy—which is as much an indication of acceptance of the viewer within the space as it could be a sign of unfriendliness. Most notable in the illustration is the lack of caricature to mark the ethnic character of the region. While the architecture and presence of peddlers' carts place the scene on the Lower East Side, Glackens depicts a range of clothing, hair color, and physiognomy; and while the English words on Patrick Nolan's shop-window sign are visible on the left side of the illustration, they are barely sketched in, included as a part of the general scene rather than a focal point.

After Denny's father Patrick Nolan returns to Ireland for a "home visit," he loses a leg in an accident, and when he finally returns to the United States, he is denied entrance at Ellis Island and is subsequently deported back to Ireland due to his inability to contribute able-bodied labor to the American economy. Denny, despondent, discovers in discussions with his new friends Ikey Seltzer and Sam Knoploch that Ikey's family had once prevailed upon the Hebrew Aid Society to help his Russian uncle—who, like Denny's father, is disabled with a wooden leg—gain admittance to the US. Denny writes to his father suggesting they do the same. The important thing, he stresses, is that they have to prove they are Jews, or "Sheenies," as he puts it:

> dear daddy bring the wooden leg but dont forget to tellem you are a sheeny and talk to them in sheeny langwids sheeny is a yid and a leg is a fus and money is gelt and kimshon is be quick about it me and minnie is sheenys already and we are going to tellem to look out for you in ellis island . . .

Patrick is slow to take up these suggestions, but Denny nevertheless is successful at convincing the Hebrew Aid Society, with all the "sheeny langwids" he knows, to help his family. The agent from the society tells Denny's wondering mother, "You see, ma'am, we Jews want to help all we can, strangers as well as our own" (54). Over the course of subsequent stories, all published in *Everybody's*, Denny, as a result of his assimilation to Jewish culture, is able to secure his father's return to the family, gets his sister Minnie enrolled in the Jewish kindergarten, obtains gainful employment as a newsboy selling Jewish newspapers, and even gets his father a job, cork leg and all—as a janitor for a synagogue (a longstanding position for the goyim in Jewish communities, because they are able to open and close the synagogue on the Sabbath).

Denny is convinced that the Nolans are able to regain their foothold in American society because they have become more Jewish. Seeing his father working at the synagogue next to his new boss, Barney Schmaltz, he thinks proudly that he "could not tell which was the real boss. . . . At last he had made a Sheenie and a man of him."[39] Though Denny doesn't realize that the Jews

THE ONLY THINGS PATRICK JOSEPH WOULD NOT GUARANTEE WERE THE SALT HERRINGS WHICH HIS YIDDISH CUSTOMERS PERSISTED IN EATING RAW. BUT THEY CAME AGAIN AND LOOKED NONE THE WORSE.

Figure 3.14. William Glackens, *The only things Patrick Joseph would not guarantee were the salt herrings which his Yiddish customers persisted in eating raw . . .* , illustration for "Denny the Jew" by Edward Raphael Lipsett. *Collier's* 27 (July 1912): 47.

Figure 3.15. William Glackens, *She sang the Hatikvah in her thin, metallic voice*. Illustration for "The Amateur Jew" by Edward Raphael Lipsett, *Collier's* 32 (June 1915): 773.

in their new community know full well that the Nolans are not Jewish, this awareness is immaterial to Lipsett's point. In 1908, Lipsett wrote in the *Jewish Chronicle* that despite the corruption of the leadership of the Jewish community in New York, they had "not yet killed the right Jewish spirit of New York. The finest gem in the crown of Jewry, Jewish charitableness, shines resplendent."[40] In the *Chronicle* and elsewhere, he wrote that this "charitableness," generosity, and hospitality were hallmarks of American Jewish culture and needed to be recognized and cultivated. "With all its faults and failings, long live New York!"[41]

Glackens's illustrations for "The Amateur Jew" (1915) underscore Lipsett's notion that the issue was not whether or not Jews could or should assimilate to

American culture—as was the predominant theme of literature of the time—but rather, the notion that the Jewish community was happy to accommodate the American. Near the end of the story, when challenged to prove his family is indeed Jewish, Denny calls on his sister Minnie to sing the Hatikvah (now the national anthem of Israel), which she has learned in school. She does so beautifully, and Glackens's illustration shows Minnie surrounded by the Jewish boys, with Denny proudly standing next to her and among them (see figure 3.15). If Lipsett sounded and amplified the "contradictory ring" of hybridized identity in his stories, Glackens naturalized these identities through his resistance to type, the casual use of sketch, and informal (but carefully constructed) composition.

In a 1931 exhibition catalog, friend and art critic Guy Pène du Bois remarked of Glackens's illustrations that they "supplemented the writer's text in a way that few illustrations have ever done. They fulfilled characters and scenes but half drawn in the text, lent color, built form, where it was but faintly suggested."[42] Yet I would argue that those suggestions, even if faint, were necessary to give Glackens's work human form in the fullest sense of the term. Writing of Glackens's large drawings for *Collier's*, Rebecca Zurier notes that their elevated perspective conveyed the "psychological distance appropriate to Glackens's vision of the city" even as they constituted the apogee of the "cartoonist's art."[43] It may have taken the imaginative power of story and speech to bring Glackens down to street level, and to fulfill his comic potential.

CHAPTER FOUR

The Black Comic Sensibility

"Why did they make it seem funny, *only* funny?"
—Ralph Ellison, *Invisible Man*[1]

Historian Ian Gordon argues that while early comic artists reveled in the shifting notions of identity that characterized the urban, "polychromatic" environments of New York City and San Francisco, their playful treatment of ethnic identity did not extend to African Americans. He writes that Jewish, Irish, and German comic artists did not simply exclude blacks from the communal intimacy enabled by the comic sensibility; they were actively "allied" against them.[2] One need merely skim the comics supplement of any major newspaper of the era to see his point. E. W. Kemble, for example, made his fortune specializing in dehumanizing depictions of "pickanninnies," "coons," and "blackberries"; William Marriner's *Sambo* came to embody the type of the gullible, unintelligible Negro, and Richard F. Outcault's *Li'l Mose* featured a "cur'ous lil coon" who, happily, "never had no work to do but only jest to play."[3] Others, including Dirks, in *The Katzenjammer Kids*, and Winsor McCay, in *Little Nemo*, portrayed blacks as primitive, tribal figures, half-naked, grass-skirted, with bones through their noses. These strips support novelist (and one-time comic strip artist) Charles Johnson's claim that "these creators knew nothing—absolutely nothing—about their black subjects."[4]

Meanwhile, comics historians would have you know that no comic strips by African Americans, about African Americans, and created expressly for African Americans were produced before the 1920s. It was only in this decade that an autonomous African American print culture coalesced in the wake of the Great

Migration and the Harlem Renaissance.[5] African American cartoonist Ollie Harrington, who emerged at this time, claimed that white cartoonists "did not envision ... black Americans as their audience. We were not part of the artist/audience equation."[6] Nevertheless, African Americans were comic strip readers from the very start. As early as 1900, black newspapers casually described characters or situations as falling under a generic "comic weekly type," and Pulitzer advertised in black newspapers during the first two decades of the twentieth century, offering the comics supplement of the *New York World* as an enticement to potential subscribers. Several newspapers also mentioned or reprinted editorials bemoaning the deleterious effects of comics on societal mores—of blacks as well as whites. The black newspaper the *Washington Bee* of September 1, 1906, for example, recommended a "timely article" in the August 18 issue of the *Literary Digest* "on the comic supplement, issued in connection with many Sunday papers," which had generated "many protests";[7] in 1908, the *Savannah Tribune* reprinted an essay by the white cultural critic Agnes Repplier titled "A Censor of the Press," where she described the comics as being "designed for the exclusive refreshment of the feeble-minded ... a blight upon the intelligence of youth" (May 9, 1908).[8] (The *Savannah Tribune*, it should be noted, was one of several black newspapers that actually published cartoons at the time.)

What did blacks find funny about the funnies? Perhaps they did not actually find them funny—except in the "peculiar" sense. Perhaps they were simply remaining conversant with contemporary mainstream popular culture. Perhaps they ignored or resigned themselves to racist depictions—racism, after all, infused nearly all aspects of American popular culture at the turn into the twentieth century. Perhaps they read *around* the racism, appreciating aspects of the comics outside of the demeaning depictions of blacks. Certainly one can enjoy the fantastic composition and lush coloring of McCay's *Little Nemo in Slumberland* at the same time that one condemns the characterization of Impy. Or perhaps black readers pushed back—read *against*—the comics. Writing specifically of the comics, Frances Gateward and John Jennings write about the ways that ink itself creates opportunities for pure signifying:

> The ink used in comics is not only physically and formally perceived to be the neutral of black; it is also the reification of "Blackness" in the modern sense. If you think of the ink container as the Black body, it completes this metaphor. The container is merely a vessel for the flexible, mutable, liminal nature of ink. It is no wonder that Rorschach tests are made with it. Ink holds vitality, potential, unpredictability, and the very nature of creation within its affordances, as does any medium for that matter. It resists being codified, tamed, or caged—Luke Cage notwithstanding.[9]

As Eric Lott has argued, demeaning representations of blacks need not represent a single power dynamic: "The blackface mask," he writes, is "less a *repetition* of power relations than a *signifier* for them—a distorted mirror, reflecting displacements and condensations and discontinuities between which and the social field there exist lags, unevennesses, multiple determinations."[10] If we think of black caricature in the early comic strip as a negotiated site of meaning, like blackface minstrelsy, it is possible to see that it, too, raises questions about what race means by virtue of its *difference* from actual black people. A space thereby opens for black readers to become active readers of the comics, solidifying and even empowering a black comics-reading audience that would eventually produce comic strips that were by, about, and for blacks.

Black caricature in early comic strips, I would suggest, is characterized by visible voids, black spaces that are not quite shapes (see figure 4.1). While black caricature occupies space in the image, it functions more as a shadow or a negation, as is the case with the blackface mask, than as a fully fleshed-out figure in and of itself. Its representation of absence or negation, or alternately as the embodiment of the "flexible, mutable, liminal nature of ink," as Gateward and Jennings write, is precisely what enables it to function as a space from which different meanings might emerge. In many ways, it functions as the inverse—a turning-inside-out rather than simply a reversal—of the white, blank gutter between the panels. Like the gutter, black caricature requires readers to enact closure. However, the kind of closure that can be achieved depends heavily on how the reader views blackness. Is caricature a way of representing the unknown and feared, as was the case for many whites? Or is it an imposition, a representation that dictates how one is seen? Nicholas Sammond attributes the appeal of racialized performances like blackface minstrelsy and black caricature to its "recourse to blackness as a fantastic primal realm and force," where readers and viewers can imagine without acting upon urges to "disrupt or rewrite the social order."[11] For black readers, the black figure also could function as a site for the enactment of double consciousness, the "peculiar sensation of looking at one's self through the eyes of others, of measuring one's soul by the tape of a world that looks on in amused contempt and pity."[12]

While double consciousness was, in large part, recognized and experienced by the reader, it also was intentionally invoked by comic strip artists. We can see this intentional invocation in the work of two early comic strip pioneers: George Herriman, a mixed-race Creole who chose to pass as white, and his friend Jimmy Swinnerton, a white Californian who gained his first professional success "blacking up" in minstrel shows. Swinnerton and Herriman turned black caricature on its head. They refused to accept its blackening annihilation of humanity, and instead offered it up as a representation of the state of

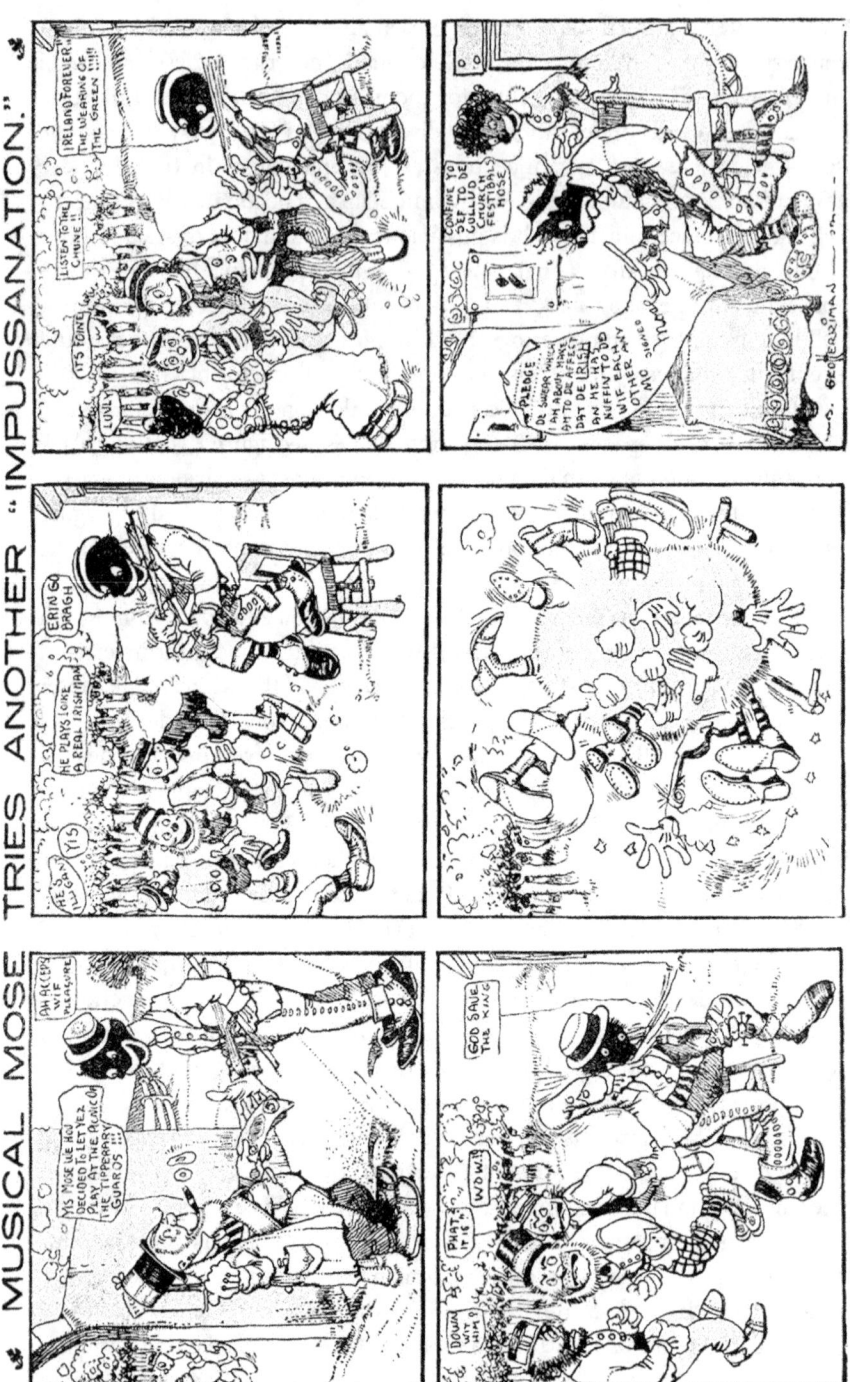

Figure 4.1. George Herriman, "Musical Mose Tries Another 'Impussonation,'" *New York World*, February 23, 1902.

double consciousness itself. In doing so, they were able to "change the joke" and thereby "slip the yoke": like Ralph Ellison's Invisible Man, they transformed laughter generated solely at the expense of blacks into a wry laughter rising out of an understanding of the absurdity of race relations in the United States, what Ellison called "the joke at the center of the American identity."[13] This laughter, elicited despite—or in the face of—worsening conditions for blacks following the 1896 *Plessy v. Ferguson* decision, forms the basis of what we might call a black comic sensibility. As Ellison said in 1970, "We couldn't escape, so we developed a style of humor which recognized the basic artificiality, the irrationality, of the actual arrangement."[14]

For Swinnerton and Herriman, black comic sensibility emerged first in comic strips and cartoons that appeared in the hurly-burly, nether regions of the newspaper, the sporting sections. On the sports page, ironically, black athletes were afforded a humanity they were denied on the front page. Later, this sensibility informed the more family-oriented fare they created for the Sunday supplements, including Swinnerton's *Sam and His Laugh* (1905–1906) and ultimately, Herriman's transcendently tragicomic *Krazy Kat* (1913–44). These manifestations of black comic sensibility exhibited a sensitive awareness of Du Boisian double consciousness that exposed the fundamental irony of American democracy, separate but nevertheless, supposedly, equal.

Jimmy, Sam, and Blackface Laughter

James Swinnerton was discovered by Hearst in San Francisco in the early 1890s. At the advanced age of sixteen, Swinnerton had already lived a colorful life: after running away from home when he was fourteen years old, he worked as an exercise boy at the San Francisco Bay District Fairgrounds Race Track, and then traveled for several months with one of W. S. Cleveland's minstrel troupes.[15] It may be that Swinnerton's unusual physiognomy, as much as his comedic talent, provided his entrée into blackface minstrelsy: friends described him as having "a face like a frog,"[16] and in an 1894 interview, Swinnerton claimed that "[b]ecause of my large mouth and peculiar face, I made quite a hit as the negro kid and had the position next to the end man, with the promise of elevation to that highest pinnacle of minstrel fame, the End Man's chair."[17] He was offered the generous salary of $20 per week but declined when his father agreed to send him to art school instead. Swinnerton related his father's view of the matter: "'I'd rather you'd become a minstrel than a lawyer,' he said, 'but it's minstrels or the art school, so pack your traps and take the morning train for the school.'"[18] Despite his turn to the higher arts, Swinnerton did not abandon

Figure 4.2. "Dear Reader, Please Permit Us to Present to You Sam!" *Chicago Sunday American*, March 1, 1905. San Francisco Academy of Comic Art Collection, Ohio State University, Billy Ireland Cartoon Library & Museum.

blackface altogether. He "blacked up" on occasion throughout his life, and the visual, verbal, and situational rhetoric of minstrelsy infused his cartoons and comic strips from the beginning of his career.

The influence of blackface minstrelsy on Swinnerton's comic sensibility is most apparent in his strip *Sam and His Laugh*, which ran in the Hearst Sunday supplements from 1905 to 1906. By this time, Swinnerton was working at Hearst's *New York Journal* and had become a bedrock member of Hearst's comics staff. The running gag of *Sam and His Laugh*—itself a concept originating in the minstrel show—is that Sam, an ungainly black man, is hired and then subsequently fired when he is unable to contain his mirth at the absurd behavior of his employers and customers. Drawn with a froglike head, an impossibly wide mouth, and garish, colorful clothing, Sam is hardly recognizable as a human figure. Yet his simultaneous aping and mocking of both white behavior and what was assumed to be "proper" black behavior replicates the multivalent form of mimicry that gave minstrelsy its problematic force.

Swinnerton establishes Sam as a knowing mirror of white behavior and perception in the very first installment of his strip. A wealthy white man hires Sam to answer the door and announce guests at a tony party and gives Sam one of his old tuxedos to wear for the occasion. In the second panel, Sam looks over his shoulder at himself at the mirror and notes that "it's lucky de boss's got d'same shape I got. His old suit fits me fine!" This observation is already suggested to the reader in the previous panel, where the two characters are drawn in profile, facing (and thus mirroring) one another, both in complementary suits, similarly styled shoes, and with rounded bellies and bald pates (see figure 4.2). He continues to mirror his social superiors throughout the strip, with his black-and-white tuxedo, white gloves, and his aforementioned shape, which is similar not only to that of his employer, but also his guests (panels 3, 5, and 8). As the strip progresses, Sam becomes increasingly indistinguishable from the guests at the party, culminating in the final few panels, where doorman and guest alike are depicted with fists flying, coattails flapping, legs jack-knifed.

This implied equality—or even superiority, in the case of the diminutive German dignitary Sam is expected to introduce—is literally upended when Sam is kicked out of the house and tumbles, head over heels, down the front steps in the penultimate frame. But Sam gets the last laugh. The mirroring and inversion of white and black characters in this strip do not simply result in a reversion to the status quo. Instead, the supposedly defeated and debased Sam finally announces the petite count with a name of his own choosing. While the owner of the mansion may remain in a position of economic and social power, Sam's laughter constitutes a rejection of that status. He begins the strip in want of employment, with a job's promise of meaningful labor and monetary compensation, and ends it in a state of amused, carefree leisure. The kind of work he is offered by the rich, he realizes, dehumanizes rather than uplifts.

Swinnerton establishes the relationship between Sam and his various employers as being much like that between the "end man" and the interlocutor of the minstrel show. The interlocutor plays the role of the "white presence" on the minstrel stage: he speaks in grammatically correct, often rhetorically inflated language, is often well dressed, and positions himself in other ways above the other members of the minstrel troupe—the endmen in particular—and the audience. Mel Watkins writes of the interlocutor that "his pompous, exaggeratedly elitist demeanor was in direct contrast to the wild antics and preposterous language of the endmen, for whom he functioned as a straight man."[19] While the endmen, Tambo and Bones, are ignorant, sensuous, and violent, their performances use those stereotypes to deflate the pretensions of those who consider themselves civilized and sophisticated. Thus, while perpetuating negative stereotypes of blacks, minstrelsy also, as W. T. Lhamon Jr. has written, "saps racism from within."[20]

Nowhere does the double edge of minstrelsy cut deeper than in "Sam as a Magician's Confederate," published on April 30, 1905 (see figure 4.3). Here, a magician hires Sam as his assistant. He loads Sam up with various props and orders him to "jump up quickly" when he asks for a volunteer. This cunning plan falls apart almost immediately, when the magician calls for a "gentleman" to "kindly step forward." Sam begins to chuckle, one assumes, because he knows the magician most certainly does not consider him a gentleman; moreover, anyone who might step forward doesn't do so in the spirit of altruistic kindness, but rather, out of a desire to be entertained, or a self-centered desire to be the focus of the audience's attention. Sam's laughter escalates when the magician declares that the audience can "plainly see" that he "is no confederate." As Sam doubles over in laughter, the magician's props spill forth, revealing Sam's incompetence as an assistant, and eliciting both delight and rage on the part of the audience. In the final panel, Sam is, of course, still laughing at the prospect of being the magician's "comfeberit." "Wow!" he exclaims, in wonder.

The strip, of course, depends on the multiple meanings of the word "confederate," highlighted through the malapropism Swinnerton introduces in the final frame. What exactly *is* a confederate—or a comfeberit, for that matter? While Sam agrees to act as the magician's confederate, it is, in fact plainly seen that the magician does not consider him an active assistant, a contributor to the act, but rather, little more than a prop, a human version of the rabbit Sam is left holding in the final panel of the strip. The magician does not hire him because he is a gentleman, because he is kind, or because he is intelligent—characteristics he highlights in the course of his act. In reality, he hires him for the unstated but

Figure 4.3: "Sam as a Magician's Confederate." *Chicago Sunday American*, April 30, 1905. San Francisco Academy of Comic Art Collection, Ohio State University, Billy Ireland Cartoon Library & Museum.

obvious reason that he is highly unlikely to be confederated with the magician in a society increasingly segregated by race. Sam is also highly unlikely to be a confederate in another sense that again called the contemporary racial environment to mind: it is plain to see that Sam was not likely to have been a Confederate, or a Confederate sympathizer, in the Civil War. To be identified as such, when the truth could be so plainly seen, is either an instance of utter obtuseness or an attempt at fraud.

Yet the magician's easy assumption that Sam will go along with the act, that he will allow the magician to "fix" him up and do whatever he is told, also reflects the presumptuousness of many whites who assumed that blacks were simply too stupid, too docile, or too incapable of independent action to resist the trickery in which they were expected to act as willing accomplices. By leaving Sam with the rabbit at the end of the strip, Swinnerton implies again that while Sam may be out of a job, he also has left behind the role of the dupe and overtaken the role of the trickster. Not only is Sam left in possession of the magician's most identifiable prop, he also mirrors the rabbit in ways that align him with another well-known trickster figure, Br'er Rabbit. Swinnerton depicts Sam *acting* like an ignorant, inarticulate buffoon (as he is perceived to be since he is, of course, black) in order to send up the *actual* buffoon, the magician.

In this strip, and throughout the run of *Sam and His Laugh*, Swinnerton's humor depends on the notion that race—whether black or white—is a role to be performed, not something embodied. In Sam's search for employment, he is asked to play a variety of roles, sometimes menial jobs commonly identified with African Americans (doorman, gardener, handyman, servant), sometimes in jobs where his racial identity appears incongruous (artist's model, stage actor). In one notable strip from July 1905, he is hired to play "The Famous Wild Man of Zanzibar" in a carnival sideshow. He is stripped of his clothes, given a false, bristly beard, a headdress, and a club, and instructed to "keep on growling all the time and look as fierce as you can." Sam is unable to sustain the fiction, as he dissolves predictably into laughter once he faces his awestruck audience. After months of taking on menial jobs, Sam is now paid to act the savage that the audience already assumes him to be. Yet when one of the audience members cries out that Sam "ain't no wild man," his growls can't help but dissolve into human—civilized—laughter. The strip ends with Sam bursting free of the carnival tent and his manacles, growling and laughing in equal measure: "Gr-r-r-r! HO! HO! HO!"[21]

As Sam takes on various roles, it becomes clear that his employers, too, are also playing roles that are sometimes as incongruous as the ones Sam is expected to play. Whether they present themselves as captains of industry, society types, artists and actors, or laborers in their own right, they are all, like Sam, performing an act, an act often wrapped up in a fraudulent self-portrayal.[22] The incongruity between his employers and the postures they adopt to enforce their positions of dominance spurs Sam's incredulous laughter. *Sam and His Laugh* provides a counterpoint to other strips running in the Hearst comics supplement during the period, including Frederick Opper's foundational strip *Happy Hooligan*, which was based on a similar conceit but with a less liberatory ending. In Opper's strip, Happy seeks out employment, but is not only fired, but jailed, when his attempts to help others go awry. While Happy's name denotes one affective state, he ends each strip in a state of confusion and despair. Swinnerton's Sam, in contrast, revels in his rejection.

In this sense, Sam functions much like the earliest versions of Jim Crow. While the character came to represent the most denigrating aspects of racial stereotyping, Lhamon writes that T. D. Rice's original performances as the character in the 1830s figured "the very opposite of the segregation he came to signify ... Jim Crow figured freedom, integration, and unity ... He lambasted a culture that could declare all men are created equal but leave multitudes in chains, disfranchised and disdained." Both Lott and Lhamon identify the black minstrel as a signifier of class as much as race, or perhaps more specifically, as signifying class *through* race, where blackness becomes a marker for both dispossession and enslavement, both literally and figuratively. As a result, Jim Crow was a figure with which the working class of the 1850s strongly identified, even loved.

Of Rice's performance, Lhamon writes, "This lumpen trickster figure, the lowest of the low, charismatically represented for disaffected white clerks and artisans, along with the white and black underclass, their mutual resentment at exclusion. His performance diagnosed their dilemma and demonstrated one way to spin free of it." Sammond notes that as the blackface minstrel continued to appear in increasingly "vestigial" forms as repeating characters in comic strips and then in animated features, he (and sometimes she) takes the representation of enslaved labor and "does his live cousin one better in this regard: he is actually created by the very forces of regulation and domination he resists."[23] The increasingly imbricated contradictions contained in the void of the blackface mask made the connection between blackface and working-class resistance more and more difficult to recognize, or perhaps, easier and easier to ignore. As Lhamon writes, the "blackface lore" surrounding the minstrel figure "comprises American winks so sublimated that even the many racist and antidemocratic Americans who are mocked within it cannot or will not read its contrarian content."[24]

And yet—and yet. It is difficult to believe that Swinnerton's readers would have been blind to Sam's winks. Not even five years earlier, in August 1900, New

York City had been rocked by race riots spurred by the perceived threat posed by the large numbers of African Americans migrating north after the failure or Reconstruction. Poor whites—especially, the Irish—competed with blacks for adequate housing, and they believed that blacks would be willing to work for less pay. During the riots, blacks were beaten with impunity, frequently at the hands of the policemen who were ostensibly tasked with their protection. James Weldon Johnson described a "brutish orgy, which, if it was not incited by the police, was, to say the least, abetted by them."[25] According to historian Gilbert Osofsky, there were "no reliable estimates of the number of persons injured in the riot," though "any Negro who happened to be on the streets of the Tenderloin that night [August 15, 1900] was attacked and beaten."[26] Blacks initially responded fearfully—many workers sought shelter at their places of employment, rather than attempt to traverse the city streets—but within the next day or two, local newspapers, including the *New York World*, reported that many took up arms to be able to defend themselves against future reprisals. Clashes between blacks and whites continued for weeks, and a coalition of prominent black and white New Yorkers formed the Citizens' Protective League in early September to bring white policemen, in particular, to justice. However, a grand jury refused to indict them, and other cases against policemen brought to trial were duly dismissed.[27]

Contemporary accounts of the riots are contradictory and predictably biased, while the historical record is filled with lacunae. One of the most interesting, yet puzzling, aspects of the race riots is how quickly they faded from public memory. Historian Martha Hodes writes that while coverage of the riots was widespread in national media, "that knowledge and its circulation did not result in justice, or in any meaningful action at all." Osofsky notes that "Negroes of 'the old Knickerbocker stamp,' . . . ('the best people,' 'aristocratic dark race circles')," felt little connection with poor black migrants from the South, and they may have very well turned a blind eye to the violence that might act as a deterrent to future black migration.[28] Still, the New York riots were not a singular event. Mob violence had erupted in New Orleans, Louisiana, and Akron, Ohio, in previous months, and continued throughout the decade. The riots, along with the dramatic rise in lynchings during this period, made racial violence a frequent topic of discussion in the popular press. Swinnerton frequented the dives and saloons in the sorts of regions where the New York riots took place and may have even experienced them at first hand.

Hodes argues that any critique of the official response to the riots "was overwhelmed and overpowered by the justifications of those who embraced and furthered Jim Crow racism."[29] One might ask, then, whether *Sam and His Laugh* constitutes an expression of these justifications, or if they offer, four and a half years after the fact, a gentle, but no less startling, rebuke to them. On the one hand, if Sam, a black man who treats whites with contemptuous amusement, could elicit laughter from readers, that could demonstrate how completely the threat of racial violence had been squelched under the white supremacist assumptions of Jim Crow. On the other, the very fact that Sam's contemptuousness was tolerated—in the popular press, no less—could be seen as evidence that white supremacy was not total or uniform.

Complicating the matter is the fact that *Sam and His Laugh* may have been an adaptation of—or inspired by—an earlier strip created by his friend George Herriman. The two certainly knew each other by 1904, when Herriman arrived at the *New York Journal*, where Swinnerton had been ensconced since 1902.[30] Early in 1902, one of Herriman's first continuing-character strips, *Musical Mose*, appeared in the pages of the *Journal*'s primary competitor, Joseph Pulitzer's *New York World*, and it's likely that Swinnerton had seen them (see figure 4.1). After Herriman joined Hearst's staff, the two artists became lifelong friends, sharing not just an occupation, but also their Californian childhoods, a love for the desert Southwest landscape (where Swinnerton would live almost exclusively after 1906), and possibly a love for the same woman (Swinnerton's wife, Louise, with whom Herriman maintained a deep friendship and intimate correspondence). Friends remember both men as outsiders. They recall Swinnerton affecting the "cowboy" image on the streets of New York, sporting leather chaps, a bandanna, and cowboy hat. And Herriman was a cipher to all of his fellow *Journal* artists. As Thomas "Tad" Dorgan, one of his closest friends at the time, recalled in 1924: "He looked like a cross between Omar the tent maker and Nervy Nat when he eased into the art room. . . . We didn't know what he was, so I named him the Greek, and he still goes by that name."[31]

Neither Greek nor Arabian, Herriman was born in New Orleans into a mixed-race family with a complicated history. While biographer Michael Tisserand describes the family as being filled with "political radicals," he also notes that Herriman's grandfather and possibly namesake enlisted in the Confederate Army during the Civil War. After witnessing the failure of Reconstruction, Herriman's parents picked up the family and moved to Los Angeles when George was ten years old, choosing to pass into what they hoped would be a better life.[32] Herriman never publicly revealed exactly "what he was." He famously wore a hat, ostensibly to cover the curly hair that would disambiguate his racial-ethnic identity. It was not until the 1980s that his mixed-race background was confirmed by historians. Since then, critics, biographers, and fans have been compelled to reassess his career.

Essentialist arguments aside, the question remains: what difference does race make in Herriman's work? Nearly all attention has focused on his best-known strip, *Krazy Kat*, which depicts the black Krazy Kat and the white Ignatz Mouse in a supremely dysfunctional love-hate relationship.[33] Before Krazy ever appeared on the boards, however, Herriman had originated over a dozen other serial strips, including *Musical Mose*, and had also drawn hundreds, if not thousands, of stand-alone strips and cartoons for the World Publishing Syndicate, the weekly humor magazine *Judge*, the *New York Daily News*, Hearst's *Journal*, and the *Los Angeles Examiner*, another Hearst publication. While the racial allegory in *Krazy Kat* is veiled, if not intentionally obscured, it appears much more clearly in the strips and cartoons Herriman produced in his early career, particularly in cartoons drawn for the sports pages of the *Los Angeles Examiner*, published in the city he considered "his only home."[34] As we will see, these comics, like *Sam and His Laugh*, present knowing, if often marginalized or suppressed, black observers who comment—often nonverbally, and always ambivalently—on racial politics in the turn-of-the-century United States; they are visual manifestations of Du Boisian double consciousness.

The gag on which *Musical Mose* was based was similar, but not identical, to that of *Sam and His Laugh*. Mose is always employed as a musician, rather than being assigned to different jobs. However, he adopts different musical styles: he pretends to be a Scottish bagpiper in one strip, an Irish fiddler or an Italian organ-grinder in others. Rather than just playing the music in different styles, Mose believes he can actually "pass" as a Scottish, Irish, or Italian *musician*; "Ise a l'il bit tanned des all," he says when a skeptical Italian questions his ethnic identity. As it turns out, he fails to execute the various ethnic "impussanations" he attempts. When the fraud is recognized, Mose is beaten and duly fired. Each installment of *Sam and His Laugh*, as we have seen, ends with Sam literally rolling on the ground in defiant laughter. Mose, in contrast, regrets his transgressions: the last panel of each strip ends with his baleful renunciation of musical impersonation and the scolding of his wife, who implores him to respect conventional ethnic-racial boundaries. "Why didn't yo impussanate a cannibal?" she asks when Mose's experiment as a Scottish bagpiper goes awry. "Confine yo sef to cullud church festibals," she chides in another strip. Mose, for his part, simply wishes "mah color would fade," even though his failures are not simply due to the audience's recognition of his physical features as belonging to a "nig," but also due to his inability to sustain a believable impersonation. When hired to play for a group of Irish nationalists, he lapses into a rendition of the British anthem "God Save the King," and suffers the predictable consequences.[35]

While *Sam and His Laugh* renders, in comic strip form, the situational and rhetorical strategies of blackface minstrel performance, Herriman in *Musical Mose* imagines a black performer who attempts to abandon the minstrel stage, to escape what Lhamon describes as the "fetish figure" of Jim Crow. However, he is unable to escape the blackface mask. He can never be anything but a "nig," the object of ridicule, recipient of blows, the lowliest of the low. Whether or not *Musical Mose* reflected Herriman's personal anxieties as a mixed-race Californian trying to succeed in New York, it conveys the very real limitations imposed on blacks who might attempt to occupy a different station in life, to sing a different sort of tune. Though the comedy here is muted at best, Herriman's Mose, like Swinnerton's Sam and the early manifestations of Jim Crow, represented the desire, the imagined possibility, of "freedom, integration, and unity," while at the same time demonstrating how far American society was from the realization of these ideals. For Mose, unfortunately, blackness was a void that in the end could be filled with nothing but its own blackness.

Aside from the short-lived *Musical Mose*, the strips that Herriman created for the Sunday supplements in the first decade or so of the twentieth century generally avoided a head-on confrontation with race. However, as Jared Gardner and Michael Tisserand have documented, the absence of explicit references to race or depictions of African Americans does not mean that Herriman excluded racial issues from his work. Instead, he appears to have masked them—in a sense, he put a mask on the blackface mask itself—by inserting a figure in his strips that embodied what might be described as the lived experience of African American double consciousness without needing to resort to blackface caricature, the socially accepted sign of African American identity. Before Krazy Kat appeared in 1911, a black cat played a recurring role as observer and mostly silent commentator in strips including *Mrs. Waitaminnit, Lariat Pete, Major Ozone's Fresh Air Campaign*, and various single-panel cartoons and illustrations.[36] The cat appearing in these strips, Gardner writes, "is for the most part a mute witness to the events set in motion by the bumbling human actors. The cat's expression changes, from amusement, to concern, to terror, but ultimately it offers no explicit commentary.... And yet, we cannot help but focus on the cat, whose movements and insights seem often more engaging and original than the predictable slapstick being played for broad effect in the center of the panel."[37]

Herriman's cats and Swinnerton's Sam, in short, offer interpretations and imply critiques of white-dominated society through nonverbal means; they operate outside "official" modes of discourse. Sam laughs; he mimics the forms and postures of his white employers. Even though he is fired for his insubordination, and thus is disciplined through official channels, his laughter is a flouting of that discipline. Black laughter, Mel Watkins reminds us, to this day produces "confusion, consternation, and bafflement among whites," constituting an unintelligible yet discernible threat to white superiority.[38] Herriman's cats also mock white behavior and postures, not just bearing silent witness but also passing silent judgment.

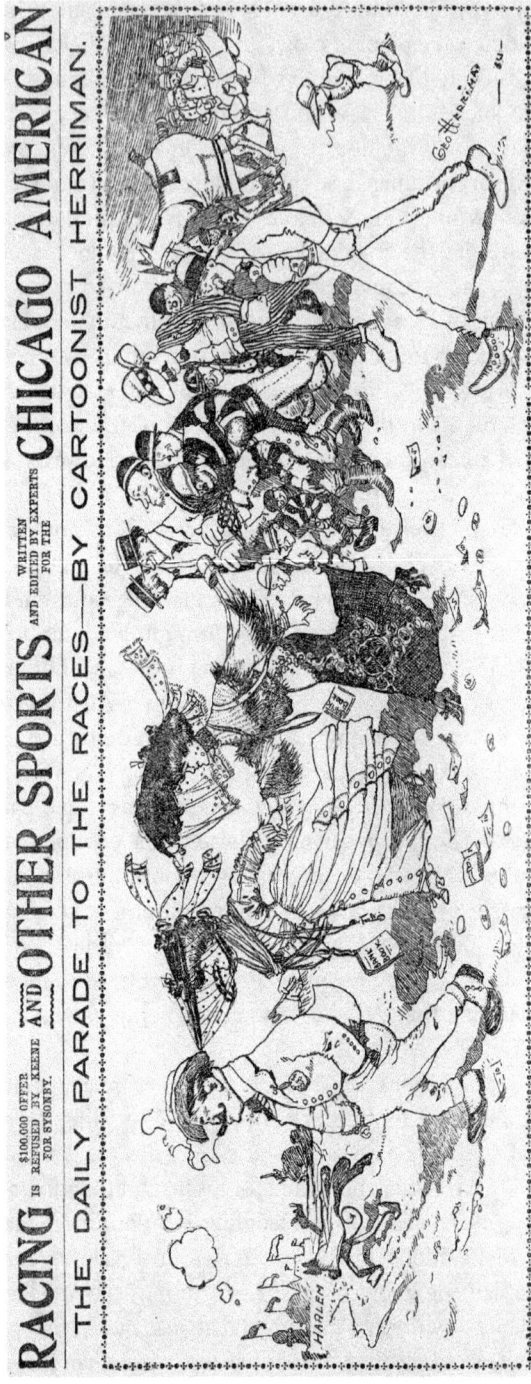

Figure 4.4. "The Daily Parade to the Races," *Chicago American*, August 3, 1904. The *Chicago American* was part of Hearst's national network of newspapers, along with the *Los Angeles Examiner*, where Herriman was employed at the time. It appears, however, that Herriman drew this cartoon for the *Chicago American*, as it depicts the Harlem Race Track located in what is now the Chicago suburb of Forest Park. San Francisco Academy of Comic Art Collection, Ohio State University, Billy Ireland Cartoon Library & Museum.

The observational role played by the family cat is played by human characters in Herriman's sporting cartoons and strips, which appeared almost daily in the *Los Angeles Examiner* and other newspapers between 1904–1910 and comprise a major, yet almost completely neglected, part of Herriman's oeuvre. In his sports-page work, Herriman frequently depicted sports fans and other observers in the margins—marginal figures in a world that was already considered marginal. Early in his tenure at the *American*, he published "The Daily Parade to the Races" (see figure 4.4), showing a polyglot amalgamation of young and old, rich and poor, men and women all headed to the track, and scenes of multiethnic crowds watching sports appeared throughout his illustrations and cartoons throughout his tenure in Los Angeles. Herriman, an avid "sport" himself, included himself in the crowd in several illustrations, and also made special note of African American, Latino, and Asian athletes. When he was picked off by the Hearst-owned *Examiner* in August 1906, Herriman continued drawing in this vein. Herriman produced only one recurring strip between 1906 and 1909, *Mr. Proones, the Plunger*, several installments of which appeared in 1907. However, his drawings, cartoons, and "one-shot" strips (strips that did not become a recurring series) filled the *Examiner* during this period, appearing on the sports pages, on the editorial page, and accompanying news pieces.

It was on the sports pages that Herriman found his comic footing—and also developed a way to represent African Americans without being forced to collapse them into blackness. In his cartoons and comic strips, black boxers, Japanese servants, and fans of different colors and stripes appear in the periphery of the images, many expressing a longing to move from the margins to the center of the action. In one, a small caricature of a black fighter plaintively asks, "Why don't he fight me?" In another strip, another boxer sighs, just as Herriman's Musical Mose did a few years earlier, "Ah wish my color would fade."[39] These marginal figures were often included in cartoons that were not themselves focused on race. Yet sports—in particular, boxing—could not to escape race as a central concern.

While boxing was perhaps the most integrated of early twentieth-century American sports, its acceptance of black athletes depended on an interrelated set of paradoxes. Considered a sport of grace and finesse in Europe, the cruder, more brutish American style of boxing emerged in Southern plantation culture, where white plantation owners and overseers would pit their strongest and most capable slaves against one another as a form of entertainment, an adaptation of "sports" like cockfighting or dogfighting. Thus, black fighters were not only part of boxing from the beginning; they made up the vast majority of fighters. At the same time, blacks were often thrown into the boxing ring to fight whites, due to the very fact of their supposed inferiority. The strength,

Figure 4.5. "Hooray!! Jeff's Coming Home Soon." *Los Angeles Examiner*, February 18, 1910: 13. San Francisco Academy of Comic Art Collection, Ohio State University, Billy Ireland Cartoon Library and Museum.

dexterity, and competitive intelligence displayed by boxing champions made them the most perfect "specimens" of a region, a nation, or a race, and boxing matches came to be perceived as contests between exemplars of national or racial manhood rather than individuals. Interracial bouts may have gestured toward integration, but they also provided perceived opportunities to demonstrate white supremacy. As a result, white fighters occasionally accepted challenges from black fighters, especially those they felt sure they could defeat.

The ascendance of the black boxer Jack Johnson to the world heavyweight title in 1908 brought racial tensions, heightened by *Plessy*, to a fever pitch. Historian Jeffrey T. Sammon writes that when Johnson defeated Canadian boxer Tommy Burns, many assumed that he would be quickly unseated, "buoyed in their confidence that white physical and intellectual superiority would prevail."[40] But it was Johnson who prevailed, defending his title five times over the next two years. Ratcheting up anxieties even further was the concomitant rise of several other black boxers, including Joe Gans, Joe Jeannette, Sam McVey, and most significantly for our purposes, Sam Langford. These boxers, writes Sammon, "made an extended black reign entirely possible"—and demanded its prevention at all costs.[41] When former world heavyweight Jim Jeffries agreed to come out of retirement to challenge Johnson, the boxing world rejoiced: the "Great White Hope" would return the sport to its formerly pristine state. The fight was announced in November 1909 and scheduled for that most patriotic of US holidays, July 4, 1910.

Herriman documented the turbulence of popular opinion in the months preceding the "Fight of the Century" in comic strips that appeared almost daily on the sports page as well as in spot illustrations for other columns. Because Jeffries was a native Californian, readers of the *Examiner* naturally aligned themselves with him. Herriman's strip from February 18, 1910, shows Los Angeleños of all stripes joyfully preparing for the arrival of the "big boss" to training camp and the return of "old times" (see figure 4.5). At the same time, the very diversity of Los Angeles also meant that Johnson also had his share of supporters; his brash showboating, stylish dress, and flagrant womanizing in the Jim Crow era made him an object of wonder, even awe, for blacks and whites alike.

Mainstream press coverage of Johnson's exploits in and out of the boxing ring would singe the ears of a twenty-first-century audience: he was regularly referred to as "the big Negro," the "dusky Texan," or simply, "the nigger," and his appetites for food, liquor, and women were commonly attributed to the natural "animal" tendencies of the black race. The *Examiner*'s coverage was not devoid of racism. Herriman's good friend H. W. "Beany" Walker claimed that "this being Jim Jeffries' home, the feeling against colored fighters has been worked up several degrees above the choking mark."[42] Herriman's own cartoons depicted Johnson and other

138 The Black Comic Sensibility

Figure 4.6a-b. George Herriman, "If Jack Johnson Wins," *Los Angeles Examiner*, May 19, 1910; and "If Jack Johnson Loses," *Los Angeles Examiner*, May 20, 1910, San Francisco Academy of Comic Art Collection, Ohio State University, Billy Ireland Cartoon Library & Museum.

black boxers with huge lips and eyes, and rendered their speech in the dialect of high minstrelsy. However, they also demonstrate a nuanced understanding of what Johnson's victory might mean for the African American community.

In a pair of strips that appeared on May 19 and May 20, 1910, he depicts in a single panel running the entire width of the sports page what the African American community might look like "If Jack Johnson Wins" and "If Jack Johnson Loses" (see figures 4.6a-b). If he won, blacks would have lives of luxury and leisure, serenaded by "self-playing banjos," nursing their babies from fancy, cut-glass bottles, shooting craps wearing tuxedos. If Johnson lost, Herriman suggests, their lives would become worse than before, with old men and children reduced from rags to "no clothes" and eating nothing but beans. (One might note that the black cat in each strip registers the level of comfort or suffering portrayed in each scenario.) Tisserand writes that in these cartoons, Herriman was "lampooning white fears of a Johnson victory," describing one where "white spectators might watch films of the fight with 'transformation glasses' to turn the blacks to whites and whites to blacks." But Herriman might also have been lampooning a black audience whose hopes far surpassed any possible outcome. One African American woman growing up at the time remembered later that for adults on that day, "the fate of an entire race hung in the balance. Today, one lone black man had the power to make us a race of champions."[43]

Herriman captures the anxious hopes and fears of both whites and blacks in "Three Put Up a Better Argument Than Two" (figure 4.7). Here, two white men express serious doubts about Jeffries's ability to stage a successful comeback. "Poor ole Jeff," one sighs. "It looks like Johnson's going to cop him—sure—." Overhearing this, a black man joyfully agrees, at which point the two white men lay into him in typical comic fashion. Leaving the black man in a starry state of confusion, the white men leave, satisfied that they have put the "dinge" in his place and confident that Jeffries will put Johnson "down for the count." The title of the strip contains the punch line, which, like so many of Herriman's comics, strikes both ways: it pokes fun of whites, who have no argument with each other, but only with the black man, who "puts up," with both his brash prognostications and by embodying racial difference, the "better" or real argument the fight raises. It also is a warning to blacks, that they should not mistake whites' doubts about Jeffries's ability for support of Johnson. Herriman's own position as a mixed-race man passing for white complicates matters further. Is he speaking for whites? Or blacks? Or neither? Or is he speaking for and to both audiences simultaneously, with the "second sight" Du Bois attributes to double consciousness?

Figure 4.7. "Three Put Up a Better Argument Than Two," *Los Angeles Examiner*, February 18, 1910: 13. San Francisco Academy of Comic Art Collection, Ohio State University, Billy Ireland Cartoon Library & Museum.

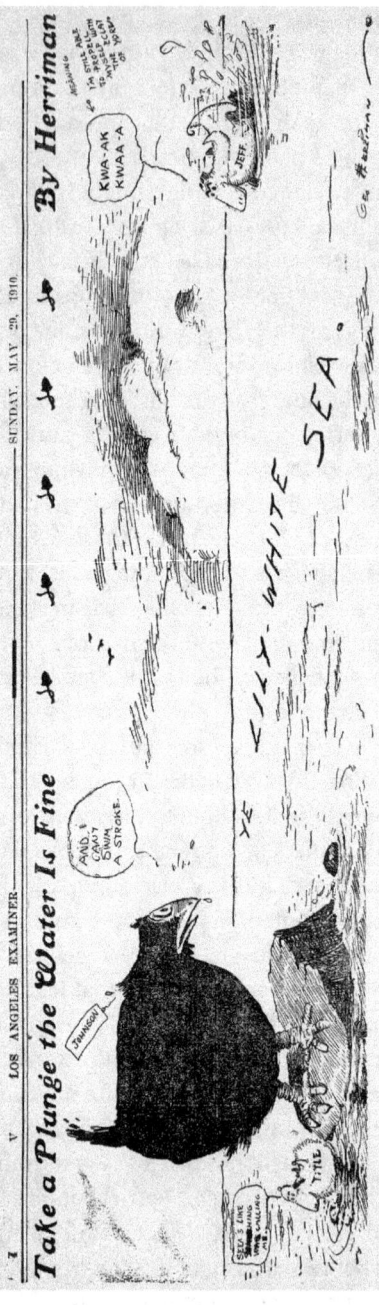

Figure 4.8. "Take a Plunge the Water Is Fine," *Los Angeles Examiner*, May 29, 1910, sporting section: 4. San Francisco Academy of Comic Art Collection, Ohio State University, Billy Ireland Cartoon Library & Museum.

Herriman's family opted to live in a white-dominated society as whites, yet they also lived in the private knowledge that if the people who surrounded them knew who they were, they would be considered black—and thus inferior. If blacks in the United States lived in a state of racial melancholia, one might describe those who chose to pass—or those like Herriman, who were swept along in a family decision to do so—as living in an even more vexed or enhanced state of melancholia, knowing they could neither attain the "ideal" of whiteness, nor publicly embrace their blackness. This melancholia may have informed Herriman's strip "Take a Plunge the Water Is Fine" (see figure 4.8). Jack Johnson is pictured as a huge black chicken, perched on a rock in the middle of "Ye Lily-White Sea." "I can't swim a stroke," he says worriedly, as he sees Jeffries, a white duck industriously swimming off in the distance, declaring proudly, "I'm still able to propell [sic] myself with the éclat of yore." This depiction of an anxious, querulous Johnson presents a stark contrast to popular representations of the boxer, who famously "took orders from no one and resolved to live always as if color did not exist."[44] Rather than expressing Johnson's fears of swimming in the Lily-White Sea, fears that he never appeared to express, perhaps they represent the inner doubts Herriman believed Johnson must have felt. At the same time, the strip's exhortation to "take a plunge the water is fine" seems either to indicate that these fears might be baseless, or to issue a sarcastic warning about the choppy seas that lay ahead.

Herriman never embraced Johnson. Three weeks before the fight, he predicted that the "Jeffries limited" would "heave a load of anthracite off the championship main line."[45] He appeared to view the fight itself as little more than a publicity stunt, a theatrical spectacle that would be a financial boon for both boxers regardless of the winner. In one strip, he depicts Johnson and Jeffries as partners in a vaudeville act that had a bigger draw than Halley's Comet, which brushed past Earth on May 19, 1910; in another, he depicts the boxing ring as a circus, with Jeffries dressed in a female circus rider's costume, and Johnson as his horse.[46] Both Jeffries and Johnson, like many boxers of the time, had performed in the vaudeville circuit. Jeffries abandoned a successful vaudeville tour to come out of retirement to fight Johnson, and Johnson, too, had staged a variety of vaudeville acts in the years preceding his fight with Jeffries to demonstrate his fighting prowess. One handbill advertised his act by declaring, seemingly without irony, "JOHNSON IS A FIGHTER NOT A SHOWMAN." The worlds of showmanship and sport were not so far removed from one another after all.[47]

Herriman's lukewarm depiction of Johnson may also have resulted from Johnson's unwillingness to engage with other black fighters once he had won the world heavyweight title in 1908. In particular, he assiduously avoided the

Canadian boxer Sam Langford, whom he had fought only twice, both times in 1906, when Langford first emerged onto the American boxing scene. While Johnson had defeated Langford both times, he did so with difficulty, despite the fact that Langford was some thirty pounds lighter and six inches shorter. In subsequent years, Johnson clearly sought to avoid a rematch with a more experienced, seasoned fighter, one whom many boxing historians now consider to be one of the greatest boxers ever. Langford's biographer, Clay Moyle, writes that Johnson "claimed that a match between two black men wouldn't draw well. Privately, [he] admitted that there were plenty of other, easier 'white hopes' for him to fight and that he had no desire to risk his title against Langford, who he felt had a chance to win against anybody." Johnson himself said in the 1940s, long after his boxing career had ended, that "Sam Langford was the toughest little son of a bitch that ever lived."[48]

If Herriman believed Johnson was a showman as much as a fighter, or a load of coal fueling the fortunes of white boxers, he depicted Langford instead as the pure essence of boxing: a force of nature, simultaneously superhuman and subhuman. Three times between 1908 and 1910, Langford fought "Fireman" Jim Flynn, himself a contender for the world heavyweight title. Flynn was known for fighting dirty and was the only boxer ever to knock out Jack Dempsey; he also was willing to fight anyone, white or black. The first time they fought, in December 1908, Langford dropped Flynn for the count in just two minutes. In their second fight, exactly one year later, a highly favored Langford was defeated by Flynn in ten rounds, by decision. Langford's manager, Joe Woodman, quickly arranged a rematch. A month later, Langford avenged his loss, crushing the Fireman in the eighth of forty-five (!) scheduled rounds. Harry Carr, of the *Los Angeles Times*, described the bout:

> It was horrible—sickening. . . . It was cold, deliberate slaughter. Langford, the cave man, would put his left hand against the white man's bleeding face and push him away to arm's length, his little red pig eyes running critically over the maimed white body, a connoisseur selecting a vital spot, then his fists would drive in with a crash. The impact of the blows so terrible they could be heard all over the pavilion. Flynn fought with the helpless ferocity of a wounded lion ... the fight was painfully unequal. It was a raw, clumsy, savage blunderer, trying to defend himself against the skill and strength of a jungle animal.

Langford's biographer, Clay Moyle, cites several other accounts describing him as a gorilla, a "throwback to the cave dwellers," and a saber-toothed tiger.[49]

Herriman's depictions of Langford in the comic strips appearing on the sports pages refracted his popular iconography (see figures 4.9 a-c). On

February 10, 1910, some six weeks before the rematch between Langford and Flynn, Herriman portrayed Langford as a wildcat tamed by the hunter Flynn, much to the amazement of various boxers who had avoided fighting him. In the week before the fight, Flynn is shown putting his now-docile housecat through his tricks but finds to his chagrin that Langford has grown back into a wildcat—foretelling the result of the rematch, as described by Carr above. After Langford's decisive victory, Herriman returned to the trained cat conceit, but he recast it in terms of Flynn's temporary removal of Langford from the "Lily-White Inn" only to be dragged back to its threshold by a resurgent wildcat with no fears of taking the plunge back in.

The brute savagery ascribed to Langford by Carr and other journalists is itself tamed through Herriman's rendering of the wildcat, who seems more amused than bloodthirsty. In fact, he seems primarily amused by the fact that he is seen as a wildcat at all. Herriman's depiction of whites' literal perception of blacks—that blacks were animals—reverses, to a degree, the effect of double consciousness, demonstrating it on the one hand to be ludicrous and on the other as being as potentially damaging to whites as it is demeaning to blacks. By depicting Langford's would-be white rivals quaking in fear at the threshold of the "Lily-White Inn," hiding in burrows outside of the wildcat's den, Herriman shows them essentially unmanned when faced with Langford's primal force.

Taken together, Herriman's strips concerning Jack Johnson, Sam Langford, and sports in general provide a crucial context for the development of Herriman's comic sensibility. It was certainly in his sports cartoons that the gloves came off, where Herriman expressed his views about race most clearly. Tad Dorgan once commented that he never understood why Herriman abandoned sports cartooning. In 1924, he wrote, "I still think George is one of the best sporting artists in the world."[50] It may be precisely because of Dorgan, however, that Herriman left the sporting arena to return to the Sunday supplements. Just a few weeks before the Johnson-Jeffries bout, Herriman was suddenly called to New York in the summer of 1910 to swap places with Dorgan, whom Hearst wanted to send West to cover the all-important fight. While Herriman continued to cover sports for the *New York Journal*, he soon turned to strips that had nothing to do with boxing, baseball, horse-racing, or football—culminating in *Krazy Kat*, which debuted as a daily strip in 1913.

As critics have shown in recent years, *Krazy Kat* subverts not just race and ethnicity but also gender and nation as categories through which one can fix identity. In Herriman's imagined universe of Coconino County, everything is, indeed crazy—"kookoo": cats love mice, mice persecute cats; a universe presented in black and white is shown to be anything but. The instability of identity is embodied most clearly in the strip's title character, the kat who is and

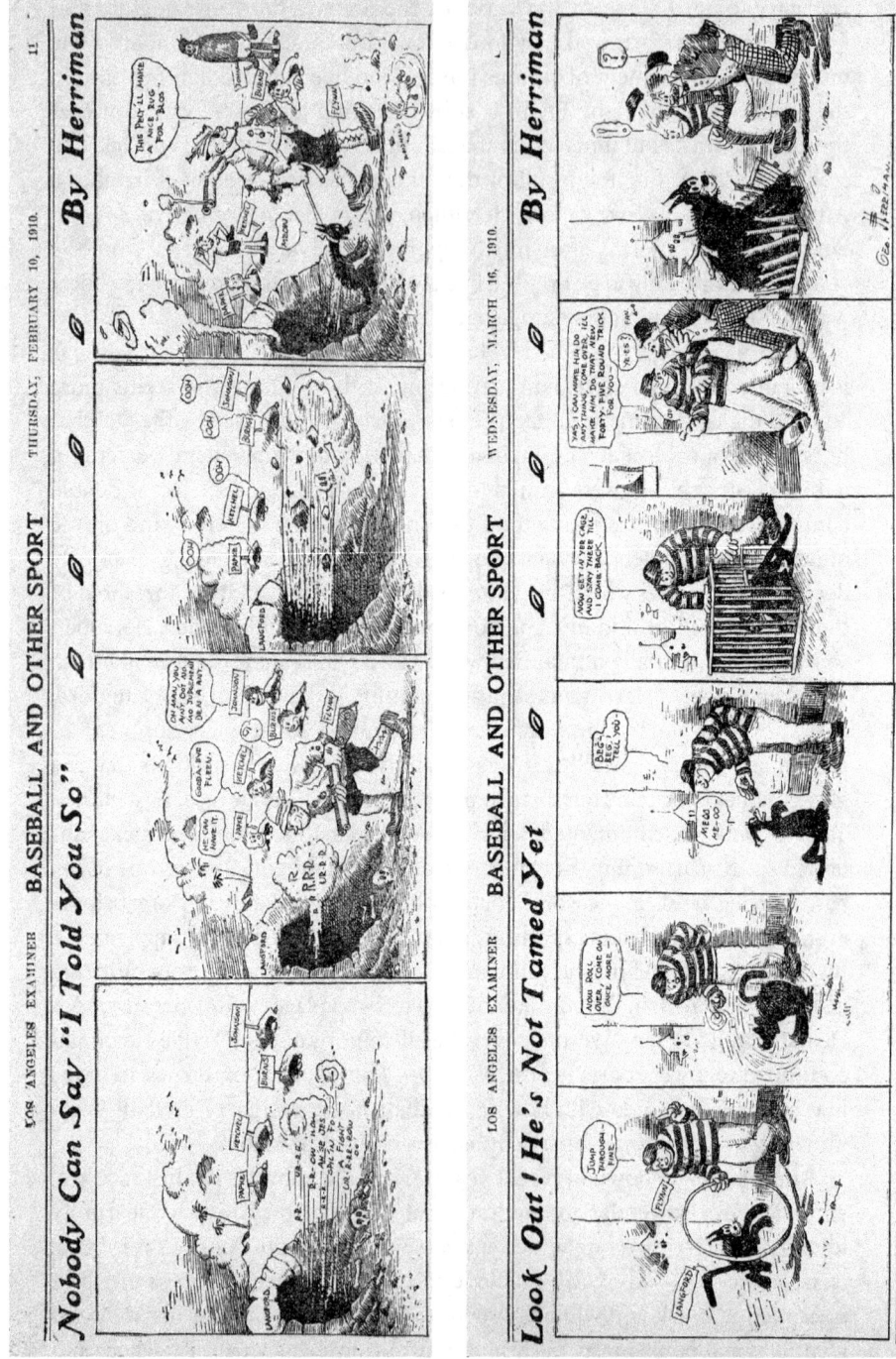

The Black Comic Sensibility

Figure 4.9 a–c. Strips depicting Sam Langford, *Los Angeles Examiner*, February 10, 1910; March 16, 1910; and March 19, 1910. Langford crushed Flynn on March 17, 1910. San Francisco Academy of Comic Art Collection, Ohio State University, Billy Ireland Cartoon Library & Museum.

isn't a cat, whose very gender—male or female?—remained in doubt during the three decades the strip ran in the funny pages. As with black caricature generally, but in more pointed, radical form here, Krazy functions as a kind of void that calls for closure but resists it at the same time, offering a paradox and a cipher to those who might attempt to attain it. Krazy's indeterminacy—as well as that of the other denizens of Coconino County—is emphasized by Herriman's use of an idiosyncratic dialect that combines the speech of different regions and groups into a transcendent goulash of sound, described by McDonnell as "an outrageous alphabet soup of . . . Spanish, French, Brooklyn Yiddish, onomatopoetic juxtapositions—and almost anything else that came to Herriman's mind."[51] Indeed, as Krazy says, "Language is that we may misunda-stend each udda," rather than attain understanding.[52]

Jeet Heer argues that Herriman's use of strong blacks and whites and a subdued color palette contributes to his subversive commentary on racial boundaries and the assumed fixity of identity. By demonstrating the very limits of binary categories, he writes, "Herriman used his strip to critique the very rigid racial thinking that drove his family out of New Orleans."[53] What Heer describes as Herriman's "subversive comedy" arose from a deep awareness of double consciousness originating from his own experience, but is not limited to or simply directed toward African Americans. As Gardner writes, "just as we do wrong to insist on the fiction that Herriman was 'white'—French or Greek (as his friends and colleagues believed him to be)—so it is wrong to insist that Herriman was in fact 'black.' All identity, Herriman knew long before academic theorists caught up with him, was fiction—a performance."[54] Like his friend Jimmy Swinnerton, Herriman, too, performed not just in newsprint, but on the boards, appearing in blackface—with Swinnerton, no less. In April 1910, just as the hysteria surrounding the Johnson-Jeffries fight was reaching its height, he participated in parades advertising an "All-Star Minstrels" benefit for Los Angeles-area actors. The *Examiner* reported that the two cartoonists, along with the minstrel performers, "other stage favorites," and "other newspapermen" would all "don the most approved minstrel costumes."[55]

In *Krazy Kat*, as well as *Musical Mose* and other early strips, Herriman shows that all identity is put on. However, he emphasizes that in some cases the costume is donned by choice, while in others, it is imposed by an audience or viewer. In a July 16, 1916, strip, Krazy's friend W. Cephus Austridge sells him a "Little Gem Vanisher" device, a tin can that he promises will render Krazy invisible if he puts it over his head (see figure 4.10). While Krazy has his doubts about the device's efficacy, he tries it and demonstrates that the device simply blinds him; he becomes visible only to himself, while remaining all too visible to everyone else. Calling Cephus—an "austridge" whose invention simply

Figure 4.10. *Krazy Kat*, July 16, 1916. San Francisco Academy of Comic Art Collection, Ohio State University, Billy Ireland Cartoon Library & Museum.

makes transportable the ostrich's stereotypical penchant for sticking his head in the sand—a "fibba" and a "robba," Krazy swears that he will never again serve as "a 'intelligent audience'" for Cephus's swindles. But the fact that he desires to attain invisibility despite his doubts reflects the racial melancholia that Krazy embodies: he knows he can never be invisible, or even not visible, even to himself, no matter how much he wishes. He will always be seen as what the "intelligent audience" believes him to be.

Herriman treats the performativity of identity with humor, but he did not, as Ralph Ellison said of Ras the Destroyer in *Invisible Man*, make it "seem funny—*only* funny." He also provides glimpses into the inner anguish experienced by the marginalized and liminal, glimpses that might pass fleetingly under the gaze of most readers of the funny papers but provided points of identification and access to the marginalized themselves. The moment of identification might elicit little more than a wry smile of recognition, or a cathartic—if helpless—laugh. The moment of understanding is, nevertheless, an affirming recognition of common humanity. Langston Hughes later wrote that "humor is laughing at what you haven't got when you ought to have it. . . . . Humor is what you wish in your secret heart were not funny. But it is, and you must laugh. Humor is your unconscious therapy."[56] The therapeutic, secret humor of *Krazy Kat* verges on comic nihilism, which appears throughout modernist art and literature. Unsurprisingly, figures ranging from Willem de Kooning to E. E. Cummings to Langston Hughes and Ralph Ellison have acknowledged Herriman's influence on their own work. One need not be black to understand black humor, and one need not be black to create black comics. What Toni Morrison identified as an abiding "Africanist presence" throughout American culture, then, is part of the comic sensibility too.

Coda

> It is very often the woman's laugh that covers a great deal more than it reveals.
> —Robert J. Burdette, "Have Women a Sense of Humor?"[1]

The veiled comic critique effected in Herriman's work is an example of what Mel Watkins has described as "private" humor, which developed in the African American community in response to the public suppression of black laughter. In a society where African Americans have been forcibly disempowered, black people's laughter, he writes, has been interpreted as "inappropriate" at best, but for whites in positions of power, as a challenge, as "insolent," as "aggressive." As a result, laughing blacks were punished with beatings, whippings, and worse.[2] Who knows how many lynchings may have been caused by a black man's (or woman's) laugh?

Private humor, in contrast to more performative, flamboyant forms of the joke, produces a quiet kind of laughter. This knowing chuckle indicates *sotto voce* agreement between the joker and their audience, protecting both from full, public exposure.[3] This humor might be more accurately described as semi-private, or perhaps, subcultural or communal, as it establishes the *einfuhling* (in-feeling) of group membership. Communal humor is recognizable to those who share a common understanding but is veiled, invisible, and inaudible to everyone else. It elicits laughter that is produced by double consciousness itself, laughter that constitutes both recognition and response. Various examples of this kind of communal humor emerged in public forms during this period: in Charles Chesnutt's conjure tales, Paul Laurence Dunbar's dialect poetry, and the Bre'r Rabbit tales popularized by Joel Chandler Harris. In all of these texts, characters perceived as weaker, subservient, or peripheral—Chesnutt's and Dunbar's "faithful old darkies," the lowly rabbit—best the strong and powerful, often through surreptitious means, feigning ignorance or "faithfulness" while actually engaging in acts of trespass and transgression. For this humor's very inappropriateness points toward violations of propriety, decorum, and business as usual.

Zora Neale Hurston represented private humor not only as a form of quiet subversion but also as a kind of psychological sustenance. In her own version of the "John and Ole Massa" story—on which Chesnutt's conjure stories too were based—she wrote of black private humor as "the source of courage that endures, and laughter":

> They heard what Massa said, and they felt bad right off. But John de Conquer took and told them, saying, " . . . You know where you got something finer than this plantation and anything it's got on it, put away. Ain't that funny? Us got all that, and he don't know nothing at all about it. Don't tell him nothing. Nobody don't have to know where us gets our pleasure from." . . .
> "Ain't that funny?" Aunt Diskie laughed and hugged herself with secret laughter. "Us got all the advantage, and Old Massa think he got us tied!"[4]

Hurston's comic vision was criticized by her contemporaries for exploiting the "chauvinistic tastes" of a white audience, for denigrating her own artistic talents by resorting to "the minstrel technique that makes the 'white folks' laugh" at the expense of limning the depths of black interiority.[5] I would suggest that Hurston's critics also objected to the fact that Hurston, like the artists and writers included in this book, made the semi-private humor of the black community public. Black humor, and the communal bonds it strengthened, were not intended for others'—especially whites'—consumption.

Yet as the United States became more diverse, pluralistic, and "transnational" in character, communal humor naturally went public. And as once-close-knit communities became fragmented and dispersed, forms of the comic sensibility appearing on the comics pages, in national magazines, and on the stage became ways for individuals to identify and feel themselves part of a larger—if imagined—community. The feeling of comic solidarity was just as important as labor unions, political parties, and churches in establishing group identity during an era of national transformation.

I had completed work on this book when I encountered Christina Sharpe's idea that black people in the United States are "living in the wake": living in the literal wake of the singular but as-yet unreckoned cataclysm of transatlantic slavery. The ripple effects from slavery continue centuries after its legal end.

More than 150 years after the Civil War supposedly ended slavery, blacks find themselves living through the wake as a dynamic, almost physiological process; living in the combined mourning and celebratory atmosphere of the wake, as affective state and as ritual; and living in wakefulness, awake, conscious that one is living in a world predicated on anti-blackness.⁶ While anti-blackness is not total, Sharpe writes, those who live in the wake understand that it is pervasive and may require lifetimes to eradicate. "At stake, then, is to stay in this wake time," she writes, and work "toward inhabiting a blackened consciousness that would rupture the structural silences produced and facilitated by, and that produce and facilitate, Black social and physical death."⁷ Living in the wake, or in "wake time," is not just a way of coping with pain and suffering, a way to keep putting one foot in front of the other. It is also important, as Sharpe argues, to recognize its generative potential: "the knowledge of this positioning avails us particular ways of re/seeing, re/inhabiting, and re/imagining the world. And we might use these ways of being in the wake in our responses to terror and the varied and various ways that our left lives are lived under occupation."⁸ Black people may have "experienced, recognized, and lived subjection," she writes, but they "did not *simply* or *only* live in subjection and *as* the subjected."⁹

Sharpe is rightly careful to distinguish the specificity of black experience. The wake she explores has very different contours and different affordances than the wakes of immigrant steamers or the trailing smoke of train cars. Yet her idea of the generative potential of trauma is applicable to a range of experiences. The comic sensibility provides a way to respond to trauma, first, as Bergson and Freud have written, through cathartic release of emotion, and second, as I argue, through shared recognition of the forces that have caused those emotions to accumulate. In response to other socially and culturally traumatic experiences (the Industrial Revolution, modernity, immigration and forced migration, the Holocaust, the Vietnam War, the Great Depression, the War on Drugs), the comic sensibility has been a sensory, physiological engagement with—and processing of—trauma. This is the kind of laughter that constitutes, as Kobena Mercer has written, "not merely a mode of survival but a manifestation of aliveness in the face of loss and dispossession."¹⁰ It is a way to *make sense* of trauma through collective feeling, feeling together.

In the preceding chapters, I have tried to offer a restorative understanding of the early newspaper comic strip. But it is important to emphasize that not all comic strip artists engaged in the comic sensibility as I have described it. Certainly, few actively sought to elicit "a physiological rather than intellectual response and . . . feelings of solidarity and community among the marginalized"¹¹ in their daily or weekly strips. And as the comic supplement gradually ossified into the two-row grid of "the funnies," and as concerns about the impact of comics on young minds led to the sanitation of comics, the ability for comics to engage in multivalent social and political critique also diminished. After a brief dalliance with E. W. Kemble-esque racist caricature in his short-lived strip *Pore Li'l Mose*, Richard Outcault turned his attention away from the rowdy world of urban street culture and toward the tame exploits of a suburban boy named Buster Brown and his dog, Tige, who became even more successful than the Yellow Kid at selling newspapers, lunch boxes, and eventually, clothes and shoes.[12] Rudolph Dirks's *Katzensjammer Kids* was taken over by Harry Knerr in 1914 and in time spent most Sundays exploring imaginary lands full of one-dimensional savages. The working-class urban magazine fiction that brought together the accented voices of Russian immigrants with the art of bohemian painters in the pages of mass-market magazines quickly disappeared in the mid-1910s; free-market capitalism, and the need for US industry and investment after European devastation in World War I, steamrolled over the earlier socialist impulses of Henry George and Edward Bellamy and propelled the US into the Roaring Twenties. It is important to distinguish the comic sensibility from what it is *not*. It is not simply comics as a genre, or laughter as a behavior. It is cultural production that generates laughter while doing "wake work."

Yet there are many avenues to explore further. The scope of this project and the difficulty of accessing scattered archival holdings prevented more expansive treatment of this history. Additional research on black comic strip artists would greatly enrich the history of comics and graphic art. George Herriman passed as white to gain access to nationally distributed comic networks, but other black comic artists developed the black comic sensibility in the black press. Black comics historians have noted the careers of artists such as Leslie Rogers, whose strip *Bungleton Green* began publication in 1920 in the *Chicago Defender*, and Ollie Harrington, whose single-panel cartoon *Bootsie* plainly and directly addressed anti-black racism in New York's *Amsterdam News* beginning in the mid-1930s; Garfield T. Haywood drew editorial cartoons for the *Indianapolis Freeman* beginning in 1902, and Fred B. Watson drew editorial and sports cartoons for the *Baltimore Afro-American* beginning in the early 1920s.[13] Earlier examples of black comic art remain to be rediscovered and situated within the national history of American comics. The same holds true for comic strips, cartoons, and illustration in the immigrant and ethnic press.

Women also engaged with the comic sensibility. Female comics, minstrels, impersonators, and burlesque performers were an important part of concertsaloon culture in the decades after the Civil War, and comic actresses including Eva Tanguay, Mae West, and Marie Dressler became some of the early female stars in American film. American newspapers also published comic strips by women, though the vast majority were restricted to the Sunday supplements, which did not require newspapers to accommodate respectable women in their rough-and-tumble, male-dominated art departments. In her Sunday strip *Naughty Toodles* (1902), Grace Gebbie Wiederseim (later Grace Drayton, creator of the Campbell's Soup Kids) presented a singularly grotesque vision of American domestic life, dominated by monstrously proportioned infants who terrorized their mothers with their hapless misbehavior (figure 5.1), while a decade later, Katherine P. Rice highlighted, in surprisingly forthright terms, the embarrassing situations encountered by the equally hapless New Woman (figure 5.2).[14]

Even within the coterie of The Eight, women practiced the comic sensibility alongside, and at times, on equal or even superior footing to their male counterparts and companions. As noted in chapter 3, Florence Scovel Shinn, first wife of Everett Shinn, and May Wilson Preston, married to William Glackens's friend James Preston and former roommate of Glackens's wife, Edith Dimock Glackens, attained professional success as comic illustrators. Even before that, however, Marjorie Organ, later married to Robert Henri, was a rare female staff comic strip artist at Hearst's *New York Journal*. There she originated several strips that spoofed the anxious conventionality of modern men and women. Like George Luks (and many others, it should be noted), Organ emphasized the replicability and uniformity of human behavior in the age of mechanization and photographic reproduction; in some of her strips, however, she revealed how patriarchy transformed women into grotesques. In one installment of her most pointedly critical strip, *Strange What Difference a Mere Man Makes*, Organ depicts a group of women, walking and conversing in casual pairs, who "distort themselves out of all semblance to human beings" the moment a "mere man" appears, marching as a group, in lockstep, breasts thrust forward and buttocks extended, chins raised at identical angles so that their faces can moon up at their male target (figure 5.3).[15] These women embody the "artificially induced pathological features" and "mutilations of unquestioned repulsiveness" that Thorstein Veblen assigned to upper-class women—the signs of uselessness, ornament, and conspicuous consumption—in his *Theory of the Leisure Class* (1890).[16]

Organ left cartooning after she married Henri, and although she continued to paint and sketch throughout her life, she became better known as the subject of his paintings and as his secretary, embellishing her correspondence with her native Irish wit and humor. Edith Dimock Glackens, like Organ, is also remembered primarily as a subject in her husband's paintings as well as the source of his financial security, being the scion of a wealthy West Hartford family. Yet she, too, carried on with her painting, and under the name Edith

Figure 5.1. Grace G. Wiederseim, *Naughty Toodles!*, St. Louis Republic, May 10, 1903: 61.

Dimock, she continued to exhibit her work throughout the 1910s and 1920s—a fact left out of virtually all biographical treatments of her husband. William Glackens, of course, was far more prolific and more widely recognized in the press. But Dimock's artistic activities also may have been overlooked because she worked in watercolor and gouache, mediums seen as less serious, even feminine, by the art establishment.

Dimock's father had once commented that she "would have made a fine comedienne."[17] In her paintings, we see the comic sensibility on display, through a visceral engagement with color and the grotesque possibilities of the human form, and a loving if humorous treatment of her subjects. In *Mrs. Roosevelt at Klein's* (figure 5.4), she depicts the semi-private chaos inside the "trying on room" of one of Manhattan's not-quite premier shopping establishments, with women of all different shapes, sizes, ages, social classes, and stages of undress united in their search for bargains. Though facial expressions are mere suggestions in this watercolor sketch, the women collectively appear to be thoroughly engaged in the scrutiny of their own bodies as well as one another; several appear to be conferring, while one looks directly at the viewer, seemingly unconcerned. It's not clear who "Mrs. Roosevelt" might be, as there is no clear

FLORA FLIRT TAKES A FOOL'S DAY JAUNT

Miss Flora Flirt, in plumage fair.
Parading goes in the April air.

The vain, proud thoughts of dress quite blind her
To the imp who's stealing up behind her

So intent is she on being matched
She never feels the sign attached.

Despite her charming lures and wiles,
All gallants pass her by with smiles.

If she can move them thus to laughter,
She thinks they'll soon be following after

Horrors! The sign has met her ey
Amid the roars of the passersby.
The Moral—Don't base your conquests on a smile
He may be laughing all the while.

Figure 5.2. K. P. Rice, "Flora Flirt Takes a Fool's Day Jaunt," *Oregon Daily Journal*, March 28, 1914: 14.

Figure 5.3. Marjorie Organ, *Strange What Difference a Mere Man Makes*, *Fort Wayne Weekly Sentinel*, August 30, 1905: 2.

Figure 5.4. Edith Dimock, *Mrs. Roosevelt at Klein's*, n.d. Watercolor, 10 x 9 1/4 inches. NSU Art Museum, Fort Lauderdale; gift of the Sansom Foundation, 92.77.

central figure. Rather, Dimock depicts an entire collective of women engaged in the same activity and implies that while they may dress for public display in the patriarchal world outside of the dressing room, in this space they are also dressing for themselves and for one another.

A recognition of the comic sensibility and its abiding presence on the margins and in the nether regions of culture and society can help us locate energies and desires that cannot be expressed in socially acceptable—"rational"—discourse. If slavery is an as-yet unreckoned cataclysm, patriarchy might well be another. As we trace the presence of the comic sensibility in other places and other times, other moments of transgression and resistance, of unstated (or suppressed) yearning and desire, will be revealed. Martha Banta describes comic periodicals in the late nineteenth century as evoking "feelings of betrayal that come about when hitherto hidden facts are revealed, trust is broken, and the familiar patterns of conduct in a knowable world are destroyed through the sudden release of the uncanniness that has been there all along,"[18] in the form of "frightening, fascinating hybrid shapes visualized as beasts on the loose ... the Irish, the Jew, the black, the restless proletariat, and the unassimilated immigrant."[19] Such moments of uncanniness are, in Banta's characterization, realizations of *Unheimlichkeit*, of feeling no longer at home in the world. Yet for the Irish, Jews, blacks, laborers, immigrants, and possibly, women, these grotesque visualizations may have functioned in the opposite fashion, confirming their sense of "home" and the reality they occupied, and perhaps, awakening them into new life.

Notes

Introduction: The Comic Sensibility

1. Colton Waugh, *The Comics* (New York: Macmillan, 1947), 8.
2. Jacob Riis, *How the Other Half Lives* (1890; New York: W. W. Norton, 2010), 81–82.
3. Riis, *How the Other Half Lives*, 79.
4. Riis, *How the Other Half Lives*, 6.
5. David Hume, "Of the Standard of Taste," in *Of the Standard of Taste and Other Essays*, ed. John Lenz (Indianapolis, IN: Bobbs-Merrill, 1965), 10; emphasis in original.
6. Daniel Wickberg, *The Senses of Humor: Self and Laughter in Modern America* (Ithaca: Cornell University Press, 1998), 64–65.
7. Thomas Carlyle, "Jean Paul Friedrich Richter," in *Critical and Miscellaneous Essays* (New York: John B. Alden, 1885), 19–20.
8. Qtd. in Wickberg, *Senses of Humor*, 65.
9. Ted Cohen, *Jokes: Philosophical Thoughts on Joking Matters* (Chicago: University of Chicago Press, 1999), 28.
10. Dorothee Schneider, *Trade Unions and Community: The German Working Class in New York City, 1870–1900* (Urbana: University of Illinois Press, 1994), 8; Stanley Nadel, *Little Germany: Ethnicity, Religion, and Class in New York City, 1845–80* (Urbana: University of Illinois Press, 1990), 42.
11. While Wilhelm Busch's *Max und Moritz* drawings are produced in a cartoon style, the *Katzenjammers* are much more roughly drawn; Busch's tales also were written in verse, while Dirks's were not. Dirks's main formal contribution to the comic strip form was the popularization of the speech balloon (c. 1900)—an innovation that further distanced the *Katzenjammer Kids* from their original source material.
12. Cohen, *Jokes*, 26–27.
13. Riis, incidentally, was himself an immigrant from Denmark.
14. Eric Lott, for example, argues that the "racial bad attitudes" evinced by the white working class in their adoption of blackface minstrelsy nevertheless contained "resistant, oppositional, or emancipatory accents" (*Love and Theft: Blackface Minstrelsy and the American Working Class* [New York: Oxford University Press, 1993], 11).

15. William Dean Howells, *Criticism and Fiction* (New York: Harper and Brothers, 1902), 73.

16. Susan Sontag, *On Photography* (1977; New York: Macmillan, 2011), 5–6.

17. Riis, *How the Other Half Lives*, 29.

18. Riis, *Children of the Poor* (New York: Charles Scribner's Sons, 1892), v.

19. Riis, *How the Other Half Lives*, 5–6, emphasis added.

20. David Shi, *Facing Facts: Realism in American Thought and Culture, 1850–1920* (New York: Oxford University Press, 1995), 6–7.

21. Shi, *Facing Facts*, 7.

22. Riis, *The Making of an American* (New York: Macmillan, 1901), 269.

23. Riis, "The Passing of Cat Alley," *Century Magazine* 57.2 (December 1898): 166, 169, 176.

24. Riis, "Midwinter in New York," *Century Magazine* 59.2 (December 1900): 527. *Century* published a number of pieces by Riis over the next decade, including "Light in Dark Places," (December 1896), "The Passing of Cat Alley" (December 1898), "Children of the People" (December 1903), and "The Snow-Babies' Christmas" (December 1905). According to biographer Tom Buk-Swienty, Riis most likely gained an entrée into the *Century*'s pages through his association with the Tenement Club established by New York City mayor William L. Strong, which was chaired by Richard Watson Gilder, *Century*'s editor and of which Riis was an "informal advisor" (*The Other Half: The Life of Jacob Riis and the World of Immigrant America*, trans. Annette Buk-Swienty [New York: W. W. Norton, 2008], 261).

25. Riis, "The Passing of Cat Alley," 176.

26. Phillip J. Barrish, *Cambridge Introduction to American Literary Realism* (Cambridge, GB: Cambridge University Press, 2011), 44. The relationship between realism and "arrangement" calls to mind the final scene of Stephen Crane's grotesquely comic story "The Monster," in which the careful arrangement of cups on the table provides a highly ironic contrast to the community's unspeakable treatment of Henry, and the insistence of Henry's deformed visage of the "monster" of racial prejudice.

27. Carrie Tirado Bramen, *The Uses of Variety: Modern Americanism and the Quest for National Distinctiveness* (Cambridge, MA: Harvard University Press, 2000), 160. Also see Sabine Haenni, "Visual and Theatrical Culture, Tenement Fiction, and the Immigrant Subject in Abraham Cahan's *Yekl*," *American Literature* 71.3 (September 1999), 493–527.

28. Richard Brodhead, *Cultures of Letters: Scenes of Reading and Writing in Nineteenth-Century America* (Chicago: University of Chicago Press, 1993), 125.

29. Bramen, *Uses of Variety*, 160.

30. Barrish, *Cambridge Introduction to American Literary Realism*, 4.

31. Matthew Frye Jacobson, *Barbarian Virtues: The United States Encounters Foreign Peoples at Home and Abroad, 1876–1917* (New York: Hill and Wang, 2000), 125. Henry Wonham applies this thinking to realism in general: "magazine realism . . . served the interests of democracy and of patriarchy at once, instituting new controls over the representation of formerly invisible subjects in the act of making them visible" (*Playing the Races*, 21).

32. Henry James, *The American Scene* (New York: Penguin, 1994), 66.

33. Henry James, *The American Scene*, 101, 102.

34. Jonathan Crary, *Suspensions of Perception: Attention, Spectacle, and Modern Culture* (Cambridge, MA: MIT Press, 1999), 12; 90–92.

35. Crary, *Suspensions of Perception*, 84.

36. Crary, *Suspensions of Perception*, 88.

37. Crary, *Suspensions of Perception*, 9. Robyn Wiegman also argues that the modern environment does not simply invite, but requires new "economies of visibility" in *American Anatomies: Theorizing Race and Gender* (Durham, NC: Duke University Press, 1995).

38. Sigmund Freud, *Jokes and Their Relation to the Unconscious*, trans. and ed. James Strachey, vol. 8 of *The Standard Edition of the Complete Psychological Works of Sigmund Freud* (London: Hogarth Press, 1960), 11.

39. Bruno Lessing (Rudolph Block), "Ingratitude of Rosenfeld," *Cosmopolitan Magazine* 41.4 (August 1906): 388–89.

40. Lessing, "Ingratitude of Rosenfeld," 390, 392.

41. Headlines from the front pages of the February 19 and March 17, 1898, issues of the *New York World*.

42. Albert F. McLean Jr., *American Vaudeville as Ritual* (Lexington: University of Kentucky Press, 1965), 107, 109.

43. Douglas Gilbert, *American Vaudeville: Its Life and Times* (New York: McGraw-Hill, 1940), 160–61.

44. Qtd. in McLean, *American Vaudeville as Ritual*, 106; Rick DesRochers traces the quote to an interview published in the *New York World* in 1909, but dates the quotation 1900. Rick DesRochers, *The New Humor in the Progressive Era: Americanization and the Vaudeville Comedian* (New York: Palgrave Macmillan, 2014), xiv.

45. Robert Clyde Allen, *Horrible Prettiness: Burlesque and American Culture* (Chapel Hill: University of North Carolina Press, 1991), especially chapter 7, "Burlesque at Century's End," 195–240.

46. Felix Isman, *Weber and Fields: Their Tribulations, Triumphs and Their Associates* (New York: Boni and Liveright, 1924), 169.

47. Gilbert, *American Vaudeville*, 12–13.

48. Filippo Tommaso Marinetti, "The Variety Theatre," in *Marinetti: Selected Writings* (New York: Farrar, Straus and Giroux, 1971), 116. Along the same lines, McLean writes that vaudeville is designed to "provoke loud laughter" throughout, and is governed by "the impulse toward hysteria" (*American Vaudeville as Ritual*, 112–13). Also see Wickberg, chapter 4, especially pages 128–30.

49. Lessing, "The Ingratitude of Rosenfeld," 388.

50. E. H. Gombrich, with Ernst Kris, "The Principles of Caricature," *British Journal of Medical Psychology* 17 (1938), 322, 324.

51. Wonham, *Playing the Races*, 9, 11.

52. Gavin Jones, *Strange Talk*, 3, 11.

53. William Dean Howells, *A Hazard of New Fortunes*, book 4, chapter 4.

54. Howells, *A Hazard of New Fortunes*, book 4, chapter 6.

55. Jones, *Strange Talk*, 11.

56. Gombrich and Kris, "Principles of Caricature," 325.

57. Qtd. in S. D. Travis, *No Applause—Just Throw Money: The Book that Made Vaudeville Famous* (New York: Farrar, Straus and Giroux, 2006), 10.

Chapter 1: The Comic Grotesque

1. Bernard De Casseres, "The Fantastic George Luks," *New York Herald Tribune Sunday Magazine*, September 10, 1933; qtd. in Rebecca Zurier, *Picturing the City: Urban Vision and the Ashcan School* (Berkeley: University of California Press, 2006), 120.

2. See, especially, the introduction and chapter 6 of Tracy Wuster, *Mark Twain: American Humorist* (Columbia: University of Missouri Press, 2016).

3. Twain, "How to Tell a Story" (1895), in *Collected Tales, Sketches, Speeches, and Essays, 1891–1910* (New York: Library of America, 1992), 201–203.

4. Daniel Wickberg, *The Senses of Humor: Self and Laughter in Modern America* (Ithaca: Cornell University Press, 1998), 134.

5. For more on the joke-making industry, see chapter four of Wickberg's *The Senses of Humor*, "The Commodity form of the Joke," 120–69.

6. Susan Gillman, *Dark Twins: Imposture and Identity in Mark Twain's America* (Chicago: University of Chicago Press, 1989), 23–25.

7. On the shift in the perception of authorship from individual to personality, see Barbara Hochman, *Getting at the Author: Reimagining Books and Reading in the Age of American Realism* (Amherst: University of Massachusetts Press, 2010), chapter 1.

8. Gillman, *Dark Twins*, 3, 5.

9. Mark Twain, *Pudd'nhead Wilson* (New York: Penguin, 1986), 225.

10. Leonard Cassuto, *The Inhuman Race: The Racial Grotesque in American Literature and Culture* (New York: Columbia University Press, 1997), 2.

11. Twain, "Three Thousand Years Among the Microbes," in *Mark Twain's Which Was the Dream and Other Symbolic Writings of the Later Years*, ed. John S. Tuckey (Berkeley: University of California Press, 1968), 436; qtd. in Wonham, *Playing the Races*, 69.

12. Wonham, *Playing the Races*, 71.

13. Cassuto, *The Inhuman Race*, 8–9.

14. Twain, *Pudd'nhead Wilson*, 302––03.

15. Twain, *Pudd'nhead Wilson*, 303.

16. Malcolm Bradbury, "Introduction" (1969), *Pudd'nhead Wilson* (New York: Penguin, 1986).

17. Gillman, *Dark Twins*, 54.

18. Gillman, *Dark Twins*. 51–52.

19. James Goodwin, *American Grotesque* (Columbus: Ohio State University Press, 2009), 18.

20. Jonathan Crary, *Techniques of the Observer: On Vision and Modernity in the Nineteenth Century* (Cambridge: MIT Press, 1990), 119–20.

21. Jennifer Greenhill elaborates on the significance of the Sliced Nations game in *Playing It Straight: Art and Humor in the Gilded Age* (Berkeley: University of California Press, 2012), 64.

22. Cassuto, *The Inhuman Race*, 16.

23. James, *The American Scene* (London: Chapman and Hall, 1907), 75.

24. Stephen Millhauser, *Martin Dressler* (New York: Vintage, 1996), 115.

25. Bennard Perlman, "Drawing on Deadline," *Art and Antiques* (October 1988): 118.

26. Luks, "Gathering News," Everett Shinn Papers, Smithsonian Archives of American Art, box 1, folder 72.

27. Qtd. in Bennard Perlman, *The Immortal Eight: American Painting from Eakin to the Armory Show, 1870-1913* (New York: Exposition Press, 1962), 87–88 (emphasis added).

28. Luks, "In Hot Pursuit of a Scout," *Philadelphia Evening Bulletin*, February 10, 1896; Robert Gambone discusses this image and other instances of Luks's manufactured reportage in *Life on the Press: The Popular Art and Illustrations of George Benjamin Luks* (Jackson: University Press of Mississippi, 2009), 89–96.

29. Joshua Brown, *Beyond the Lines: Pictorial Reporting, Everyday Life, and the Crisis of Gilded Age America* (Berkeley: University of California Press, 2002), 55.

30. In *Picturing the City*, Zurier recounts the story, likely apocryphal, that "arriving in New York from Cuba—having been fired by the *Bulletin* for drunkenness and missing deadlines—he spent the night on a park bench and landed a job the next day as an illustrator for the *New York World*."

31. *New York World* (March 15, 1896), 21.

32. In Philadelphia, he had also made the acquaintance of Robert Henri, John Sloan, and Everett Shinn—like Luks, they were future members of The Eight and the Ashcan School, and they would exert a profound influence on Luks's work as a painter.

33. Perlman, *The Immortal Eight*, 71–73.

34. Perlman, *The Immortal Eight*, 72; technological innovations made it possible for large-circulation daily newspapers to quickly and accurately reproduce drawings made by artist-reporters, replacing the painstakingly produced composite-woodblock engraving process developed at *Frank Leslie's Illustrated Newspaper* in the 1850s and described by Joshua Brown in chapter 2 of *Behind the Lines*.

35. I discuss the emergence of the photographer-reporter in "The Hideous Obscure of Henry James," *American Periodicals* 20.2 (2010): 190–215. Also see Perlman, "Drawing on Deadline."

36. The integration of visual and textual expressions of the grotesque was the hallmark and invention of Brisbane's editorial predecessor, Morris Goddard. William Randolph Hearst had hired Goddard away from the *New York World* just weeks before Luks joined the staff, but Brisbane ably carried on where Goddard left off. See Sorrentino, *Stephen Crane: A Life of Fire* (Cambridge, MA: Harvard University Press, 2014), 194; and Ferdinand Lundberg, *Imperial Hearst* (New York: Modern Library, 1936), 54–55.

37. Douglas Gilbert, *American Vaudeville: Its Life and Times* (New York: McGraw Hill, 1940), 11.

38. Everett Shinn, essay included in *The Eight* exhibition catalog (Brooklyn, NY: Brooklyn Museum of Art, 1944) and included in George Luks papers (Archives of American Art, Film 95).

39. "At a 'Select' and 'Special' with Artists, Actors and Newspapermen at a Popular Uptown Café," *New York World*, February 26, 1905 (Archives of American Art, Film 95, Frame 119). Luks's drawing *The Orator* (c. 1920) was similar in style and composition to de Fornaro's cartoon, though he apparently was depicting a different performer; the drawings suggest that tabletop performance was not uncommon in the bohemian world of turn-of-the-century New York City. A letter from Luks to Shinn contains a sketch of a "Buzzy and Anstock" act, where Luks as Buzzy, in blackface, cowers when faced by "the wolf at the door" (Shinn Papers, MF 952, frames 911–912; Smithsonian Archives of American Art).

40. Bill Blackbeard claims that the Luks and Outcault "formed a fast friendship" at *Truth*. Bill Blackbeard, *R. F. Outcault's The Yellow Kid: A Centennial Celebration of the Kid Who Stated the Comics* (Princeton, WI: Kitchen Sink Press, 1995), 42.

41. Blackbeard, "Laughing on the Outside: The Slum Kids of M. A. Woolf (1893–1896)," in Blackbeard, *R. F. Outcault's The Yellow Kid*, 17–19. Luks's cartoons featured African Americans, Jews, Irish, and Germans; Gambone writes that Luks drew cartoons addressing "the theme of race and ethnicity over sixty-eight times" in *Truth* (Gambone, *Life on the Press*, 53, 78–79).

42. Blackbeard, *R. F. Outcault's The Yellow Kid*, 23.

43. See figure 2.1 in chapter 2 for an example.

44. Blackbeard, *R. F. Outcault's The Yellow Kid*, 46, 49. Gambone writes that prototypes of the Yellow Kid appeared in *Truth* as early as 1893–94, while Blackbeard locates his emergence in a series of drawings completed in 1892 (*R. F. Outcault's The Yellow Kid*, 21). The Blackbeard volume contains color facsimiles of the majority of Outcault's Sunday Yellow Kid strips, including those published in the *World* as *Hogan's Alley*, at the *Journal* under the titles *McFadden's Flats* and *Ryan's Arcade*; and the *Yellow Kid's Diary* strip that ran on the *Journal's* editorial page from November 9, 1896–May 7, 1897. Because of the widespread availability of Outcault's work both in print and online, I have chosen (for the most part) not to reproduce his work in this

volume. His work in *Truth* is discussed in chapters 3 and 4 of Blackbeard's *R. F. Outcault's The Yellow Kid* (21–29), as well as in Gambone's chapter on Luks in *Truth* in *Life on the Press*.

45. To see the development of Outcault's comic sensibility, see "Feudal Pride in Hogan's Alley" (*Truth*, June 2, 1894, rpt. in Blackbeard's *R. F. Outcault*, p. 26), a single-panel cartoon; the half-page "The Horse Show as Reproduced in Shantytown" (*New York World*, November 17, 1895, rpt. in Blackbeard, plate 7); and "An Old-Fashioned Fourth of July in Hogan's Alley" (*New York World*, July 5, 1896, rpt. in Blackbeard, plate 25). The latter two cartoons are also available in high-res versions online at http://cartoons.osu.edu/digital_albums/yellowkid/.

46. He also contributed cartoons to the comics supplement nearly every week. Most of them are unremarkable, conventionally depicting the foibles of New York society ("Wedding Trousseau of a Young Man of To-Day," April 12, 1896; "The Different Kinds of Fun to be Had at a Chowder Party," July 26, 1896; "The Great American 'Introducing' Habit," September 20, 1896).

47. Shinn, "Plush and Cut Glass," unpublished t.s., Everett Shinn Papers, Archives of American Art, box 1, folder 80, 17–18.

48. According to some accounts, it was Pulitzer who initially wanted to feature a character based on one drawn by the English *Punch* artist Peter May, making Outcault, perhaps, a kind of handmaiden to Pulitzer's genius. For example, an article appearing in the *New York Tribune* on June 11, 1922, attributed the idea for the strip to Pulitzer (hand-dated clipping, George Luks scrapbook, Archives of American Art, NLU-1, frame 119). The questions raised by the ownership of the strip were not unlike the questions raised regarding the culpability of the Capellos in Twain's *Those Extraordinary Twins*. The case depends on whether just Luigi, whom everyone agrees kicks Tom Driscoll offstage during a political rally, is guilty, or if both Luigi and Angelo are guilty, because the leg that kicked Tom belongs to both men. Does the strip belong just to Outcault, or to both Outcault and Pulitzer? Or to Outcault and Luks? Or all three? I do not pursue the question here due to considerations of length.

49. Meredith McGill, *American Literature and the Culture of Reprinting, 1834–1853* (Philadelphia: University of Pennsylvania Press, 2003).

50. George Luks, "Hogan's Alley Attacked by the Hoboken Pretzel Club," *New York World*, May 31, 1896. Viewable online at the Cartoon Image Database at the Ohio State University Libraries, https://cartoonimages.osu.edu.

51. In this drawing, Luks is also parodying Outcault, who included the dancing Riccadonna sisters in several strips from late 1896; on October 25, they appeared in tutus and are advertised as being able to provide "plain & fancy dancing to beat the band," including "lessons in couché-couché" (hootchy-kootchy was a suggestive, sexual dance popularized in dance halls at the end of the nineteenth century); in a November 22 strip, they shown dressed in very skimpy costumes, revealing a great deal leg and are referred to—by a goat, no less—as "de naughty Riccadonnas."

52. Blackbeard, *R. F. Outcault's The Yellow Kid*, 55.

53. Gambone, *Life on the Press*, 148–52.

54. For examples of sentimental depictions of the slums, see "Moving Day in Hogan's Alley," May 3, 1896; and "Merry Xmas Morning in Hogan's Alley," December 15, 1895.

55. Robert C. Evans, "A Sharp Eye for the Grotesque in Flannery O'Connor's 'Good Country People,'" in *The Grotesque*, ed. Harold Bloom and Blake Hobby (New York: Chelsea House, 2009), 76.

56. Mikhail Bakhtin, *Rabelais and His World*, trans. Helene Iswolsky (Bloomington: Indiana University Press, 1984), 62.

57. Shinn, "Plush and Cut Glass," 11–12.

58. *Mose's Incubator* was an offshoot of another series Luks developed for the *World, Mose the Trained Chicken*, which showed the titular character behaving in distinctly human—and subversive—ways, often taking advantage of his dimwitted African American owners, the Kalsomine family. *Mose the Trained Chicken* stands as clear evidence of Luks's inability to grasp the more inclusive aspects of the racial grotesque.

59. Gambone, *Life on the Press*, 120.

60. George Luks, "The Chicks and Chinks Find Names and Mose Celebrates," *New York World* comic supplement, February 20, 1898.

61. William McKinley, proclamation dated December 21, 1898, reprinted in James M. Blount, *The American Occupation of the Philippines, 1898–1912* (New York: G. Putnam Sons, 1913), 149.

62. The last *Mose's Incubator* strip appeared on April 17. Allan Holtz, *American Newspaper Comics: An Encyclopedic Reference Guide* (Ann Arbor University of Michigan Press, 2012), 277.

63. According to Perlman, before 1899, Luks "knew no media but pencil, charcoal, and pen and ink" (*Immortal Eight*, 103). Perlman's assertion, it should be noted, disregards Luks's newspaper and magazine work.

64. Shinn, "Plush and Cut Glass," 22.

65. C. de Fornaro, "At a 'Select' and 'Special' with Artists, Actors and Newspapermen at a Popular Uptown Café," *New York World*, February 26, 1905 (AAA Film 95, Frame 119).

66. James Huneker, "George Luks," *New York Sun*, December 28, 1906. Clipping from George Luks Papers, Smithsonian Archives of American Art, FILM 95, frame 125.

67. Qtd. in Perlman, *The Immortal Eight*, 90.

68. Perlman, *The Immortal Eight*, 108–109.

69. William Dean Howells, "Mark Twain," *Century* 24.5 (September 1882), 780.

70. Tracy Wuster, *Mark Twain, American Humorist* (Columbia: University of Missouri Press, 2016), 10; 2; 21. Wuster quotes a letter from Twain to Andrew Lang in 1890 (not sent): "I have never tried in even one single instance, to help cultivate the cultivated classes. I was not equipped for it, either by native gifts or training. And I never had any ambition in that direction, but always hunted for bigger game—the masses. . . . Yes, you see, I have always catered for the Belly and the Members, but have been served like the others—criticised from the culture-standard—to my sorrow and pain; because, honestly, I never cared what became of the cultured classes; they could go to the theatre and the opera, they had no use for me and the melodeon." Twain to Andrew Lang (draft), reprinted in Frederick Anderson, *Mark Twain: The Critical Heritage* (London: Routledge and K. Paul, 1971), 336; qtd. in Wuster, 12.

Chapter 2: Rising from the Gutter

1. Paul Levitz, "Inside the Editorial Process: *Mad* Veterans Jaffee and Meglin Look at Their Editors" *Studies in American Humor* 30 (2014): 10.

2. David Nasaw, in his definitive biography of William Randolph Hearst, claims that Hearst hired Block away from Pulitzer in fall 1897; Maurice Horn claims that it was Block, not Hearst, who encouraged Rudolph Dirks to model a strip on the German *Max und Moritz* books. David Nasaw, *The Chief: The Life of William Randolph Hearst* (Boston: Houghton Mifflin, 2000), 110; Maurice Horn, *100 Years of Newspaper Comics: An Illustrated Encyclopedia* (New York: Gramercy Books, 1996), 163. Rick Marschall provides the most detailed description of Block's actual work at the *Journal*, claiming that Rudolph Dirks quit the *Journal* because of Block's "autocratic attitude"; he continues, "Through the years other leading cartoonists, including

Opper, Outcault, and Frank Willard, also expressed disgust with Block, and it seems amazing that Hearst retained him" (Rick Marschall, *The Great American Comic-Strip Artists* [New York: Abbeville Press, 1989], 46).

3. Meyer Waxman's comprehensive *A History of Jewish Literature* (1941) and Josh Lambert's revisionist *JPS Guide: American Jewish Fiction* (2009) include Lessing, but only discuss *Children of Men*. William Burling's entry on Lessing in the *Dictionary of Literary Biography* volume on *Twentieth-century Jewish American Fiction* (1984) also discusses, briefly, Lessing's work after 1903. Lessing is excluded altogether from *Jewish American Literature: A Norton Anthology* (2000), eds. Jules Chametzky, et al., as well as, more predictably, Irving Howe's *Jewish American Stories* (1977) and Theodore L. Gross's *The Jew in American Literature* (1973).

4. In his entry on Lessing in *JPS Guide: American Jewish Fiction*, Josh Lambert notes that Lessing "does not seem to have been Jewish himself," based on the fact that his depiction of East Side Jews "is not quite realistic or historically accurate" (Josh Lambert, *JPS Guide: American Jewish Fiction* [Philadelphia: Jewish Publication Society, 2009], 19–20). Daniel Walden, editor of the *Dictionary of Literary Biography*'s volume on *Twentieth-Century American-Jewish Fiction Writers*, clearly believed he was, since he explicitly restricted the volume to Jewish authors, writing that the authors included "deal with or come out of their American-Jewish experience . . . it is the importance of the American-Jewish experience in shaping a writer's fictional world that has been crucial in my determination to include that author" (Daniel Walden, "Foreword," *Twentieth-Century American-Jewish Fiction Writers* [Detroit: Gale, 1984], xiii). In his comprehensive five-volume work, *A History of Jewish Literature*, Meyer Waxman also includes Lessing in his discussion of fiction by the "American Jewry," even singling him out above Cahan, Herman Bernstein, and others as writing "stories [that] really reflect the tragedy of Jewish life at the time"; Lessing "expresses the best that there was in this Anglo-Jewish fiction during its early stage" (Waxman, *History of Jewish Literature*, vol. 4, part 2, 965).

5. Michael Kramer explores this history in several trenchant essays, especially, "The Wretched Refuse of Jewish American Literary History," *Studies in American Jewish Literature* 31.1 (2012): 61–67.

6. Block's religious affiliation is unclear even to his descendants, according to the family historian, Jean Maier, Block's great-great grand-niece (email correspondence, March 5, 2015).

7. Benjamin Schreier, "Editor's Introduction," *Studies in American Jewish Literature* 31.1 (2012): 3.

8. Simon J. Bronner, "Daniel Walden and the Jewish Subject in American Studies," talk delivered at the Northeast Modern Language Association, Harrisburg, PA (April 3–5, 2014), "American Jewish Literature: Retrospective and Prospective" roundtable. See also Schreier's *The Impossible Jew: Identity and the Reconstruction of Jewish American Literary History* (New York: New York University Press) and Julian Levinson, *Exiles on Main Street: Jewish American Writers and American Literary Culture* (Bloomington: Indiana University Press, 2008), 2.

9. Edwin G. Burrows and Mike Wallace, *Gotham: A History of New York City to 1898* (New York: Oxford University Press, 1999), 737–45; Ronald Sanders, *The Downtown Jews: Portraits of an Immigrant Generation* (New York: Harper & Row, 1969), 1–6. Burrows and Wallace write that Kleindeutschland included a Jewish sector ("in the area bounded by Grand, Stanton, Ludlow, and Pitt"), and also notes that German Jews remained largely invisible to non-Germans because "most found it hard to distinguish German Jews from other Germans, and when they did, it was apparent that the newcomers were intent on fashioning a brand of Judaism that would be 'acceptable' to the gentile majority" (Burrows and Wallace, *Gotham*, 745, 749). Stanley Nadel confirms this statement when he writes that "German Jews were a conspicuous portion of Kleindeutschland's population. . . . German Jews were also reported as participants in all kind of community activities (though they were frequently identified only as Germans).

Their numbers, however, are difficult to ascertain," he writes; he puts the number as somewhere between 7,000 and over 20,000 for the year 1860, which he claims is still "probably too low" (Stanley Nadel, *Little Germany: Ethnicity, Religion, and Class in New York City, 1845–80* [Urbana: University of Illinois Press, 1990], 99).

10. George Block is listed as working for the *New Yorker Volkszeitung* beginning in 1881 (until an unknown date), and the *Deutsch-Amerikanische Bäcker-Zeitung* from 1885–1889, in Hartmut Keil's "Appendix: List of Editors/Journalists of German-American Radical Papers, 1865–1914," in *The German-American Radical Press: The Shaping of a Left Political Culture, 1850–1940* (Urbana: University of Illinois Press, 1992), 213–19. Census data and family members indicate that George Block may have worked in other occupations as well, including the manufacture of leather goods and liquor sales.

11. "Bruno Lessing," *The Bookman* 18 (January 1904), 468–69.

12. Peter Conolly-Smith, *Translating America: An Immigrant Press Visualizes American Popular Culture, 1895–1918* (Washington: Smithsonian Books, 2004), n. 32, p. 318.

13. Conolly-Smith, *Translating America*, 20. Conolly-Smith notes that the publishers' copy of the entire run was destroyed by fire in 1911, and no other copies of the newspaper from this time have been recovered. As a result, he writes, "few historians even acknowledge its existence" (91).

14. Ian Gordon attributes many stylistic and formal innovations to cartoonist F. M. Howarth, who later created the strip *Lulu and Leander* for the *Journal*, where it ran for several years starting in 1902 (*Comic Strips and Consumer Culture, 1890–1945* [Washington: Smithsonian Institution Press, 1998], 15–24). Alex Beringer, meanwhile, has shown that forms of graphic narrative appeared much earlier, in the 1840s (Alex Beringer, "Transatlantic Picture Stories: Experiments in the Antebellum American Comic Strip," *American Literature* 87.3 [2015]: 455–88).

15. Qtd. in Thierry Smolderen, *The Origins of Comics: From William Hogarth to Winston McCay*, trans. Bart Beaty and Nick Nguyen (Jackson: University Press of Mississippi, 2014), 106.

16. Gordon, *Comic Strips and Consumer Culture*, 38–41.

17. David Kunzle defines the early comic strip along these lines, though he also emphasizes that it is "moral and topical," and not necessarily humorous (David Kunzle, *The Early Comic Strip: Narrative Strips and Picture Stories in the European Broadsheet from c. 1450–1825* [Berkeley: University of California Press, 1973], 2). Note that I am speaking specifically here about the comic *strip*, not comics in general, which Will Eisner defines using the term "sequential art" and which Scott McCloud defines as "juxtaposed pictorial and other images in a deliberate sequence intended to convey information and/or produce an aesthetic response in a reader (Will Eisner, *Comics and Sequential Art* [New York: W. W. Norton, 2008]; Scott McCloud, *Understanding Comics: The Invisible Art* [New York: William Morrow, 1993], 20).

18. Conolly-Smith, *Translating America*, 16–18.

19. Frederick Adolph Herman Leuchs, *The Early German Theatre in New York, 1840–1872* (New York: Columbia University Press, 1928).

20. Stephen Crane, chapter 7 of *Maggie: Girl of the Streets* (New York: Bantam, 1986), 25–28.

21. Thanks to Richard Blum for assistance with translation and interpretation.

22. Conolly-Smith, *Translating America*, 84. Conolly-Smith restricts his use of the term *translation* to one of exchange, "in which a word or phrase is exchanged for its equivalent"; cultural translation, then, "sees ethnic traditions and rituals replaced by an American cultural equivalent" (17).

23. Henry B. Wonham, *Playing the Races: Ethnic Caricature and American Literary Realism* (New York: Oxford University Press, 2004), 26.

24. Gavin Jones, *Strange Talk: The Politics of Dialect Literature in Gilded Age America* (Berkeley: University of California Press, 1995), 8.

25. McCloud, *Understanding Comics*, 32–33.

26. McCloud, *Understanding Comics*, 36; Jared Gardner, *Projections: Comics and Twenty-First Century Storytelling* (Stanford: Stanford University Press, 2012), 14, emphasis added.

27. Gordon also describes the mediating role played by comic strips from a class perspective in *Comic Strips and Consumer Culture*, 14–18.

28. Jones, *Strange Talk*, 7.

29. Jones, *Strange Talk*, 11.

30. There were, of course, significant exceptions to this basic plot. One was Opper's *And Her Name Was Maud!*, which reversed this trajectory by having the recalcitrant mule, Maud, kick her owner to kingdom come as a reward for his schemes to rid himself of her. Moving in the opposite direction, Outcault's *Buster Brown* portrayed a white, well-to-do little boy who, like his immigrant counterparts, also suffered spankings at the end of the strip.

31. Gardner, *Projections*, 9–11. Scholars since Janice Radway have defended genre fiction for providing readers with consoling and sometimes restorative depictions of the disempowered; of romance fiction, for example, Radway writes, "By picturing the heroine in relative positions of weakness, romances are not necessarily endorsing her situation, but examining an all-too-common state of affairs in order to display possible strategies for coping with it" (Janice Radway, *Reading the Romance: Women, Patriarchy, and Popular Literature* [Chapel Hill: University of North Carolina Press, 1984], 75).

32. Jones, *Strange Talk*, 163.

33. Qtd. in Jones, *Strange Talk*, 170.

34. Henry Jenkins, *What Made Pistachio Nuts? Early Sound Comedy and the Vaudeville Aesthetic* (New York: Columbia University Press 1992), 61–63.

35. Albert F. McLean Jr., *American Vaudeville as Ritual* (Lexington: University of Kentucky Press, 1965), 109.

36. According to David A. Cook, the term *persistence of vision* was "first described scientifically" in 1824, referring to the perception of "after-images on the retina of the eye after an object is removed from sight" (David A. Cook, *A History of Narrative Film*, 5th ed. [New York: Norton, 2016], 3).

37. Smolderen, *Origins of Comics*, 123. Smolderen attributes the first use of the "Muybridgean grid" in pictorial storytelling to A. B. (Arthur Burdett) Frost beginning in the mid- to late 1880s.

38. Agnes Repplier, "A Censor of the Press," *Savannah Tribune*, May 9, 1908; reprinted from *Life*.

39. McCloud, *Understanding Comics*, chapter 3. French critic Thierry Groënsteen argues that images are linked not just in a linear progression but in a network of multiple directions across the page and across pages, a process and technique he calls *braiding*. In the *Katzenjammer Kids*, one might note, for example, the ways that Dirks uses mirroring, symmetry, and inversion in composition between the top and bottom row of panels to underscore the repetitive gag of prank-planning, prank execution, and just deserts that occurred in each strip (Thierry Groënsteen, *The System of Comics*, trans. Bart Beaty and Nick Nguyen [Jackson: University of Mississippi Press, 2007], 145–49).

40. "Literature and Art: Sounding the Doom of the Comics," *Current Literature* 14.6 (December 1908), 632–33. The journal's Block names are all either British or German.

41. "Successful Fiction of 1903," *The Bookman* 18 (January 1904), 481.

42. "Magazine Shop-Talk," *Cosmopolitan* 40.2 (December 1905), 243.

43. The only year where Lessing published fewer than six stories was in 1912, when he was embroiled in a lawsuit regarding the ownership rights of Rudolph Dirks's *The Katzenjammer*

Kids. Beginning in 1913, Lessing's publications shifted to *Hearst's Magazine*, formerly titled the *World Today*, which Hearst purchased in 1911, and *Puck*, after World War I.

44. For a discussion of the *schnorrer*, *shadchen*, and the *schlemiel* in Jewish humor see Irving Howe, "The Nature of Jewish Laughter," in *Jewish Wry: Essays on Jewish Humor*, ed. Sarah Blacher Cohen (Bloomington, IN: Indiana University Press, 1987), 22–23. Howe's essay was originally published in *American Mercury* in 1951.

45. Lessing, "The Big Tree," *Cosmopolitan* 41.5 (September 1906), 549.

46. Jones, *Strange Talk*, 139.

47. Block did not hone his dialect-writing skills just as an editor of the comic supplement. He also wrote a number of Irish dialect pieces in the first-person voice of the Yellow Kid, Mickey Dugan, to accompany Outcault's series, "Around the World with the Yellow Kid," which ran in the *Journal* from January to June of 1898.

48. Lawrence Venuti, *The Scandals of Translation: Towards an Ethics of Difference* (London and New York: Routledge, 1998), 12, 10.

49. Editor's head note to "A Trifle Light as Air," *Cosmopolitan* 51.5 (October 1911), 777.

50. Wonham, *Playing the Races*, 9.

51. It's possible that Block may have been working at the Sunday *World* at the time Howells's review was published. Even if the two writers knew each other personally, however, a friendship between the two was unlikely. Cahan was famously prickly, and moreover, shared many East-siders' resentment toward the "uptown" German Jews, who often looked down their noses at their Eastern European counterparts. Block, certainly, did not share Cahan's commitment to socialism, despite his sympathetic treatment of the working class.

52. Hana Wirth-Nesher, *Call It English: The Languages of Jewish American Literature* (Princeton: Princeton University Press, 2006), 33.

53. Jones, *Strange Talk*, 154.

54. Abraham Cahan, *Yekl and The Imported Bridegroom and Other Stories* (New York: Dover, 1979), 89.

55. Cahan, *Yekl*, 187, 223.

56. Jones, *Strange Talk*, 160.

57. For the *Commercial Advertiser* pieces, see *Grandma Never Lived in America: The New Journalism of Abraham Cahan*, ed. Moses Rischer (Bloomington: University of Indiana Press, 1985). Cahan's work for the newspaper, it should be noted, almost always appeared without a byline; Rischin relies on stylistic analysis in determining the authorship of the articles included in the volume.

58. Bruno Lessing, "Monahan's Musical Education," *Cosmopolitan* 42.4 (February 1907), 414.

59. Lessing, "Monahan's Musical Education," 416.

60. Lessing, "Monahan's Musical Education," 420.

61. Bruno Lessing, "The Parrot of Uncle Hurwitz," *Cosmopolitan* 41.6 (October 1906), 584, 584–85, 586.

62. Lessing, "The Parrot of Uncle Hurwitz," 588.

Chapter 3: Illustration and the Narrative Quality of Appeal

1. Qtd. in *City Life Illustrated, 1890–1940* (Wilmington: Delaware Art Museum, 1980), 34.

2. William Dean Howells, "American Literary Centers," in *Literature and Life* (New York: Harper Bros., 1902), 175.

3. Judy L. Larson, *American Illustration, 1890–1925: Romance, Adventure and Suspense* (Calgary, Alberta: Glenbow Museum, 1986), 65.

4. Michele H. Bogart, *Artists, Advertising, and the Borders of Art* (Chicago: University of Chicago Press, 1995), 12.

5. Ira Glackens, "Author's Note," in *William Glackens and the Ashcan Group* (New York: Grosset and Dunlap, 1957), vii.

6. Avis Berman, "Introduction," *William Glackens*, ed. Avis Berman (New York: Skira Rizzoli in association with the Barnes Foundation, 2014), 17.

7. Larson, 31.

8. For an invaluable catalogue of the thousand-plus illustrations Glackens produced in magazines, see Nancy Allyn and Elizabeth Hawkes, *William Glackens: Book and Magazine Illustrations* (Wilmington: Delaware Art Museum, 1987). Glackens was arguably the most successful illustrator among the Ashcan group. John Sloan was also prolific (Elizabeth Hawkes has documented nearly a thousand illustrations he published), but his illustrations were produced over a much longer time span and also appeared in more obscure periodicals (many of them politically oriented) and for less prominent writers. Catalogues for other successful illustrators in the Ashcan group—especially, May Wilson Preston, who published over a thousand illustrations for the *Saturday Evening Press* alone (and, I would argue, was as important as Norman Rockwell in defining the visual ethos of that magazine)—remain to be compiled. See Elizabeth H. Hawkes, *John Sloan's Illustrations in Magazines and Books* (Wilmington: Delaware Art Museum, 1993).

9. Rebecca Zurier, *Picturing the City: Urban Vision and the Ashcan School* (Berkeley: University of California Press, 2006), 182.

10. Avis Berman, "Urban Arcadia," in *William Glackens*, 81. Berman cites a single interview from 1907 in which Glackens stated his desire to separate his illustration work from his painting; it's not clear however that Glackens sought that separation because he believed his illustration work was inferior to his painting, as Berman argues; rather, based on other statements he made at the time, he sought to dissociate his illustration work from the negative judgments applied to the field of illustration as a whole.

11. "American Illustrators." *Art and Progress* 5.3 (January 1914): 99–100.

12. These volumes, appropriately titled *American Beauties* and *Bachelor Belles*, may have served as samples for his own illustrations depicting society types and the American girl next door, which Fisher, along with Charles Gibson, helped develop into a distinct visual type.

13. Qtd. in Bogart, *Arts, Advertising, and the Borders of Art*, 319, n. 85.

14. William Glackens, "The American Section: The National Art," *Arts and Decoration* 3.5 (March 1913): 159, 160. Further citations given in text.

15. Qtd. in Ira Glackens, *William Glackens and the Ashcan Group*, 162.

16. Another example, drawn for his daughter Lenna (c. 1910?), bears a distinct resemblance in both form and style to Rudolph Dirks's *Katzenjammer Kids*, including the final panel where Oscar, the "bad little boy," gets his just deserts, much to his horror (and the delight of the reader). William Glackens Collection, Nova Southeastern Museum of Art.

17. Zurier, *Picturing the City*, 184.

18. Two installments of "The Merry-Go-Rounders" appeared in the *World*, on January 23 and February 6, both in the Sunday color comics supplement. Several other "one-shot" (i.e., strips without a repeating concept or characters) appeared in the Sunday comic supplement on the days of February 6, 13, and 20.

19. Heather Coyle Campbell writes that despite the high quality of Glackens's war illustrations, only a few were actually published; "The war was short, and it was difficult getting the drawings

to New York to accommodate the magazine's production schedule" (Campbell, "The Character and Rhythm of Modern Life" in *William Glackens*, ed. Avis Berman, 47). She lists six published illustrations that accompanied the following essays and articles on the war: Stephen Bonsal, "The Fight for Santiago: The Account of an Eye Witness," *McClure's* 11 (October 1898): 499–518; Bonsal, "The Night after San Juan: Stories of the Wounded on the Field and in the Hospital," *McClure's* 12 (December 1898): 118–28; Stephen Crane, "Marines Signaling under Fire at Guantanamo," *McClure's* 12 (February 1899): 332–36; Richard Titherington, "Our War with Spain, Part 6," *Munsey's* 20 (March 1899): 895–916; Titherington, "Our War with Spain, Part 7," *Munsey's* 21 (April 1899), 40–59; and Titherington, "Our War with Spain, Part 8," *Munsey's* 21 (May 1899): 258–78.

20. Regina Armstrong, "The New Leaders in American Illustration, IV The Typists: McCarter, Yohn, Glackens, Shinn, and Luks" (*The Bookman* 11.3 [May 1900]): 247. In her analysis of Armstrong's judgment, Campbell focuses on Glackens's illustrations for Albert White Vorse's story "The Play's the Thing" (*Scribner's* 26.2 [August 1899]), which I examine later in the chapter as an example of Glackens's narrative style. This story is in fact somewhat atypical of the illustrations Glackens produced for *Scribner's* during this year.

21. Regina Armstrong, "The New Leaders in American Illustration: III: The Story-tellers," *The Bookman* 11.2 (April 1900): 140.

22. Zurier, *Picturing the City*, 195, 197.

23. Carrie Tirado Bramen, "The Urban Picturesque and the Spectacle of Americanization," *American Quarterly* 52.3 (1990): 446.

24. Zurier, *Picturing the City*, 193.

25. Campbell, "Character and Rhythm of Modern Life," 52.

26. Campbell, "Character and Rhythm of Modern Life," 44.

27. Marion Hill, "A Tune in Court," *McClure's* June 1900: 174.

28. Larson claims that during this period, artists had a great deal of control over image placement and page composition (*American Illustration, 1890–1925*, 25) If that is true, it would certainly be even more likely for an illustrator of Glackens's stature. Regardless, effective page composition of the type I am describing was common in the tabloid-size periodicals such as the *Saturday Evening Post* and *Collier's*, and is as much a testament to the art editors as the illustrators themselves.

29. Glackens used the device of the casually placed, empty chair in numerous illustrations, including the other story by Lessing that he illustrated, "Tempus Fugit" (*Cosmopolitan* 46.4 [March 1909]: 422).

30. Myra Kelly, "The Wiles of the Wooer," *McClure's* 29.5 (September 1907): 537–46. Subsequent citations in text.

31. William Glackens, "Esther Mogilewsky's golden head rested against a pile of 'flannel opportunities' as she listened," *McClure's* 29.5 (September 1907): 538.

32. I. K. (Isaac Kahn) Friedman, *The Autobiography of a Beggar, Prefaced by Some of the Humorous Adventures and Incidents Related in the Beggars' Club* (Boston: Small, Maynard, 1903). The book included eighteen illustrations by Glackens (I believe all appeared in the serialized version published in the *Saturday Evening Post*).

33. Qtd. in Catherine Hezser, "'Are You Protestant Jews or Roman Catholic Jews?': Literary Representations of Being Jewish in Ireland," *Modern Judaism* 25.2 (May 2005): 188, n. 59.

34. Halitvack (Edward Raphael Lipsett), "Jews in the South of Ireland," *Jewish Chronicle*, September 7, 1906: 27.

35. Halitvack (Edward Raphael Lipsett), "The Judaism of the New York Ghetto," *Jewish Chronicle* March 3, 1908: 11.

36. Halitvack (Edward Raphael Lipsett), "The Jewish Press of America," *Jewish Chronicle*, July 31, 1908: 10. All subsequent quotations from the same page.

37. Halitvack (Edward Raphael Lipsett), "Baer's Last Rosh Hashana," *Jewish Chronicle*, September 1, 1907.

38. Edward Raphael Lipsett, "Denny the Jew," *Everybody's* 27 (July 1912): 45. Subsequent citations given in text.

39. Edward Raphael Lipsett, "The Amateur Jew," *Everybody's* 32 (June 1915): 765.

40. Halitvack (Edward Raphael Lipsett), "About Passover in the New York 'Ghetto,'" *Jewish Chronicle*, May 1, 1908: 21.

41. Halitvack (Edward Raphael Lipsett), "About Passover in the New York 'Ghetto,'" *Jewish Chronicle*, May 1, 1908: 21.

42. Guy Pène du Bois, *William Glackens* (New York: Whitney Museum of American Art, 1931), 12.

43. Zurier, *Picturing the City*, 211.

Chapter 4: The Black Comic Sensibility

1. Ralph Ellison, *Invisible Man* (New York: Vintage, 1995), 564.

2. Ian Gordon, *Comic Strips and Consumer Culture, 1890–1945* (Washington, DC: Smithsonian Institution, 1998), 60.

3. *New York Herald*, December 2, 1900, qtd. in Gordon, 65.

4. Charles R. Johnson, "Foreword," in Fredrik Strömberg, *Black Images in the Comics: A Visual History* (New York: Fantagraphics Books), 11. Strömberg's book contains numerous examples of racist representations of Africans and African Americans in the early comics.

5. Most histories name the first black comic strip as Leslie Rogers's *Bungleton Green*, which appeared in the *Chicago Defender* beginning in 1920, and the first black comic book as *All-Negro Comics #1* (1947). Sheena C. Brown defines the black comics as those "created by Black artists and featuring Black characters" (Sheena C. Brown, "Brief History of the Black Comic," in *Black Comics: Politics of Race and Representation*, ed. Sheena C. Brown and Ronald L. Jackson [New York: Bloomsbury, 2014], 11). Historians of black comics generally presume that these comics were and are created for a black audience. As early as the late 1880s, topical cartoons appeared in the *Indianapolis Freeman* and other black newspapers; Frances Gateward and John Jennings note that if one adopts Scott McCloud's very broad definition of comics as "juxtaposed pictorial and other images in deliberate sequence, intended to convey information and/or to produce an aesthetic response in the viewer," then "black people have been making comics and seeing themselves as subjects for comics for thousands of years," in forms such as "Ghanaian Andinkra stamps, the geometric patterns of the Ndebele, . . . the Igbos' Nsibidi symbols," and African American quilts (Frances Gateward and John Jennings, "Introduction: The Sweeter the Christmas," in *The Blacker the Ink: Constructions of Black Identity in Comics and Sequential Art*, eds. Gateward and Jennings [New Brunswick, NJ: Rutgers University Press, 2015], 2). For definitions of the comic strip, see Scott McCloud, *Understanding Comics: The Invisible Art* (New York: William Morrow, 1993), Will Eisner, *Comics and Sequential Art* (New York: W. W. Norton, 2008), and Thierry Groënsteen, *The System of Comics*, trans. Bart Beaty and Nick Nguyen (Jackson: University of Mississippi Press, 2009).

6. Qtd. in Johnson, "Foreword," 8.

7. "Daughter on Stage," *Washington Bee* 19.26 (November 24, 1900): 6; "Paradise for the Lazy," *Chicago Broad Ax*, December 28, 1901: 4. Ads for the *World* appearing in black newspapers as early as 1908 declared its Sunday comic supplement "the foremost thing in America," and offered joke books containing popular comic strips as premiums for new subscribers. These advertisements continued to appear in the same newspapers into the 1910s.

8. Agnes Repplier, "A Censor of the Press," *Savannah Tribune*, May 9, 1908, 2.

9. Gateward and Jennings, "Introduction: The Sweeter the Christmas," 3.

10. Eric Lott, *Love and Theft: Blackface Minstrelsy and the American Working Class* (New York: Oxford University Press, 1994), 8.

11. Nicholas Sammond, *Birth of an Industry: Blackface Minstrelsy and the Rise of American Animation* (Raleigh, NC: Duke University Press, 2015), 17, 27.

12. *The Souls of Black Folk* (New York: Dover, 1994), 2. Mel Watkins writes that double consciousness is in fact the basis of much African American humor (*On the Real Side: Laughing, Lying, and Signifying—the Underground Tradition of African American Humor that Transformed American Culture from Slavery to Richard Pryor* [New York: Touchstone Books, 1994], 27); Ralph Ellison also describes African American representation in Hollywood cinema in similar ways in his essay "Shadow and Act," in the book of the same title (New York: Random House, 1953). See also Shawn Michelle Smith, *Photography on the Color Line: W.E.B. Du Bois, Race, and Visual Culture* (Durham: Duke University Press, 2004).

13. Ellison, "Change the Joke and Slip the Yoke," *Shadow and Act*, 54.

14. Ellison, "Change the Joke," 54; 1970 speech qtd. in Watkins, *On the Real Side*, 31.

15. Harold G. Davidson, *Jimmy Swinnerton: The Artist and His Work* (New York: Hearst Books, 1985), 18.

16. Qtd. in Jerry A. Schefcik, "James G. Swinnerton (1880–1974)," *Nevada Historical Society Quarterly* 33.2 (June 1990), 105.

17. Qtd. in Davidson, *Jimmy Swinnerton*, 18.

18. Qtd. in Davidson, *Jimmy Swinnerton*, 19.

19. Watkins, *On the Real Side*, 90. Sammond writes that animators including Winsor McCay, Max Fleischer, and Walter Lantz frequently figured themselves as interlocutors "drawing" or otherwise framing the actions and utterances of their minstrel characters (27). Swinnerton, with his experience as a performer aspiring to the "end man's chair" and with his physical resemblance to Sam, appears to identify instead with the end man himself.

20. W. T. Lhamon Jr., *Raising Cain: Blackface Performance from Jim Crow to Hip Hop* (Cambridge: Harvard University Press, 2000), 6.

21. *Detroit Free Press*, July 9, 1905.

22. For example, see "And Sam Jes' Roared," where Sam is hired to play a doorman on stage for an acting troupe (Jimmy Swinnerton, *Sam and His Laugh* [New York: American-Journal-Examiner, 1906], 19); and a strip published in the *Detroit Free Press* on August 20, 1905, where Sam is hired by a black waiter to be another black waiter.

23. Sammond, *Birth of an Industry*, 4.

24. W. T. Lhamon Jr., "Turning around Jim Crow," in *Burnt Cork: Traditions and Legacies of Blackface Minstrelsy*, ed. Stephen Johnson (Amherst: University of Massachusetts Press, 2012), 26–27, 24.

25. James Weldon Johnson, *Black Manhattan* (New York: Arno Press, 1968), 127.

26. Gilbert Osofsky, *Harlem, the Making of a Ghetto* (New York: Oxford University Press, 1969), 48.

27. Osofsky, *Harlem*, 50–51.

28. Martha Hodes, "Knowledge and Indifference in the New York City Race Riot of 1900: An Argument in Search of a Story," *Rethinking History* 15.1 (March 2011): 78; Osofsky, *Harlem*, 43.

29. Hodes, 78.

30. Patrick McDonnell, Karen O'Connell, and Georgia Riley de Havenon, *Krazy Kat: The Comic Art of George Herriman* (New York: Abrams, 1999), 41; Davidson, *James Swinnerton*, 41.

31. TAD (Theodore A. Dorgan), "This Is About Garge Herriman," reproduced in McDonnell, et al., *Krazy Kat*, 40.

32. Michael Tisserand, "Birth of the Krazy," in *Scenes of My Infint-hood: Celebrating the Birth of Krazy Kat* (exhibition catalog), Ohio State University, Billy Ireland Cartoon Library & Museum and the Wexner Center for the Arts (Columbus: Ohio State University Libraries, 2010), 14; Tisserand, *Krazy: George Herriman, a Life in Black and White* (New York: HarperCollins, 2016), 17.

33. The most surprising thing, perhaps, about the revelation of Herriman's ethnic-racial heritage is the fact that it remained unrecognized for so long.

34. McDonnell, et al., *Krazy Kat*, 30.

35. Herriman, "Musical Mose 'Impussonates' a Scotchman, with Sad Results," *New York World*, February 16, 1902; "Musical Mose Tries Another 'Impussanation,'" *New York World*, February 23, 1902; "Scotchman"; "Another 'Impussanation." Other installments appeared in the *World* on January 19 and March 9, 1902, though the character in the January 19 strip is named "Sam" and does not engage in ethnic impersonation.

36. Jared Gardner reproduces examples of *Lariat Pete* and *Major Ozone* in "Becoming Krazy," *Scenes of My Infint-hood: Celebrating the Birth of Krazy Kat* (exhibition catalog), Ohio State University, Billy Ireland Cartoon Library & Museum and the Wexner Center for the Arts (Columbus: Ohio State University Libraries, 2010), 24–26. For reproductions of *Mrs. Waitaminnit*, see *Krazy + Ignatz: "At Last My Drim of Life Has Come True," 1922–1924*, ed. Bill Blackbeard (New York: Fantagraphics Books, 2012).

37. Gardner, "Becoming Krazy," 26–27.

38. Watkins, *On the Real Side*, 17.

39. "The New Colossus," *Los Angeles Times*, April 8, 1906; *Los Angeles Times*, February 4, 1906.

40. Jeffrey T. Sammon, *Beyond the Ring: The Role of Boxing in American Society* (Urbana and Chicago: University of Illinois Press, 1988), 35.

41. Sammon, *Beyond the Ring*, 37.

42. "Flynn and Langford Drew $11,046 to Box Office; Pueblo Boy Got $3313; Negro $2761," *Los Angeles Examiner*, February 10, 1910, p. 11.

43. Tisserand, "The Birth of the Krazy," 19; Ruby Goodwin, qtd. in Thomas R. Hietala, *The Fight of the Century: Jack Johnson, Joe Louis, and the Struggle for Racial Equality* (Armonk, NY, and London: M. E. Sharpe, 2002), 14. Herriman depicted a sentiment similar to that expressed by Goodwin in "Mammy's Latest Lullaby" (May 4, 1910).

44. Geoffrey C. Ward, *Unforgivable Blackness: The Rise and Fall of Jack Johnson* (New York: Knopf, 2004), 4.

45. Qtd. in McDonnell, et al., 51.

46. "Back in the Spotlight Again," *Los Angeles Examiner*, May 23, 1910, p. 11; "Ready to Enter the Ring," *Los Angeles Examiner* sporting section, p. 4. TAD relied on a similar conceit in his strip "That's What They All Say" (*Los Angeles Examiner*, January 9, 1910).

47. Ward, *Unforgivable Blackness*, 111. Many boxers, including nearly all of those mentioned in this chapter, performed on the vaudeville circuit to supplement their prize earnings. Most

engaged in boxing demonstrations (Ward relates one of Johnson's acts where he would send an entire punching bag into the audience with a single blow), but many, including Johnson, also sang, acted in sketches, and danced.

48. Qtd. in Glenn Stout, "Fighting Blind," *Boston Magazine* 79.3 [March 1987], 95. Also see Sammons, 37; "The Boston Tar Baby," *Time Magazine* (January 23, 1956), 75.

49. Carr, *Los Angeles Times*, March 18, 1910, qtd. in Clay Moyle, *Sam Langford: Boxing's Greatest Uncrowned Champion* (Seattle: Bennett and Hastings, 2012), chapter 10. Moyle gives February 10, 1910, as the date of the second bout, but newspaper coverage in the *Examiner* clearly shows that the two fought on December 21, 1909.

50. Qtd. in McDonnell, et al., *Krazy Kat*, 44.

51. McDonnell, et al., *Krazy Kat*, 63.

52. *Krazy Kat* daily strip, January 6, 1918, reprinted in McDonnell, et al., 61.

53. Jeet Heer, "Afterword," in Brown, ed., *Black Comics*, 252.

54. Gardner, "Becoming Krazy," 34.

55. "All-Star Minstrels Ready for Great Actors' Benefit," *Los Angeles Examiner*, April 11, 1910, p. 10.

56. Hughes, preface from 1962 ed. of *Book of Negro Folklore*, qtd. in Watkins, *On the Real Side*, 16.

Coda

1. Robert J. Burdette, "Have Women a Sense of Humor?," *Harper's Bazaar* 36.7 (July 1902): 597.

2. Mel Watkins, *On the Real Side: Laughing, Lying and Signifying—the Underground Tradition of African-American Humor that Transformed American Culture, from Slavery to Richard Pryor* (New York: Simon and Schuster, 1994), 17.

3. Watkins, *On the Real Side*, 11–12.

4. Zora Neale Hurston, "High John de Conquer," *The Book of Negro Folklore*, eds. Langston Hughes and Arna Bontemps (New York: Dodd, Mead, and Co., 1958), 102, 101.

5. Alain Locke, review of *Their Eyes Were Watching God*, *Opportunity* (June 1, 1938); Richard Wright, "Between Laughter and Tears" (review of *Their Eyes Were Watching God*), *New Masses* (October 5, 1937), 25.

6. Christina Sharpe, *In the Wake: Blackness and Being* (Durham, NC: Duke University Press, 2016), 19–20.

7. Sharpe, *In the Wake*, 22.

8. Sharpe, *In the Wake*, 22.

9. Sharpe, *In the Wake*, 4.

10. Kobena Mercer, "Carnivalesque and Grotesque: What Bakhtin's Laughter Tells Us about Art and Culture," in *No Laughing Matter: Visual Humor in Ideas of Race, Nationality, and Ethnicity*, ed. Angela Rosenthal (Hanover, NH: Dartmouth College Press, 2016), 9.

11. See p. <000> of introduction to this volume.

12. See Ian Gordon, *Comic Strips and Consumer Culture* (1993), for a definitive exploration of the role Outcault played in the development of modern American consumer culture.

13. On the *Indianapolis Freeman*, see Andreá N. Williams, "Cultivating Black Visuality: The Controversy over Cartoons in the Indianapolis Freeman," *American Periodicals* 25.2 (2015): 124–38; and Aleen J. Ratzlaff, "Illustrated African American Journalism: Political Cartooning in the *Indianapolis Freeman*," in *Seeking a Voice: Images of Race and Gender in the Nineteenth-Century Press*, eds. David B. Sachsman, S. Kittrell Rushing, and Roy Morris Jr. (West Lafayette, IN: Purdue University Press, 2009), 131–40.

14. Trina Robbins provides a brief but useful—and heavily illustrated—survey of these and several other female cartoonists and comic strip artists in "The Queens of Cute," chapter 1 of *Pretty in Ink: North American Women Cartoonists, 1896–2013* (Seattle: Fantagraphics Books, 2013), 7–28.

15. According to Allan Holtz, *Strange What Difference a Man Makes* ran in the *New York Evening Journal* and was distributed by the *New York Evening Journal* syndicate from February 24 to August 17, 1905.

16. Thorstein Veblen, *Theory of the Leisure Class* (Mineola, NY: Dover, 1994), 91.

17. Qtd. in Ira Glackens, *William Glackens and the Ashcan Group*, 48.

18. Martha Banta, *Barbaric Intercourse: Caricature and the Culture of Conduct, 1841–1936* (Chicago: University of Chicago Press, 2003), 8.

19. Banta, *Barbaric Intercourse*, 5.

Works Consulted

Archival

Billy Ireland Cartoon Library & Museum, Ohio State University Libraries, Columbus, OH.
William and Ira Glackens Papers, Archives of American Art, Smithsonian Institution, Washington, DC.
William Glackens Collection, Nova Southeastern Museum of Art, Fort Lauderdale, FL.
George Luks Papers, Delaware Museum of Art, Wilmington, DE.
George Luks Papers, Archives of American Art, Smithsonian Institution, Washington, DC.
John Sloan Collection, Delaware Museum of Art, Wilmington, DE.
Everett Shinn Papers, Delaware Museum of Art, Wilmington, DE.
Everett Shinn Papers, Archives of American Art, Smithsonian Institution, Washington, DC.

Primary and Secondary Sources

Allen, Robert Clyde. *Horrible Prettiness: Burlesque and American Culture.* Chapel Hill: University of North Carolina Press, 1991.
Allyn, Nancy E. *William Glackens: Illustrator in NY, 1897–1919.* Wilmington: Delaware Art Museum, 1985.
Allyn, Nancy, and Elizabeth Hawkes. *William Glackens: Book and Magazine Illustrations.* Wilmington: Delaware Art Museum, 1987.
"American Illustrators." *Art and Progress* 5.3 (January 1914): 99–101.
Appel, Joseph H. *John Wanamaker: A Study.* Rodman Wanamaker, 1927 (2nd ed.). New York Public Library. 103 pages.
Armed Forces radio interview with James Swinnerton, 1963. https://www.youtube.com/watch?v=eeNKnxeR_mM
Armstrong, Regina. "The New Leaders in American Illustration I: The Academicians: Loeb, Sterner, Clark and Christy." *The Bookman* 10 (February 1900): 548–55.
Armstrong, Regina. "The New Leaders in American Illustration II: The Decorative Workers: Wright, Fisher, Hutt and Parrish." *The Bookman* 11 (March 1900): 49–56.

Armstrong, Regina. "The New Leaders in American Illustration III: The Story-Tellers: Pape, Keller, Hitchcock, Clinedinst and Ashe." *The Bookman* 11 (April 1900): 140–48.

Armstrong, Regina. "The New Leaders in American Illustration IV: The Typists: McCarter, Yohn, Glackens, Shinn and Luks." *The Bookman* 11 (May 1900): 244–51.

Armstrong, Regina. "The New Leaders in American Illustration V: The Humorous Men: Newell, Kemble, Sullivant, Zimmerman and Hamilton." *The Bookman* 11 (June 1900): 334–41.

Bakhtin, Mikhail. *Rabelais and His World*. Trans. Helene Iswolsky. Bloomington: Indiana University Press, 1984.

Banta, Martha. *Barbaric Intercourse: Caricature and the Culture of Conduct, 1841–1936*. Chicago: University of Chicago Press, 2003.

Barrish, Phillip J. *The Cambridge Introduction to American Literary Realism*. Cambridge, GB: Cambridge University Press, 2011.

Bean, Annemarie, James V. Hatch, and Brooks McNamara, eds. *Inside the Minstrel Mask: Readings in Nineteenth-Century Blackface Minstrelsy*. Middletown, CT: Wesleyan University Press, 1996.

Bell, Michael Davitt. *The Problem of American Realism: Studies in the Cultural History of an Idea*. Chicago: University of Chicago Press, 1993.

Beringer, Alex. "Transatlantic Picture Stories: Experiments in the Antebellum American Comic Strip." *American Literature* 87.3 (2015): 455–88.

Berman, Avis, ed. *William Glackens*. New York: Rizzoli, 2014.

Bhabha, Homi K. *The Location of Culture*. New York: Routledge Classics, 2004.

Birmingham, Stephen. *Our Crowd: The Great Jewish Families of New York*. New York: Dell, 1968.

Birmingham, Stephen. *"The Rest of Us": The Rise of America's Eastern European Jews*. Syracuse, NY: Syracuse University Press, 1984.

Blackbeard, Bill. *R. F. Outcault's The Yellow Kid: A Centennial Celebration of the Kid Who Started the Comics*. Princeton, WI: Kitchen Sink Press, 1995.

Bloom, Harold and Blake Hobby, eds. *The Grotesque*. New York: Chelsea House, 2009.

Blount, James M. *The American Occupation of the Philippines, 1898–1912*. New York: G. Putnam Sons, 1913.

Bogart, Michele H. *Artists, Advertising, and the Borders of Art*. Chicago: University of Chicago Press, 1995.

Boskin, Joseph. "Beyond *Kvetching* and *Jiving*: The Thrust of Jewish and Black Folkhumor." In *Jewish Wry: Essays on Jewish Humor*. Ed. Sarah Blacher Cohen. Bloomington: Indiana University Press, 1986: 53–79.

"The Boston Tar Baby." *Time Magazine* (January 23, 1956): 75.

Bourne, Randolph. "Transnational America." *The Atlantic*, July 1916. Accessed January 20, 2019. https://www.theatlantic.com/magazine/archive/1916/07/trans-national-america/304838/.

Bramen, Carrie Tirado. "The Urban Picturesque and the Spectacle of Americanization." *American Quarterly* 52 (September 2000): 444–77.

Bramen, Carrie Tirado. *The Uses of Variety: Modern Americanism and the Quest for National Distinctiveness*. Cambridge: Harvard University Press, 2000.

Brod, Harry. *Superman Is Jewish? How Comic Books Came to Serve Truth, Justice, and the Jewish-American Way*. New York: Free Press, 2012.

Brodhead, Richard. *Cultures of Letters: Scenes of Reading and Writing in Nineteenth-Century America*. Chicago: University of Chicago Press, 1993.

Bronner, Simon J. "Daniel Walden and the Jewish Subject in American Studies," talk delivered at NEMLA, Harrisburg, PA (April 3–5, 2014), "American Jewish Literature: Retrospective and Prospective" roundtable.

Brown, Joshua. *Beyond the Lines: Pictorial Reporting, Everyday Life, and the Crisis of Gilded Age America*. Berkeley: University of California Press, 2002.

Brown, Sheena C., and Ronald L. Jackson II, eds. *Black Comics: Politics of Race and Representation*. London: Bloomsbury Books, 2013.

"Bruno Lessing." *The Bookman* 18 (January 1904): 468-69.

Buhle, Paul, ed. *Jews and American Comics: An Illustrated History of an American Art Form*. New York: New Press, 2008.

Buhle, Paul, ed. *Jews and American Popular Culture*. Westport, CT: Praeger, 2007. 3 vols.

Bullard, E. John. "George Luks and William Glackens in Cuba." William and Ira Glackens Papers. 5-page t.s. Smithsonian Institution, Microfilm Reel 4709 (frames 646-650).

Burrows, Edwin G., and Mike Wallace. *Gotham: A History of New York City to 1898*. New York: Oxford University Press, 1999.

Burrows, Stuart. *A Familiar Strangeness: American Fiction and the Language of Photography, 1839-1945*. Athens: University of Georgia Press, 2008.

Cahan, Abraham. *Grandma Never Lived in America: The New Journalism of Abraham Cahan*. Ed. Moses Rischer. Bloomington: University of Indiana Press, 1985.

Cahan, Abraham. *Yekl and The Imported Bridegroom and Other Stories* (New York: Dover, 1979.

Carlyle, Thomas. "Jean Paul Friedrich Richter." *Critical and Miscellaneous Essays*, vol. 1. New York: Charles Scribner Sons, 1900: 1-25.

Cassuto, Leonard. *The Inhuman Race: The Racial Grotesque in American Literature and Culture*. New York: Columbia University Press, 1997.

Chametzky, Jules. *From the Ghetto: The Fiction of Abraham Cahan*. Amherst: University of Massachusetts Press, 1977. 161 pp. JHU PQ3505.C13 Z6 1977

Chute, Hillary L. *Graphic Women: Life Narrative and Contemporary Comics*. New York: Columbia University Press, 2010.

Cloutier, Jean-Christophe. "The Comic Book World of Ralph Ellison's *Invisible Man*." *Novel* 43.2 (2010): 294-319.

Cohen, Sarah Blacher, ed. *Jewish Wry: Essays on Jewish Humor*. Bloomington: Indiana University Press, 1987.

Cohen, Ted. *Jokes: Philosophical Thoughts on Joking Matters*. Chicago: University of Chicago Press, 1999.

Cole, Jean Lee. "The Hideous Obscure of Henry James." *American Periodicals* 20.2 (2010): 190-215.

Coleman, Harry J. *Give Us a Little Smile, Baby*. New York: E. P. Dutton & Co., 1943.

Conolly-Smith, Peter. *Translating America: An Immigrant Press Visualizes American Popular Culture, 1895-1918*. Washington: Smithsonian Books, 2004.

Cook, David A. *A History of Narrative Film* (5th ed.). New York: Norton, 2016.

Coyle, Heather Campbell, ed. *Howard Pyle: An American Master Rediscovered*. Wilmington: Delaware Art Museum, 2011.

Crary, Jonathan. *Suspensions of Perception: Attention, Spectacle, and Modern Culture*. Cambridge: MIT Press, 1999.

Crary, Jonathan. *Techniques of the Observer: On Vision and Modernity in the Nineteenth Century*. Cambridge: MIT Press, 1990.

Cuba, Stanley L., Nina Kasanof, and Judith O'Toole. *George Luks: An American Artist*. Sordoni Art Gallery, Delaware Art Museum, The Hunter Museum, Kraushaar Gallery, 1988.

Davidson, Harold G. *James Swinnerton: The Artist and His Work*. New York: Hearst Books, 1985.

Dahn, Eurie. "'Unashamedly Black': Jim Crow Aesthetics and the Visual Logic of Shame." *MELUS* 39.2 (Summer 2014): 93-113.

DesRochers, Rick. *The New Humor in the Progressive Era: Americanization and the Vaudeville Comedian*. New York: Palgrave Macmillan, 2014.
Du Bois, W. E. B. *The Souls of Black Folk*. New York: Dover, 1994.
Duffy, Damian, and John Jennings. *Black Comix: African American Independent Comics Art and Culture*. New York: Mark Batty Publishers, 2010.
The Eight (exhibition catalog). Brooklyn, NY: Brooklyn Museum of Art, 1944.
Eisner, Will. *Comics and Sequential Art*. New York: W. W. Norton, 2008.
Eisner, Will. *Graphic Storytelling and Visual Narrative*. New York: W. W. Norton, 2008.
Elliott, Michael A. *The Culture Concept: Writing and Difference in the Age of Realism*. Minneapolis: University of Minnesota Press, 2002.
Ellison, Ralph. "Change the Joke, and Slip the Yoke." In *Shadow and Act*. New York: Random House, 1953.
Ellison, Ralph. "Shadow and Act." *Shadow and Act*. New York: Random House, 1953: 273–81.
Elzea, Rowland. "The Golden Age of American Illustration and Its Sources." In *The Golden Age of American Illustration, 1880–1914*. Wilmington: Wilmington Society of the Fine Arts, 1972.
Farrar, Hayward. *The Baltimore Afro-American, 1892–1950*. Westport, CT: Greenwood Press, 1998.
Friedman, I. K. (Isaac Kahn). *The Autobiography of a Beggar*. Boston: Small, Maynard, 1903.
Foster, William H. III. *Looking for a Face Like Mine: The History of African Americans in Comics*. Waterbury, CT: Fine Tooth Press, 2005.
Freud, Sigmund. *Jokes and Their Relation to the Unconscious*. Trans. and ed. James Strachey. Vol. 8 of *The Standard Edition of the Complete Psychological Works of Sigmund Freud*. London: Hogarth Press, 1960.
Fulton, Joe B. *Mark Twain's Ethical Realism: The Aesthetics of Race, Class and Gender*. Columbia: University of Missouri Press, 1997.
Gambone, Robert L. *Life on the Press: The Popular Art and Illustrations of George Benjamin Luks*. Jackson: University Press of Mississippi, 2009.
Gardner, Jared. "Becoming Krazy." *Scenes of My Infint-hood: Celebrating the Birth of Krazy Kat* (exhibition catalog), Ohio State University, Billy Ireland Cartoon Library & Museum and the Wexner Center for the Arts. Columbus: Ohio State University Libraries, 2010: 23–35.
Gardner, Jared. *Projections: Comics and Twenty-First-Century Storytelling*. Stanford: Stanford University Press, 2012.
Garvey, Ellen Gruber. *The Adman in the Parlor: Magazines and the Gendering of Consumer Culture, 1880s–1910s*. New York: Oxford University Press, 1996.
Gateward, Francis, and John Jennings, eds. *The Blacker the Ink: Constructions of Black Identity in Comics and Sequential Art*. New Brunswick, NJ: Rutgers University Press, 2015.
Gibbons, Herbert Adams. *John Wanamaker*. New York: Harper & Brothers, 1926.
Gilbert, Douglas. *American Vaudeville: Its Life and Times*. New York: McGraw-Hill, 1940.
Gillman, Susan. *Dark Twins: Imposture and Identity in Mark Twain's America*. Chicago: University of Chicago Press, 1989.
Glackens, Ira. *William Glackens and the Ashcan Group*. New York: Grosset and Dunlap, 1957.
Glackens, William. "The American Section: The National Art." *Arts and Decoration* 3.5 (March 1913): 159–64.
Glass, Montague. *Potash and Perlmutter: Their Copartnership Ventures and Adventures*. New York: Grosset and Dunlap, 1909.

Glenn, Susan A. *Female Spectacle: The Theatrical Roots of Modern Feminism.* Cambridge: Harvard University Press, 2002.
Golden, Catherine J., ed. *Book Illustrated: Text, Image, and Culture, 1770–1930.* New Castle, DE: Oak Knoll Press, 2000.
Gombrich, E. H., and Ernst Kris. "The Principles of Caricature." *British Journal of Medical Psychology* 17 (1938): 319.
Goodwin, James. *American Grotesque.* Columbus: Ohio State University Press, 2009.
Gordon, Ian. *Comic Strips and Consumer Culture, 1890–1945.* Washington, DC: Smithsonian Institution, 1998.
Greenhill, Jennifer. *Playing It Straight: Art and Humor in the Gilded Age.* Berkeley: University of California Press, 2012.
Groënsteen, Thierry. *The System of Comics.* Jackson: University Press of Mississippi, 2007.
Gross, Theodore L. *The Jew in American Literature.* New York: Free Press, 1973.
Guttmann, Allen, *The Jewish Writer in America: Assimilation and the Crisis of Identity* (1971).
Grunwald Center for the Graphic Arts. *The American Personality: The Artist-Illustrator of Life in the United States, 1860–1930.* Los Angeles: Grunwald Center for the Graphic Arts, 1976.
Haenni, Sabine. "Visual and Theatrical Culture, Tenement Fiction, and the Immigrant Subject in Abraham Cahan's *Yekl*." *American Literature* 71.3 (September 1999), 493–527
Hancock, La Touche. "American Caricature and Comic Art." *The Bookman* 16.2 (October 1902): 120–32; 16.3 (November 1902): 263–74.
Harris, Susan K. "Problems of Representation in Turn-of-the-Century Immigrant Fiction." In *American Realism and the Canon.* Eds. Tom Quirk and Gary Scharnhorst. Newark: University of Delaware Press, 1994: 127–42
Hawkes, Elizabeth H. *John Sloan's Illustrations in Magazines and Books.* Wilmington: Delaware Art Museum, 1993.
Henken, David. *City Reading: Written Words and Public Spaces in Antebellum New York.* New York: Columbia University Press, 1998.
Herriman, George. *Krazy & Ignatz: "A Kind, Benevolent and Amiable Brick." Convening the Full-Page Comic Strips, 1919–1921.* Ed. Bill Blackbeard. Seattle: Fantagraphics Books, 2011.
Herriman, George. *Krazy & Ignatz: "Love in a Kestle or Love in a Hut." Convening the Full-Page Comic Strips, 1916–1918.* Ed. Bill Blackbeard. Seattle: Fantagraphics Books, 2010.
Hezser, Catherine. "'Are You Protestant Jews or Roman Catholic Jews?': Literary Representations of Being Jewish in Ireland." *Modern Judaism* 25.2 (May 2005): 188.
Hietala, Thomas R. *The Fight of the Century: Jack Johnson, Joe Louis, and the Struggle for Racial Equality.* Armonk, NY: M. E. Sharpe, 2004.
Hills, Patricia. *Turn of the Century America: Paintings, Graphics, Photographs, 1890–1910* (exhibition catalog). New York: Whitney Museum of American Art, 1977.
Hodes, Martha. "Knowledge and Indifference in the New York City Race Riot of 1900: An Argument in Search of a Story." *Rethinking History* 15.1 (March 2011): 61–89.
Hoffman, Arthur Sullivant. "Who Writes the Jokes?" *The Bookman* 26 (October 1907): 171–81.
Holtz, Allan. *American Newspaper Comics: An Encyclopedic Reference Guide.* Ann Arbor: University of Michigan Press, 2012.
Hooper-Greenhill, Eilean. *Museums and the Interpretation of Visual Culture.* London: Routledge, 2000.
Horn, Maurice. *100 Years of Newspaper Comics: An Illustrated Encyclopedia.* New York: Gramercy Books, 1996.
Howe, Irving, ed. *Jewish-American Stories.* New York: Signet, 1977. Print.

Howe, Irving. *The World of Our Fathers*. New York: Schocken Books, 1989.
Howe, Irving, and Eliezer Greenberg, eds. *A Treasury of Yiddish Stories*. New York: Meridian, 1958.
Howells, William Dean. "American Literary Centers." *Literature and Life*. New York: Harper Bros., 1902, 175.
Howells, William Dean. *Criticism and Fiction*. New York: Harper and Brothers, 1902.
Hume, David. "Of the Standard of Taste." In *Of the Standard of Taste and Other Essays*. Ed. John Lenz. Indianapolis, IN: Bobbs-Merrill, 1965.
Inge, Thomas. *Dark Laughter: The Satiric Art of Oliver W. Harrington*. Jackson: University Press of Mississippi, 2009.
Jacobson, Matthew Frye. *Barbarian Virtues: The United States Encounters Foreign Peoples at Home and Abroad*. New York: Hill and Wang, 2000.
Jacobson, Matthew Frye. *Special Sorrows: The Diasporic Imagination of Irish, Polish, and Jewish Immigrants in the United States*. Cambridge, MA: Harvard University Press, 1995.
James, Henry. *The American Scene*. London: Chapman and Hall, 1907.
Jameson, Fredric. *The Antinomies of Realism*. New York: Verso, 2013.
Jarenski, Shelly. *Narrating Vision, Visualizing Nation: The American Nineteenth Century After 1839*. PhD diss., Loyola University Chicago, 2007.
Jarman, Baird. "The Graphic Art of Thomas Nast." *American Periodicals* 20.2 (2010): 156.
Jay, Martin. "Scopic Regimes of Modernity." In *Vision and Visuality*. Ed. Hal Foster. Seattle: Bay Press, 1988: 3–27.
Jenkins, Henry. *What Made Pistachio Nuts? Early Sound Comedy and the Vaudeville Aesthetic*. New York: Columbia University Press, 1992.
Johnston, Patricia, ed. *Seeing High and Low: Representing Social Conflict in American Visual Culture*. Berkeley: University of California Press, 2006.
Johnson, Stephen, ed. *Burnt Cork: Traditions and Legacies of Blackface Minstrelsy*. Amherst and Boston: University of Massachusetts Press, 2012.
Johnson, James Weldon. *Black Manhattan*. 1930. New York: Arno Press, 1968.
Jones, Gavin. *Strange Talk: The Politics of Dialect Literature in the United States*. Berkeley: University of California Press, 1999.
Kandiyoti, Dalia. "What Is the 'Jewish' in 'Jewish American Literature'?" *Studies in American Jewish Literature* 31.1 (2012).
Kaplan, Arie. *From Krakow to Krypton: Jews and Comic Books*. Philadelphia: Jewish Publication Society, 2008.
Kauvar, Elaine M. "Warring Desires: The Future of Jewish American Literature." *American Literary History* 21.4 (Winter 2009): 877–90.
Keil, Hartmut. "Appendix: List of Editors/Journalists of German-American Radical Papers, 1865–1914." In *The German-American Radical Press: The Shaping of a Left Political Culture, 1850–1940*. Urbana: University of Illinois Press, 1992: 213–19.
Kelly, Myra. "A Christmas Present for a Lady." *McClure's* 20.2 (December 1902): 195–200.
Kelly, Myra. "The Gifts of the Philosophers: A Christmas Kindergarten Story." *Ladies' Home Journal* 22.1 (December 1904): 9, 55.
Kelly, Myra. "H.R.H. The Prince of Hester Street." *McClure's* 23.1 (May 1904): 103–112.
Kelly, Myra. "In Loco Parentis." *McClure's* 25.4 (August 1905): 366–75.
Kelly, Myra. "The Land of Heart's Desire." *McClure's* 23.3 (July 1904): 240–52
Kelly, Myra. *Little Aliens*. New York: Charles Scribner's Sons, 1910.
Kelly, Myra. "Little Bo-Peep." *McClure's* 28.2 (December 1906): 1–10.
Kelly, Myra. *Little Citizens: The Humors of School Life*. New York: McClure, Phillips, 1904.

Kelly, Myra. "A Little Matter of Real Estate." *McClure's* 21.2 (June 1903): 130–36.
Kelly, Myra. "Love Among the Blackboards." *McClure's* 20.5 (March 1903): 485–92.
Kelly, Myra. "Morris and the Honorable Tim." *McClure's* 21.5 (September 1903): 464–72.
Kelly, Myra. "The Mothers of Edward: The Story of a Mother's Meeting." *Ladies' Home Journal* 23.11 (October 1906): 8, 60.
Kelly, Myra. "A Passport to Paradise." *McClure's* 24.1 (November 1904): 53–62.
Kelly, Myra. "A Perjured Santa Claus." *McClure's* 28.3 (January 1907): 299–306.
Kelly, Myra. "A Soul Above Buttons." *McClure's* 27.4 (August 1906): 337–45.
Kelly, Myra. "Star of Bethlehem." *Century Illustrated Magazine* 26.2 (December 1905): 179–86.
Kelly, Myra. "The Teacher's Side of It." *Harper's Bazaar* 42.11 (November 1908): 1064–70.
Kelly, Myra. "The Touch of Nature." *McClure's* 22.3 (January 1904): 249–58.
Kelly, Myra. "When a Man's Widowed." *McClure's* 22.5 (March 1904): 517–25. Reprinted in *Current Literature* 37.1 (July–December 1904): 49–54.
Kelly, Myra. "The Wiles of the Wooer." *McClure's* 29.5 (September 1907): 537–46.
Kelly, Myra. "The Youth of Ireland." *Outlook* (June 26, 1909): 486–498.
Kramer, Michael P. "Acts of Assimilation." *Jewish Quarterly Review* 103.4 (Fall 2013): 556–579.
Kramer, Michael P. "The Wretched Refuse of Jewish American Literary History." *Studies in American Jewish Literature* 31.1 (2012): 61–79.
Kunzle, David. *The Early Comic Strip: Narrative Strips and Picture Stories in the European Broadsheet from c. 1450–1825*. Berkeley: University of California Press, 1973.
Laird, L. K. R. "New York's Comic Papers." *Hamilton Literary Monthly* 30 (April 1896): 284–89.
Lambert, Joshua N. *JPS Guide: American Jewish Fiction*. Philadelphia: Jewish Publication Society, 2009.
Landers, James. *The Improbable First Century of* Cosmopolitan Magazine. Columbia: University of Missouri Press, 2010.
Lang, Arne K. *The Nelson-Wolgast Fight and the San Francisco Boxing Scene, 1900–1914*. Jefferson, NC: McFarland, 2012.
Larsen, Susan, ed. *Wondrous Strange: The Wyeth Tradition (Howard Pyle, N. C. Wyeth, Andrew Wyeth, James Wyeth)*. Boston and New York: Bullfinch Press, in association with the Delaware Art Museum and the Farnsworth Art Museum, 1998.
Larson, Judy L. *American Illustration, 1890–1925: Romance, Adventure and Suspense*. Calgary, Alberta: Glenbow Museum, 1986.
Leuchs, Frederick Adolph Herman. *The Early German Theatre in New York, 1840–1872*. New York: Columbia University Press, 1928.
Levinson, Julian. *Exiles on Main Street: Jewish American Writers and American Literary Culture*. Bloomington: Indiana University Press, 2008.
Levine, Lawrence W. *Highbrow/Lowbrow: The Emergence of Cultural Hierarchy in America*. Cambridge: Harvard University Press, 1988.
Levitz, Paul. "Inside the Editorial Process: Mad Veterans Jaffee and Meglin Look at Their Editors." *Studies in American Humor* 30.3 (2014): 7–24.
Lewis, Paul. *Comic Effects: Interdisciplinary Approaches to Humor in Literature*. Albany: SUNY Press, 1989.
Lhamon, W. T., Jr. *Raising Cain: Blackface Performance from Jim Crow to Hip Hop*. Cambridge: Harvard University Press, 1998.
Lhamon, W. T., Jr. "Turning around Jim Crow." In *Burnt Cork: Traditions and Legacies of Blackface Minstrelsy*. Ed. Stephen Johnson. Amherst and Boston: University of Massachusetts Press, 2012: 18–50.

Lipsett, Edward Raphael. "Denny the Jew," *Everybody's* 27 (July 1912): 45. Subsequent citations given in text.
Lipsett, Edward Raphael. "The Amateur Jew," *Everybody's* 32.6 (June 1915): 765–74.
Lipsett, Edward Raphael. "Denny the Jew." *Everybody's Magazine* 27.1 (July 1912): 45–53.
Lipsett, Edward Raphael. "Denny the Jew from Ballintemple," *Everybody's Magazine* 29.1 (July 1913): 87–96.
Lipsett, Edward Raphael. "Denny Nolan, Man of Affairs." *Everybody's Magazine* 31.5 (November 1914): 652–60.
Lipsett, Edward Raphael. "Denny, Sweet Singer in Israel." *Everybody's Magazine* 31.4 (October 1914): 527–36.
Lipsett, Edward Raphael. "Izzie the Sabbath-Breaker." *McClure's* 41.2 (June 1913): 196, 199–200, 203.
Lipsett, Edward Raphael (as Halitvack). "About Passover in the New York 'Ghetto.'" *Jewish Chronicle*, May 1, 1908: 21.
Lipsett, Edward Raphael (as Halitvack). "Baer's Last Rosh Hashana." *Jewish Chronicle*, September 1, 1907.
Lipsett, Edward Raphael (as Halitvack). "Chanukah as I Knew It: A Reminiscence." *Jewish Chronicle*, December 22, 1905.
Lipsett, Edward Raphael (as Halitvack). "Chanukah That Used to Be." *Jewish Chronicle*, December 14, 1906: 32.
Lipsett, Edward Raphael (as Halitvack). "The Dreamer's Burden." *Reform Advocate* 37.3 (March 6, 1909): 74–75.
Lipsett, Edward Raphael (as Halitvack). "The Feast of 'Weeks' as I Knew It: A Reminiscence." *Jewish Chronicle*, June 9, 1905: 22.
Lipsett, Edward Raphael (as Halitvack). "A Few Impressions." *Jewish Chronicle*, November 19, 1909: 10.
Lipsett, Edward Raphael (as Halitvack). "The First Great Purim Spiel of Pavonda." *Jewish Chronicle*, March 13, 1908: 12–13.
Lipsett, Edward Raphael (as Halitvack). "First Impressions of the New York Ghetto." *Jewish Chronicle*, December 20, 1907: 14–15.
Lipsett, Edward Raphael (as Halitvack). "Impressions and Reflections." *Reform Advocate* 36.22 (January 16, 1909): 621–22.
Lipsett, Edward Raphael (as Halitvack). "The Jewish Press of America," *Jewish Chronicle*, July 31, 1908: 10.
Lipsett, Edward Raphael (as Halitvack). "A Jewry Trust." *Jewish Chronicle*, August 20, 1909: 12.
Lipsett, Edward Raphael (as Halitvack). "Jews in Ireland." *Jewish Chronicle*, December 21, 1906: 29.
Lipsett, Edward Raphael (as Halitvack). "Jews in the South of Ireland," *Jewish Chronicle*, September 7, 1906: 27.
Lipsett, Edward Raphael (as Halitvack). "The Judaism of the New York Ghetto." *Jewish Chronicle*, March 3, 1908: 11.
Lipsett, Edward Raphael (as Halitvack). "Mayer the Sinner." *Jewish Chronicle*, April 24, 1908: 24–25.
Lipsett, Edward Raphael (as Halitvack). "The New York Ghetto in a Heat Wave." *Jewish Chronicle*, September 18, 1908: 4–5.
Lipsett, Edward Raphael (as Halitvack). "A Peace Offering." *Jewish Chronicle*, October 4, 1907: 24.
Lipsett, Edward Raphael (as Halitvack). "Reb Sender's Waterloo." *Jewish Chronicle*, October 8, 1909: 19–20.
Lipsett, Edward Raphael (as Halitvack). "Rival Hod-Carriers." *Jewish Chronicle*, July 3, 1908: 28.

Lipsett, Edward Raphael (as Halitvack). "Scenes from the Beth Hamidrash." *Jewish Chronicle*, January 11, 1907: 28.
Lipsett, Edward Raphael (as Halitvack). "The Shaaloh." *Jewish Chronicle*, January 10, 1908: 23.
Lipsett, Edward Raphael (as Halitvack). "Simchah's Torah as I Knew It: A Remembrance." *Jewish Chronicle*, October 20, 1905.
Lipsett, Edward Raphael (as Halitvack). "A Spoilt Shevuoth." *Jewish Chronicle*, June 5, 1908: 9.
Lipsett, Edward Raphael (as Halitvack). "Succoth as I Knew It: A Reminiscence." *Jewish Chronicle*, October 13, 1905: 26.
Lipsett, Edward Raphael (as Halitvack). "Vill You Buy Sponzes?" *Reform Advocate* 37.2 (February 27, 1909): 41–42.
Lipsett, Edward Raphael (as Halitvack). "Yom Kippur as I Knew It: A Reminiscence." *Jewish Chronicle*, October 6, 1905: 16.
Lipsett, Edward Raphael (as Halitvack). "Yom Kippur in the Bygone." *Jewish Chronicle*, September 29, 1906: 33.
Lipsky, Seth. *The Rise of Abraham Cahan*. New York: Nextbook/Schocken, 2013.
Lott, Eric. *Love and Theft: Blackface Minstrelsy and the American Working Class*. New York: Oxford University Press, 1994.
Masson, Thomas. "How I wrote 50,000 Jokes in 20 Years." *American Magazine* 89 (June 1920): 234.
McCloud, Scott. *Understanding Comics: The Invisible Art*. New York: Harper Perennial/Kitchen Sink Press, 1992.
McDonnell, Patrick, Karen O'Connell, and Georgia Riley de Havenon. *Krazy Kat: The Comic Art of George Herriman*. New York: Harry N. Abrams, 1986.
McGill, Meredith. *American Literature and the Culture of Reprinting, 1834–1853*. Philadelphia: University of Pennsylvania Press, 2003.
McLean, Albert F., Jr. *American Vaudeville as Ritual*. Lexington: University of Kentucky Press, 1965.
McNamara, Brooks. *The New York Concert Saloon: The Devil's Own Nights*. New York: Cambridge University Press, 2002.
Macy, John Albert. "The Career of the Joke." *Atlantic Monthly* 96 (October 1905): 498–510.
Marinetti, Filippo Tommaso. "The Variety Theatre." *Marinetti: Selected Writings*. New York: Farrar, Straus and Giroux, 1971.
Marschall, Rick. *The Great American Comic-Strip Artists*. New York: Abbeville Press, 1989.
May, Jill P., and Robert E. *Howard Pyle: Imagining an American School of Art*. Urbana and Chicago: University of Illinois Press, 2011.
Miller, Stuart Creighton. *"Benevolent Assmilation": The American Conquest of the Philippines, 1899–1903*. New Haven: Yale University Press, 1982.
Mitchell, W. J. T. *Iconology: Image, Text, Ideology*. Chicago: University of Chicago Press, 1986.
Mitchell, W. J. T. *Picture Theory: Essays on Verbal and Visual Representation*. Chicago: University of Chicago Press, 1995.
Mitchell, W. J. T. "Showing Seeing: A Critique of Visual Culture." *Journal of Visual Culture*, 1.2 (2002): 165–81.
Moyle, Clay. *Sam Langford: Boxing's Greatest Uncrowned Champion*. Seattle: Bennett and Hastings, 2012.
Nadel, Stanley. *Little Germany: Ethnicity, Religion, and Class in New York City, 1845–80*. Urbana: University of Illinois Press, 1990.

Nasaw, David. *The Chief: The Life of William Randolph Hearst*. Boston: Houghton Mifflin, 2000.
Nama, Adilifu. *Super Black: American Pop Culture and Black Superheroes*. Austin: University of Texas Press, 2011.
Osofsky, Gilbert. *Harlem, the Making of a Ghetto*. New York: Oxford University Press, 1969.
Panofsky, Erwin. *Perspective as Symbolic Form* (1924).
Parkin, John, and John Phillips, eds. *Laughter and Power*. Bern: Peter Lang, 2006.
Pekar, Harvey, and Paul Buhle, eds. *Yiddishkeit: Jewish Vernacular and the New Land*. New York: Abrams ComicArts, 2011.
Pène du Bois, Guy. *William Glackens*. New York: Whitney Museum of American Art, 1931.
Perlman, Bennard B. "Drawing on Deadline." *Art and Antiques* (October 1988): 115–20.
Perlman, Bennard B. *The Immortal Eight. American Painting from Eakin to the Armory Show* (1870–1913). New York: Exposition Press, 1962.
Pinsker, Shachar. "What is Jewish Literature?" *New Republic*, December 8, 2011 (online).
Prieto, Laura R. *At Home in the Studio: The Professionalization of Women Artists in America*. Cambridge: Harvard University Press, 2001.
Radway, Janice. *Reading the Romance: Women, Patriarchy, and Popular Literature*. Chapel Hill: University of North Carolina Press, 1984.
Ratzlaff, Aleen J. "Illustrated African American Journalism: Political Cartooning in the *Indianapolis Freeman*." In *Seeking a Voice: Images of Race and Gender in the Nineteenth-Century Press*. Eds. David B. Sachsman, S. Kittrell Rushing, and Roy Morris Jr. West Lafayette, IN: Purdue University Press, 2009: 131–40.
Reed, Walt, and Roger Reed. *The Illustrator in America, 1880–1980: A Century of Illustration*. New York: The Society of Illustrators, 1984.
Repplier, Agnes. "A Censor of the Press." *Savannah Tribune*, May 9, 1908.
Riis, Jacob. *Children of the Poor*. New York: Charles Scribner's Sons, 1892.
Riis, Jacob. *How the Other Half Lives* (1890). New York: W. W. Norton, 2010.
Riis, Jacob. *The Making of an American*. New York: Macmillan, 1901.
Rischin, Moses. *Grandma Never Lived in America: The New Journalism of Abraham Cahan*. Bloomington: University of Indiana Press, 1985.
Rischin, Moses. *The Promised City: New York Jews, 1870–1914*. Cambridge: Harvard University Press, 1962.
Robbins, Trina. *Pretty in Ink. Women Cartoonists, 1896–2013*. Seattle: Fantagraphics Books, 2013.
Roeder, Katherine. *Awake in Slumberland: Fantasy, Mass Culture, and Modernism in the Art of Winsor McCay*. Jackson: University Press of Mississippi, 2014.
Rogin, Michael. "Francis Galton and Mark Twain: The Natal Autograph and *Pudd'nhead Wilson*." In *Mark Twain and Pudd'nhead Wilson: Race, Conflict, and Culture*. Eds. Susan Gillman and Forrest G. Robinson. Durham and London: Duke University Press, 1990: 73–85.
Royal, Derek Parker. "Jewish Comics; Or, Visualizing Current Jewish Narrative." *Shofar* 29.2 (Winter 2011): 1–12.
Rosenthal, Angela, ed. *No Laughing Matter: Visual Humor in Ideas of Race, Nationality, and Ethnicity*. Hanover, NH: Dartmouth College Press, 2016.
Rourke, Constance. *American Humor: A Study of the American Character* (1931). Tallahassee: University Presses of Florida, 1986.
Rosenthal, Angela, ed. *No Laughing Matter: Visual Humor in Ideas of Race, Nationality, and Ethnicity*. Hanover, NH: Dartmouth College Press, 2016.

Rubinstein, Charlotte Streifer. *American Women Artists: From Early Indian Times to the Present*. New York: Avon Books, 1982.
S. D., Trav (Donald Travis Stewart). *No Applause—Just Throw Money: The Book that Made Vaudeville Famous*. New York: Farrar, Straus and Giroux, 2006.
Sammon, Jeffrey T. *Beyond the Ring: The Role of Boxing in American Society*. Urbana and Chicago: University of Illinois Press, 1988.
Sammond, Nicholas. *Birth of an Industry: Blackface Minstrelsy and the Rise of American Animation*. Durham: Duke University Press, 2015.
Sanders, Ronald. *The Downtown Jews: Portraits of an Immigrant Generation*. New York: Harper & Row, 1969.
Sharpe, Christina. *In the Wake: Blackness and Being*. Durham, NC: Duke University Press, 2016.
Schefcik, Jerry A. "James G. Swinnerton (1880–1974)." *Nevada Historical Society Quarterly* 33.2 (June 1990): 105.
Schneider, Dorothee. *Trade Unions and Community: The German Working Class in New York City, 1870–1900*. Urbana: University of Illinois Press, 1994.
Schreier, Benjamin. "Editor's Introduction." *Studies in American Jewish Literature* 31.1 (2012): 1–5.
Schreier, Benjamin. *The Impossible Jew: Identity and the Reconstruction of Jewish American Literary History*. New York: New York University Press, 2015.
Shi, David E. *Facing Facts: Realism in American Thought and Culture, 1850–1920*. New York: Oxford University Press, 1995.
Shreiber, Maeera Y. *Singing in a Strange Land: A Jewish American Poetics*. Stanford: Stanford University Press, 2007.
Smith, Shawn Michelle. *Photography on the Color Line: W. E. B. Du Bois, Race, and Visual Culture*. Durham: Duke University Press, 2004.
Smolderen, Thierry. *The Origins of Comics: From William Hogarth to Winston McCay*. Trans. Bart Beaty and Nick Nguyen. Jackson: University Press of Mississippi, 2014
Sontag, Susan. *On Photography*. 1977. New York: Macmillan, 2011.
Sorrentino, Paul. *Stephen Crane: A Life of Fire*. Cambridge, MA: Harvard University Press, 2014.
Stout, Glenn. "Fighting Blind." *Boston Magazine* 79.3 (March 1987): 95.
Strömberg, Fredrik. *Black Images in the Comics: A Visual History*. Seattle: Fantagraphics Books, 2003.
Strömberg, Fredrik. *Jewish Images in the Comics: A Visual History*. Seattle: Fantagraphics Books, 2012.
Swanberg, W. A. *Pulitzer*. New York: Charles Scribner Sons, 1967.
Taylor, William. *In Pursuit of Gotham: Culture and Commerce in New York*. New York: Oxford University Press, 1992.
Tebbel, John, and Mary Ellen Zuckerman. *The Magazine in America, 1741–1990*. New York: Oxford University Press, 1991.
Tisserand, Michael. "Birth of the Krazy." *Scenes of My Infint-hood: Celebrating the Birth of Krazy Kat* (exhibition catalog), Ohio State University, Billy Ireland Cartoon Library & Museum and the Wexner Center for the Arts. Columbus: Ohio State University Libraries, 2010: 13–20.
Tisserand, Michael. *Krazy: George Herriman, a Life in Black and White*. New York: HarperCollins, 2016.
Toll, Robert C. *Blacking Up: The Minstrel Show in Nineteenth-Century America*. New York: Oxford University Press, 1974.

Trachtenberg, Alan. *The Incorporation of America: Culture and Society in the Gilded Age*. New York: Hill and Wang, 1982.

Trivedi, Harish. "Translating Culture vs. Cultural Translation." *91st Meridian* 4.1 (Spring 2005). Iowa City: University of Iowa International Writing Program. Accessed March 13, 2015.

Twain, Mark. "How to Tell a Story" (1895). *Collected Tales, Sketches, Speeches, and Essays, 1891–1910*. New York: Library of America, 1992: 201–203.

Twain, Mark. *Pudd'nhead Wilson* and *Those Extraordinary Twins*. New York: Penguin, 1986.

Twain, Mark. "Three Thousand Years Among the Microbes." In *Mark Twain's Which Was the Dream and Other Symbolic Writings of the Later Years*. Ed. John S. Tuckey. Berkeley: University of California Press, 1968), 436.

Venuti, Lawrence. *The Scandals of Translation: Towards an Ethics of Difference*. London and New York: Routledge, 1998.

Walden, Daniel, ed. *Dictionary of Literary Biography: Vol. 28, Twentieth-Century Jewish American Fiction*. Detroit: Gale, 1984.

Waugh, Colton. *The Comics*. New York: Macmillan, 1947.

Ward, Geoffrey C. *Unforgivable Blackness: The Rise and Fall of Jack Johnson*. New York: Knopf, 2004.

Watkins, Mel. *On the Real Side: Laughing, Lying, and Signifying—the Underground Tradition of African-American Humor that Transformed American Culture, from Slavery to Richard Pryor*. New York: Simon & Schuster, 1994.

Waxman, Meyer. *A History of Jewish Literature*. vol. 4, part II. Cranberry, NJ: Yoseloff, 1941, 1960.

Wertheim, Stanley. *A Stephen Crane Encyclopedia*. Westport, CT: Greenwood Press, 1997.

Wertheim, Stanley, and Paul Sorrentino. *The Crane Log: A Documentary Life of Stephen Crane, 1871–1900*. New York: G. K. Hall, 1994.

West, Richard Samuel. *Satire on Stone: The Political Cartoons of Joseph Keppler*. Urbana and Chicago: University of Illinois Press, 1988.

Wickberg, Daniel. *The Senses of Humor: Self and Laughter in Modern America*. Ithaca: Cornell University Press, 1998.

Wiegman, Robyn. *American Anatomies: Theorizing Race and Gender*. Durham, NC: Duke University Press, 1995.

Wilkerson, Isabel. *The Warmth of Other Suns: The Epic Story of America's Great Migration*. New York: Random House, 2010.

Williams, Andreá N. "Cultivating Black Visuality: The Controversy over Cartoons in the Indianapolis Freeman." *American Periodicals* 25.2 (2015): 124–38.

Williams, Jason Richard. *Competing Visions: Women Writers and Male Illustrators in the Golden Age of Illustration*. PhD diss., University of New Hampshire, 2011.

Wirth-Nesher. *Call It English: The Languages of Jewish American Literature*. Princeton: Princeton University Press, 2006.

Wonham, Henry B. *Playing the Races: Ethnic Caricature and American Literary Realism*. New York: Oxford University Press, 2004.

Wuster, Tracy. *Mark Twain: American Humorist*. Columbia: University of Missouri Press, 2016.

Yochelson, Bonnie, and Daniel Czitrom. *Rediscovering Jacob Riis: Exposure Journalism and Photography in Turn-of-the-Century New York*. New York: New Press, 2007.

Zurier, Rebecca. *Art for the Masses: A Radical Magazine and Its Graphics, 1911–1917*. Philadelphia: Temple University Press, 1988.

Zurier, Rebecca. *Picturing the City: Urban Vision and the Ashcan School*. Berkeley: University of California Press, 2006.

Index

Page numbers in italics refer to figures.

accuracy, 38
aesthetics, vaudeville, 81
Africanism, 148
Africans and African Americans, 28, 150–51; African American humor, 121–23, 173n12; African American quilts, 172n5; Great Migration, 119–20, 129–30; print culture, 119–20; private humor, 149–50; racist representations of, 119–21, 137–39, 172n4
Akron, Ohio, 130
alienation, 24; comic, 74–85
Allen Street (Luks), 62
alleys: *Bone Alley* (Hambidge), 14–15, *16*, 52; *Hogan's Alley* (Luks), 49–54, *51*, *53*; *Hogan's Alley* (Outcault), *47*, *48*, 52, 54, 163n44; "The Passing of Cat Alley" (Riis), 14
All-Negro Comics #1 (1947), 172n5
"Amateur Jew, The" (Lipsett), 117, *117*
Amateurs, The (Luks), 62
American Beauties (Fisher), 170n12
American Committee for the International Exhibition (1913), 97–98
American Hebrew and Jewish Messenger, 114
American literary realism, 11–18, 24–25
American Scene, The (James), 17
Amsterdam News, 152
And Her Name Was Maud! (Opper), 168n30
Andinkra stamps, 172n5
"And Sam Jes' Roared," 173n22

animation, 173n19
anti-blackness, 151
appeal, narrative quality of, 93–118
Aristotle, 6, 12
Armory Show (1913 International Exhibition), 10, 36, 94, 97–98
Armstrong, Regina, 102, 171n20
Arnold, Matthew, 8
"Around the World with the Yellow Kid" (Outcault), 169n47
artist-reporters, 41
Ashcan School, 97, 163n32, 170n8. *See also* Eight, The
assimilation, cultural, 75–79, 115
Atlantic Monthly, 6, 94, 113
At Mouquin's (Glackens), 9, *10*
authenticity, 38
authorship, 162n7
Autobiography of a Beggar, The (Friedman), 98, 107, *108*

Bachelor Belles (Fisher), 170n12
"Bad Boys' Santa Claus, The" (Luks), 54, *55*
"Baer's Last Rosh Hashana" (Lipsett), 113
Bakhtin, Mikhail, 54–55
Baltimore Afro-American, 152
Banta, Martha, 158
Barnes, Albert C., 97, 99–100
Barnes Collection, 97

Barrish, Phillip, 15
Baudrillard, Jean, 18
Beggar's Club, The (Friedman), 110–11
Bellamy, Edward, 152
Bellows, George, 9–10
Beringer, Alex, 167n14
Berman, Avis, 98, 170n10
Bernstein, Herman, 166n4
"Big Tree, The" (Lessing), 87, 89
binocular vision, 34
Blackbeard, Bill, 44–47, 52, 163n40
black caricature, 121–23, *122*
black comics, 28, 152, 172n5
black comic sensibility, 28, 119–48, 152
blackface minstrelsy, 121, 123–48, 159n14; "Buzzy and Anstock" (Luks), 43–44, *45*, 163n39; "Dear Reader, Please Permit Us to Present to You Sam!" (Swinnerton), *124*, 125; *Sam and His Laugh* (Swinnerton), 28, 123, *125*; "Sam as a Magician's Confederate" (Swinnerton), 126–28, *127*; *Turn About Is Fair Play* (Ladendorf), 37
black humor, 149–50
black laughter, 133, 149
black newspapers, 120
Block, George, 70, 167n10
Block, Rudolph, 8–9, 21–22, 26–27, 67–74, 85–86, 92, 165n2, 166n6, 169n47, 169n51. *See also* Lessing, Bruno
blue performances, 23
Bogart, Michele H., 94
Bohemian Cigarmakers at Work in Their Tenement (Riis), 3–5, *4*, 12–13
Bone Alley (Hambidge), 14–15, *16*, 52
Bonsal, Stephen, 100, 171n19
Bookman, The, 86
books: comic books, 54, 172n5; joke books, 173n7
Bootsie (Harrington), 152
Bourne, Randolph, 103
boxers and boxing, 135–39; demonstrations, 141, 174n47; "If Jack Johnson Loses" (Herriman), *138*, 139; "If Jack Johnson Wins" (Herriman), *138*, 139; strips depicting Sam Langford, 142–43, *144–45*; "Take a Plunge the Water Is Fine" (Herriman), *140*, 141; "Three Put Up a Better Argument Than Two" (Herriman), 139, *140*

Bradbury, Malcolm, 32
braiding, in comics, 168n39
Bramen, Carrie Tirado, 15, 104
Br'er Rabbit, 128, 149–50
Bringing Up Father (McManus), 75–79, *78*
Brisbane, Arthur, 38–39, 70
Broadway, 93
Brodhead, Richard, 15
Bronner, Simon J., 68–69
Bronxer Literaten Club, 74
Brown, Joshua, 163n34
Brown, Sheena C., 172n5
Brueghel, Pieter, the Elder, 106
Buk-Swienty, Tom, 160n24
Bungleton Green (Rogers), 152, 172n5
Burdette, Robert J., 149
burlesque, 22
Burling, William, 166n3
Burns, Tommy, 137
Busch, Wilhelm, 75
Buster Brown (Outcault), 168n30
"Buzzy and Anstock" (Luks), 43–44, *45*, 163n39

Café Francis, 9, 44, *46*
Café Mouquin, 9–10, *10*
Cahan, Abraham, 88–89, 113, 166n4, 169n51, 169n57; "Circumstances," 89; "Dumitru and Sigrid," 88; *The Imported Bridegroom and Other Stories*, 89; "A Providential Match," 89; "Rabbi Eliezer's Christmas," 102, *104*; *The Rise of David Levinsky*, 88–89; *Yekl*, 88–89
Campbell, Heather Coyle, 104–6, 170n19, 171n20
caricature, 7, 11, 24–25, 77; black, 121–23, *122*; in early comic strips, 77, 121, *122*
Carlyle, Thomas, 6
Carr, Gene, 71
Carr, Henry, 142
Cassuto, Leonard, 30–31
Cather, Willa, 95
censorship, 120
Century Magazine, 15, 88, 94, 97, 113, 160n24; *Bone Alley* (Hambidge), 14–15, *16*; "Light in Dark Places" (Riis), 14–15, *16*
Chametzky, Jules, 166n3
"Charity Begins at Home" (Luks), 60, *61*

Chesnutt, Charles, 149–50
chewing gum, 47
Chicago American: "The Daily Parade to the Races" (Herriman), *134*, 135; "Dear Reader, Please Permit Us to Present to You Sam!" (Swinnerton), *124*, 125; "Sam as a Magician's Confederate" (Swinnerton), 126, *127*; Sunday comic supplement, 70–71, 73, *124*, 125, 126, *127*
Chicago Defender, 152, 172n5
Children of Men (Lessing), 68, 86
children's pages, 54, *55*
cigarmakers, 3–5, *4*, 12–13
"Circumstances" (Cahan), 89
Cleveland, Grover, 38–39, *40*
Cleveland, W. S., 123
closure, 83
Cohen, Ted, 7–8
collectibles, 47
Collier's, 8, 94–95, 171n28; cover illustrations and stand-alone interior cartoons, 102–6, *105*, 118; *Far from the Fresh Air Farm* (Glackens), 102–4, *105*
comedy, visual, 94–106
Comedy of Those Extraordinary Twins, The (Twain), 30–32, 164n48
comic actresses, 152–53
comic alienation, 74–85
comic books, 54, 172n5; joke books, 173n7
comic grotesque, 29–65, *37*, 158, 160n26
comic illustrators, 153
comics and comic strips: black, 152; Block's defense of, 85–86; caricature in, 77, 121–23, *122*; conventions, 70–71, 73; definition of, 167n17, 172n5; development of, 26–27, 70–71, 73, 75, 92; early, 77, 83–85, 82, 121–23, *122*, 152, 167n17, 172n4; film-like action in, 82, 83; ownership of, 49–50; racist representations in, 121, *122*, 172n4; regularized format, 70–71, 73; Sunday supplements, 35–36, 47, 67–74, *72*, 100, *101*. See also specific comics
comic sensibility, 3–12, 18–28, 149–58; black, 28, 119–48, 152
comic strip artists, 153. See also individual artists
Commercial Advertiser, 89

commercialism, 94, 98
communal humor, 149–50
composite images, 38
Connolly-Smith, Peter, 70, 74–75, 79
Conrad, Joseph, 86
Cook, David A., 168n36
Cosmopolitan Magazine, 8, 22, 27, 67, 86–88, 93–95, *95*, 113; "The Big Tree" (Lessing), 87, 89; "Dumitru and Sigrid" (Cahan), 88; "Gimplovitz brought his fist down on the table with a crash" (Oberhardt), 94, *96*; "The Ingratitude of Rosenfeld" (Lessing), 19–21, *21*, 107–8, *109*; "Jablinowsky" (Lessing), 94, *95*; "A Trifle Light as Air" (Lessing), 88; "Under His Nose" (Lessing), 94, *96*; *With an expression of mournful resentment, he turned and left the room* (Dirks), 94, *95*
Crane, Stephen, 38, 95, 100, 171n19; *Maggie: Girl of the Streets*, 74; "The Monster," 160n26
Crary, Jonathan, 17–18, 34
Critic, The, 64
Cuba, 36–40, 60, 100; *The Garrote for Cuban Patriots* (Luks), 39–40; "Look Between the Fingers of That Concealing Hand, Mr. Cleveland!" (Luks), 38–39, *40*
cultural assimilation, 75–79, 115
cultural translation, 74–86, 167n22
Cummings, E. E., 28, 148

Dadaism, 86
"Daily Parade to the Races, The" (Herriman), *134*, 135
Damon and Pythias (1914), 74
Daumier, Honoré, 98
Davies, Arthur, 9
Davis, Richard Harding, 38, 86
"Dear Reader, Please Permit Us to Present to You Sam!" (Swinnerton), *124*, 125
de Kooning, Willem, 28, 148
Dempsey, Jack, 142
"Denny the Jew from Ballintemple" stories (Lipsett), 27–28, 98, 111, 114–17, *116*
DesRochers, Rick, 161n44
Detroit Free Press, 173n22
Deutsch-Amerikanische Bäcker-Zeitung, 167n10

Devine, Catherine (Little Egypt, Ashea Wabe), 52, *53*
dialect, 24–25, 77, 79–80, 88–91
Dickens, Charles, 64
Die gesellschaftliche Erziehung des Herrn Gradmichel (*The Societal Education of Mr. Gradmichel*) (McManus), 75–79, *78*
Dimock, Edith, 100, 153–57, *157*
Dimock, Irene, 9
Dirks, Rudolph, 5–10, 68, 75, 165n2; "Delia and Maggie—Katzenjammer Kids," 83–85, *84*; *The Katzenjammer Kids*, 4–7, *5*, 22, 75, 80, 119, 152, 168n39, 168n43; *With an expression of mournful resentment, he turned and left the room*, 94, *95*; "Yellow Kid? Ach, No! It's Only the Katzenjammer Kid—(and His Brudder)," 75, *76*
Dorgan, Thomas "Tad," 131, 143
double consciousness, 121–23, 173n12
Doubling His Pace, Flew Down Alley (Glackens), 107, *108*
Dove, Arthur, 94
Drayton, Grace, 153
Dreiser, Theodore, 5, 8
Dressler, Marie, 152–53
Du Bois, W. E. B., 28
Dugan, Mickey (the Yellow Kid). *See* Yellow Kid, the
"Dumitru and Sigrid" (Cahan), 88
Dunbar, Paul Laurence, 149–50

early comics, 83–85; caricature in, 77, 121–23, *122*; definition of, 167n17; dialect in, 77; early black comic art, 152; film-like action, 82, 83; racist representations in, 121, *122*, 172n4
Edison, Thomas, 44
Eight, The, 9–10, 36, 62, 97, 153, 163n32
"Eight Queer Facts," 41
einfuhlung (in-feeling or empathy), 7, 149
Eisner, Will, 167n17, 172n5
Ellis Island, 17
Ellison, Ralph, 28, 119, 123, 148, 173n12
empathy, 7, 149
"End of the Task, The" (Lessing), 88
ethnic identification, 74–85
Evans, Robert, 54
Everybody's Magazine, 27, 111, 115

factual accuracy, 38
Far from the Fresh Air Farm (Glackens), 102–4, *105*
"Fashion's Display in the Easter Parade" (Gordon), 42
fiction: genre, 168n31; ghetto stories, 11, 15–17, 27–28, 67–95; illustrated stories, 75, 93–95, *95*
Fields, Lew: Mike and Meyer, 22–24, 81, 83; Pool Room Sketch (Weber and Fields), 22–23
film, 93
Fisher, Harrison, 98, 170n12
Fitzgerald, Chas, 9
Fleischer, Max, 173n19
"Flora Flirt Takes a Fool's Day Jaunt" (Rice), 153, *155*
Flying Karamazov Brothers, 26
Flynn, "Fireman" Jim, 142
football, 50, *51*
Forbes, Johnny, 23
Fornaro, C. de, 44, *46*
Fort Wayne Weekly, 153, *156*
Forverts, 88
Frank Leslie's Illustrated Newspaper, 41, 163n34
freaks, 31, 41
Freud, Sigmund, 6, 12, 18–19, 151
Friedman, I. K. (Isaac Kahn), 93, 98, 171n32; *The Autobiography of a Beggar*, 98, 107, *108*; *The Beggar's Club*, 110–11
funny pages: Sunday comic supplements, 35–36, 47, 67–74, *72*, 100, *101*. *See also* comics and comic strips; *and individual publications*
Furniss, Harry, 103

Gambone, Robert, 38, 52, 162n28
games, 34, *35*, 47
Gans, Joe, 137
Gardner, Jared, 77, 80, 133, 174n36
Garrote for Cuban Patriots, The (Luks), 39–40
Gateward, Frances, 120, 172n5
George, Henry, 152
German Dialect Comedians (Glackens), 102, *103*
Germans and German Americans, 74–80
Ghana, 172n5

ghetto fiction, 11, 15–17, 27–28, 67–92; illustrated, 75, 93–95, *95*; sentimental stories, 164n54
Gibson, Charles, 170n12
"Gifts of the Philosophers, The" (Kelly), 110
Gilbert, Douglas, 22
Gilded Age, 3–4, *4*
Gilder, Richard Watson, 160n24
Gillman, Susan, 30, 32–34
Gilpin, William, 52
Gimplovitz brought his fist down on the table with a crash (Oberhardt), 94, *96*
Glackens, Edith Dimock, 9–10, 97, 153–54
Glackens, Ira, 97
Glackens, Louis, 100
Glackens, William, 8–10, 21–22, 61–62, 95–106, 153–54, 170n8; "The Amateur Jew" (E. R. Lipsett), 117, *117*; *At Mouquin's*, 9, *10*; *Doubling His Pace, Flew Down Alley*, 107, *108*; empty chairs, 108, *109*, 171n29; *Far from the Fresh Air Farm*, 102–4, *105*; *German Dialect Comedians*, 102, *103*; illustrations, 20, 27–28, 94–111, *103*, *117*, 171n29, 171n32; "Ingratitude of Rosenfeld" (Bruno Lessing), 19, *21*, 107–8, *109*; *Irish Comedians*, 102, *103*; *The Merry-Go-Rounders*, 100, *101*, 170n18; narrative strategies, 106, 171n20; *The only things Patrick Joseph would not guarantee were the salt herrings which his Yiddish customers persisted in eating raw*, 114–15, *116*; "Rabbi Eliezer's Christmas," 102, *104*, 106; *She sang the Hatikvah in her thin, metallic voice*, *117*, 118; "Sherwood Sisters," 100; *Singing Soubrettes*, 102, *103*; theatricals, 99, *99*; war illustrations, 100, 170n19; "Wiles of the Wooer" (Myra Kelly), 108–9, *110*; *With a brewer-driver's huge hand between her two slender ones*, 109, *111*; *A young doctor . . .*, 106, *107*
Glass, Montague, 93
Goddard, Morris, 38, 163n36
Gombrich, Ernest, 24–25
Goodwin, James, 34
Gordon, Bessie Moser, *42*
Gordon, Ian, 119, 175n11
Great American Simoleon Sextette, The (Luks), 62, *63*

Great Migration, 119–20, 129–30
Greenhill, Jennifer, 34, 162n21
Groënsteen, Thierry, 168n39, 172n5
Gross, Theodore L., 166n3
grotesque: comic, 29–65, *37*, 158, 160n26; purpose of, 54; racial, 30–32, 160n26
group identification, 11

Haenni, Sabine, 160n27
Halitvack (Edward Raphael Lipsett), 111–14; "About Passover in the New York 'Ghetto,'" 117; *Two Pair of Misfits: A Romance of Old Pavonda*, 114; "When Yenkel Was King," 114
Hambidge, Jay, 14–18, *16*, 52
Happy Hooligan (Opper), 71, *73*, 80, 129
Harlem Renaissance, 119–20
Harper's Monthly, 41, 94
Harrigan, Edward "Ned," 22
Harrington, Ollie, 120, 152
Harris, Joel Chandler, 149
Harvard University, 50
Hawai'i, 60
Hawkes, Elizabeth H., 170n8
Haywood, Garfield T., 152
Hazard of New Fortunes, A (Howells), 25
Hearst, William Randolph, 8, 20, 49, 67–74, 123, 163n36, 165n2
Hearst's Magazine (formerly *World Today*), 169n43
Heer, Jeet, 146
Henri, Robert, 9–10, 36, 62, 93–94, 97–99, *99*, 153, 163n32
Herriman, George, 8–9, 28, 71, 75, 121–23, 131–48, 152, 174n33; "The Daily Parade to the Races," *134*, 135; depictions of Sam Langford, 142–43, *144–45*; "Hooray!! Jeff's Coming Home Soon," *136*, 137; "If Jack Johnson Loses," *138*, 139; "If Jack Johnson Wins," *138*, 139; *Krazy Kat*, 28, 123, 131–32, 143–48, *147*; *Lariat Pete*, 133; *Major Ozone's Fresh Air Campaign*, 133; *Mr. Proones, the Plunger*, 135; *Mrs. Waitaminnit*, 133; *Musical Mose*, 131–33; "Musical Mose Tries Another 'Impussonation,'" 121, *122*; "Take a Plunge the Water Is Fine," *140*, 141; "Three Put Up a Better Argument Than Two," 139, *140*

High Rollers Extravaganza Company, 22
Hill, Marion, 106, *107*
Hochman, Barbara, 162n7
Hodes, Martha, 130
Hogan's Alley (Luks), 49–54; "A Seeley Dinner in Hogan's Alley," 52, *53*; "Training for the Football Championship Game in Hogan's Alley," 50, *51*
Hogan's Alley (Outcault), 47, 50, 52, 54, 163n44; "Hogan's Alley Folk Have a Trolley Party in Brooklyn," 47, *48*; "Yellow Kid? Ach, No! It's Only the Katzenjammer Kid—(and His Brudder)" (Dirks), 75, *76*
Holmes, Henry Howard, 49
Holtz, Allan, 176n14
home, 158
Homer, Winslow, 38
"Hooray!! Jeff's Coming Home Soon" (Herriman), *136*, 137
Horns, Maurice, 165n2
Howarth, F. M., 167n14
Howe, Irving, 166n3, 169n44
Howells, William Dean, 6, 11–12, 25, 64, 88, 93, 169n51
How the Other Half Lives (Riis), 3–5, *4*, 13–14, 25
"How to Tell a Story" (Twain), 29
Hughes, Langston, 28, 148
humor, 6; African American, 121–23, 173n12; black, 149–50; communal, 149–50; Jewish, 67, 87, 169n44; New Humor, 8, 22, 29, 54; private, 149–50; subjective, 6; tendentious, 6; as therapy, 148; visual comedy, 95–106. *See also* laughter
Huneker, James, 62
Hungarians, 89–90
Hurston, Zora Neale, 150

identification, 24; ethnic, 74–85; group, 11
"If Jack Johnson Loses" (Herriman), *138*, 139
"If Jack Johnson Wins" (Herriman), *138*, 139
Igbos, 172n5
illustration(s), 38, 44, 49, 93–118; comic, 94, 153; cover illustrations and stand-alone interior cartoons, 102–6, *105*; ghetto, 75, 93–95, *95*. *See also individual artists*
immigrants, 15–17, 92, 93

Imported Bridegroom and Other Stories, The (Cahan), 89
Indianapolis Freeman, 152, 172n5, 175n12
in-feeling (*einfuhling*), 7, 149
"Ingratitude of Rosenfeld" (Lessing), 19–24, *21*, 89, 107–8, *109*
International Exhibition (1913 Armory Show), 10, 36, 94, 97–98
intimacy, 7
Irish, 90
Irish Comedians (Glackens), 102, *103*

"Jablinowsky" (Lessing), 94, *95*
Jacobson, Matthew Frye, 15–17
Jaffee, Al, 67
James, Henry, 17–18, 36, 94–95
Jeannette, Joe, 137
Jeffries, Jim, 137, 141; "Take a Plunge the Water Is Fine" (Herriman), *140*, 141; "Three Put Up a Better Argument Than Two" (Herriman), 139, *140*
Jenkins, Henry, 81
Jennings, John, 120, 172n5
Jewett, Sarah Orne, 25
Jewish Advocate, 113
Jewish Americans, 91–92
Jewish Chronicle, 111–13, 117
Jewish humor, 67, 87, 169n44
Jim Crow, 129–33, 137
jingoism, 60
"John and Ole Massa" (Hurston), 150
Johnson, Jack, 137–39, 141–42, 175n47; "If Jack Johnson Loses" (Herriman), *138*, 139; "If Jack Johnson Wins" (Herriman), *138*, 139; "Take a Plunge the Water Is Fine" (Herriman), *140*, 141; "Three Put Up a Better Argument Than Two" (Herriman), 139, *140*
Johnson, James Weldon, 130
joke books, 173n7
joke-making industry, 29–30, 162n5
jokes, 18–19, 29–30
Jones, Gavin, 25, 79–81, 88–89

Katzenjammer Kids, The (Dirks), 5–7, 22, 68, 80, 119, 152, 159n11, 168n39, 168n43; "Bang! Ach!," 4–5, *5*; "Delia and

Maggie—Katzenjammer Kids," 83–85, 84; "Yellow Kid? Ach, No! It's Only the Katzenjammer Kid—(and His Brudder)," 75, 76

Keene, Charles, 98, 103

Kelly, Myra, 93, 98, 109–10, 113; "The Gifts of the Philosophers," 110; "Love Among the Blackboards," 110, 112; "The Wiles of the Wooer," 108–9, 111

Kemble, E. W., 32, 33, 119, 152

Kessler, Joseph, 75

Kleindeutschland (Little Germany), 69, 166n9

Knerr, Harry, 152

Kramer, Michael, 166n5

Krazy Kat (Herriman), 28, 71, 123, 131–32, 143–48, 147

Kuhn, Walt, 9–10, 94

Kunzle, David, 167n17

labels and labeling, 58

Ladendorf, Frank H., 37

Ladies' Home Journal, 110

Lady Bountiful (Carr), 71

Lambert, Josh, 166nn3–4

Lang, Andrew, 165n70

Langford, Sam, 137, 142–43, 144–45

language: dialect, 24–25, 77, 79–80, 88–91; vernacular, 77, 79

Lantz, Walter, 173n19

Lariat Pete (Herriman), 133

Larson, Judy L., 171n28

Laughlin, Carter, 58

laughter, 12, 25–26; black, 133, 149; superiority theory of, 6. *See also* humor

Lessing, Bruno, 9, 27–28, 67–69, 86–92, 95, 98, 166nn3–4, 168n43; "The Big Tree," 87, 89; *Children of Men*, 68, 86; "The End of the Task," 88; "The Ingratitude of Rosenfeld," 19–24, 89; "Jablinowsky," 94, 95; "Monahan's Musical Education," 89–90; "The Parrot of Uncle Hurwitz," 90–92; "A Swallow-Tailer for Two," 86; "Tempus Fugit," 171n29; "A Trifle Light as Air," 88; "Under His Nose," 94, 96

Lhamon, W. T., Jr., 126, 129

Life magazine, 47

"Light in Dark Places" (Riis), 14–15, 16

Li'l Mose (Outcault), 119

linguistics, 91

Lipps, Theodor, 7, 149

Lipsett, Edward Raphael, 93, 111–14; "The Amateur Jew," 117, 117; "Baer's Last Rosh Hashana," 113; "Denny the Jew from Ballintemple" stories, 27–28, 98, 111, 114–17, 116; "Mayer the Sinner," 113

Literary Digest, 120

literary realism, American, 11–18, 24–25

Little Egypt (Ashea Wabe [Catherine Devine]), 52, 53

Little Germany (Kleindeutschland), 69, 166n9

Little Nemo (McCay), 119

Little Nemo in Slumberland (McCay), 120

Little Nippers, The (Luks), 26, 50–52

local color, 14–15

Loeb, Louis, 32

London, Jack, 85

"Look Between the Fingers of That Concealing Hand, Mr. Cleveland!" (Luks), 38–39, 40

Los Angeles Examiner, 132, 135–39, 175n49; "Hooray!! Jeff's Coming Home Soon" (Herriman), 136, 137; "If Jack Johnson Loses" (Herriman), 138, 139; "If Jack Johnson Wins" (Herriman), 138, 139; strips depicting Sam Langford, 142–43, 144–45; "Take a Plunge the Water Is Fine" (Herriman), 140, 141; "Three Put Up a Better Argument Than Two" (Herriman), 139, 140

Lott, Eric, 121, 159n14

"Love Among the Blackboards" (Kelly), 110, 112

Luks, George, 8–10, 26–29, 36–47, 100, 153; *Allen Street*, 62; *The Amateurs*, 62; "The Bad Boys' Santa Claus," 54, 55; in "Buzzy and Anstock," 43–44, 45, 163n39; cartooning, 47, 163n41; "Charity Begins at Home," 60, 61; *The Garrote for Cuban Patriots*, 39–40; *The Great American Simoleon Sextette*, 62, 63; *Hogan's Alley*, 49–54; *The Little Nippers*, 26, 50–52; "Look Between the Fingers of That Concealing Hand, Mr. Cleveland!," 38–39, 40; "Modern Heroes," 60; "More Twins Born But There Are

Others to Come," 58, 59; *Mose's Incubator*, 26, 56–60, 57, 165n58, 165n62; "Mose's In-Cuba-tor," 60; *Mose the Trained Chicken*, 165n58; "One A.M. at a 'Select and Special' with Artists, Actors and Newspapermen at a Popular Uptown Café" (Fornaro), 44, 46; *The Orator*, 163n39; painting, 61–62; "A Seeley Dinner in Hogan's Alley," 52, 53; "A Street Parade to Advertise Mose's Incubator Show," 56–58, 57; "Tragic Rites of the Penitentes," 41–42, 42–43; training and education, 44; "Training for the Football Championship Game in Hogan's Alley," 50, 51; "Two Sketches of Human Driftwood," 41; "Will the Military Spirit Have This Effect on Our Future?," 60; *Woman and Macaw*, 62; world view, 54–56, 61

Luks, Will, 26, 43–44, 45

Lulu and Leander (Howarth), 167n14

Lundberg, Ferdinand, 163n36

Macbeth Gallery, 97

magazine realism, 160n31

magazines, smart, 94. *See also individual publications*

Mager, Gus, 10

Maggie: Girl of the Streets (Crane), 74

Maier, Jean, 166n6

Major Ozone's Fresh Air Campaign (Herriman), 133

Marinetti, F. T., 23

Marriner, William, 119

Marschall, Rick, 165n2

mass-market periodicals, 93–95

Max und Moritz (Busch), 75, 159n11, 165n2

May, Peter, 164n48

"Mayer the Sinner" (Lipsett), 113

McCardell, Ray, 71

McCarthy, Dan, 106

McCay, Winsor, 173n19; *Little Nemo*, 119; *Little Nemo in Slumberland*, 120

McCloud, Scott, 77, 167n17, 172n5

McClure, Samuel, 20

McClure's, 8, 27, 95–97; "The End of the Task" (Lessing), 87; "Love Among the Blackboards" (Kelly), 110, 112; "A Tune in Court" (Hill), 106, 107; With a brewer-driver's huge hand between her two slender ones (Glackens), 109, 111; "A young doctor ..." (Glackens), 106, 107

McFadden's Flats (Outcault), 49, 163n44

McGill, Meredith, 49–50

McLean, Albert, 22, 81, 83

McManus, George, 75–79, 78

McVey, Sam, 137

Meeber, Carrie (character), 5

Mercer, Kobena, 151

Merry-Go-Rounders, The (Glackens), 100, 101, 170n18

Mike and Meyer, 22–24, 81, 83

militarism, 60

Millhauser, Stephen, 36

minoritizing translation, 88

minstrelsy: blackface, 43–44, 45, 121–48, 124, 127, 163n39; end man's chair, 123

"Modern Heroes" (Luks), 60

modernism, 10, 85, 94, 175n11

"Monahan's Musical Education" (Lessing), 89–90

"Monster, The" (Crane), 160n26

Moore, James B., 9

"More Twins Born But There Are Others to Come" (Luks), 58, 59

Morgen Journal, 70, 74–79, 78

Morrison, Toni, 28, 148

Mose's Incubator (Luks), 26, 56–60, 57, 165n58, 165n62; "More Twins Born But There Are Others to Come," 58, 59; "Mose's In-Cuba-tor," 60; "A Street Parade to Advertise Mose's Incubator Show," 56–58, 57

"Mose's In-Cuba-tor" (Luks), 60

Mose the Trained Chicken (Luks), 165n58

Moyle, Clay, 142, 175n49

Mr. Proones, the Plunger (Herriman), 135

Mrs. Roosevelt at Klein's (Dimock), 154–57, 157

Mrs. Waitaminnit (Herriman), 133

Mrs. Wiggs of the Cabbage Patch (Rice), 110

Munkittrick, R. K., 100

Musical Mose (Herriman), 131–33; "Musical Mose Tries Another 'Impussonation,'" 121, 122

Muybridge, Eadweard, 83

Index

Nadel, Stanley, 166n9
names and naming, 58
narratives, 93–118
National Academy of Design, 94
Naughty Toodles! (Wiederseim), 153, *154*
Ndebele, 172n5
negative stereotypes, 90
New Humor, 8, 22, 29, 54
New Journalism, 8, 20–22
New Orleans, Louisiana, 130
newspaper comic strips. *See* comics and comic strips
newspapers, 95. *See also individual papers*
New Woman, 153, *155*
New York City, New York, 36; Gilded Age, 3–4, *4*; Kleindeutschland (Little Germany), 69, 166n9; race riots, 129–30
New Yorker Volkszeitung, 70, 167n10
New Yorkese, 87
New York Evening Journal, 176n14
New York Evening Post, 93
New York Evening Sun, 9
New York Herald, 94
New York Journal, 9, 21, 26, 49, 125, 143, 153, 165n2; Block and, 69–74; *Bringing Up Father* (McManus), 75–79, *78*; comics, 35–36, 67–71, *72*, 75, 76, 82, 83; "Yellow Kid? Ach, No! It's Only the Katzenjammer Kid—(and His Brudder)," 75, *76*
New York Recorder, 70
New York Sun, 70
New York Tribune, 164n48
New York World, 9, 21–22, 26, 34–39, 70, 100, 130, 161n44, 162n30, 163n36, 174n35; advertisements, 173n7; artist-reporters, 41; "The Bad Boys' Santa Claus" (Luks), 54, *55*; "Charity Begins at Home" (Luks), 60, *61*; children's pages, 54, *55*; comic supplements, 35–36, 47–52, *48*, *51*, *53*, 56–58, *57*, *59*, 100, *101*, 120; "Eight Queer Facts," 41; "Hogan's Alley Folk Have a Trolley Party in Brooklyn" (Outcault), *47*, *48*; "Look Between the Fingers of That Concealing Hand, Mr. Cleveland!" (Luks), 38–39, *40*; *The Merry-Go-Rounders* (Glackens), 100, *101*, 170n18; "More Twins Born But There Are Others to Come" (Luks), 58, *59*; *Musical Mose* (Herriman), 131; "Musical Mose Tries Another 'Impussonation'" (Herriman), 121, *122*; "One A.M. at a 'Select and Special' with Artists, Actors and Newspapermen at a Popular Uptown Café" (Fornaro), 44, *46*; "A Seeley Dinner in Hogan's Alley" (Luks), 52, *53*; "A Street Parade to Advertise Mose's Incubator Show" (Luks), 56–58, *57*; *Sunday Magazine*, 41–42, *42*–*43*; "Training for the Football Championship Game in Hogan's Alley" (Luks), 50, *51*; "Two Sketches of Human Driftwood" (Luks), 41
Nsibidi symbols, 172n5

Oberhardt, William, 94, *96*
"One A.M. at a 'Select and Special' with Artists, Actors and Newspapermen at a Popular Uptown Café" (Fornaro), 44, *46*
O'Neill, Rose Cecil, 94
only things Patrick Joseph would not guarantee were the salt herrings which his Yiddish customers persisted in eating raw, The (Glackens), 114–15, *116*
Opper, Frederick, 75, 166n2; *Happy Hooligan*, 71, *73*, 80, 129; *And Her Name Was Maud!*, 168n30
optical technology, 17
optical toys, 34
Orator, The (Luks), 163n39
Organ, Marjorie, 9–10, 153–54, *156*
Oregon Daily Journal, 153, *155*
Osofsky, Gilbert, 130
Outcault, Richard F. (R. F.), 8, 44–47, 71, 75, 106, 164n45, 164n48, 164n51, 166n2, 175n11; "Around the World with the Yellow Kid," 169n47; *Buster Brown*, 168n30; *Hogan's Alley*, 47, 50, 52, 54, 163n44; "Hogan's Alley Folk Have a Trolley Party in Brooklyn," *47*, *48*; *Li'l Mose*, 119; *McFadden's Flats*, 49, 163n44; *Pore Li'l Mose*, 152; Riccadonna sisters, 164n51; *Ryan's Arcade*, 163n44; *Yellow Kid*, 26, 163n44; *Yellow Kid's Diary*, 163n44

"Parrot of Uncle Hurwitz, The" (Lessing), 90–92
"Passing of Cat Alley, The" (Riis), 14

Patterson, Howard Jay, 26
Pène du Bois, Guy, 118
Penitentes, 41–42, *42–43*
Pennsylvania Academy of Fine Arts, 44
persistence of vision, 83, 168n36
Philadelphia Evening Bulletin, 36–38
Philadelphia Press, 21–22, 100
Philippines, 60
photographer-reporter(s), 163n35
pictorial news, 38
Playing the Races (Wonham), 31
pluralism, 93, 150
Pool Room Sketch (Weber and Fields), 22–23
Pore Li'l Mose (Outcault), 152
Prendergast, Maurice, 9–10
Preston, James, 9–10
Preston, May Wilson, 9–10, 153, 170n8
Princeton University, 50
private humor, 149–50
"Providential Match, A" (Cahan), 89
Puck, 100, 169n43
Pulitzer, Joseph, 8, 20, 49, 70–74, 100, 131, 164n48
Pyle, Howard, 94

quilts, 172n5

"Rabbi Eliezer's Christmas" (Cahan), 102, *104*, 106
race relations, 123, 150–51, 159n14; Jim Crow racism, 129–33, 137; riots, 129–31
racial grotesque, 30–32, 160n26
racist representations, 119–21, 137–39, 172n4
Radway, Janice, 168n31
Ratzlaff, Aleen J., 175n12
realism, 6, 12–18, 88, 93, 160n26; American literary realism, 11–18, 24–25; local color, 14–15; magazine, 160n31
Reform Advocate, 114
Repplier, Agnes, 120
Riccadonna sisters (characters), 164n51
Rice, Alice Hegan, 110
Rice, Katherine P., 153, *155*
Rice, T. D., 129
Richmond Times-Dispatch, 83, *84*

Riis, Jacob A. (Jacob August), 13–18, 160n24; *Bohemian Cigarmakers at Work in Their Tenement*, 3–5, *4*, 12–13; *How the Other Half Lives*, 3–5, *4*, 13–14, 25; "Light in Dark Places," 14–15, *16*; "The Passing of Cat Alley," 14
Rise of David Levinsky, The (Cahan), 88–89
Robbins, Trina, 176n13
Rockwell, Norman, 170n8
Rogers, Leslie, 152, 172n5
Romani, 90
Roosevelt, Theodore, 14
Rose Hill English Folly Company, 22
Roxy Harvesting Among the Kitchens (Kemble), 32, *33*
Russell, Charles, 70
Ryan's Arcade (Outcault), 163n44

Sam and His Laugh (Swinnerton), 28, 123–33; "And Sam Jes' Roared," 173n22; "Dear Reader, Please Permit Us to Present to You Sam!" (Swinnerton), *124*, 125; "Sam as a Magician's Confederate" (Swinnerton), 126–28, *127*
Sambo (Marriner), 119
Sammon, Jeffrey T., 137
Sammond, Nicholas, 121, 173n19
Saturday Evening Post, 8, 27, 94–97, 110–11, 170n8, 171n28, 171n32; "The Autobiography of a Beggar" (Friedman), 107, *108*; *Doubling His Pace, Flew Down Alley* (Glackens), 107, *108*
Savannah Tribune, 120
schematic, 38
Schiller, Friedrich, 74
Schreiber, Benjamin, 68
Scott, Walter, 54
Scribner's Magazine, 88, 94, 97, 113; "Rabbi Eliezer's Christmas" (Cahan), 102, *104*; "The Vaudeville Theater," 102, *103*
Seeley, Herbert, 52, *53*
"Seeley Dinner in Hogan's Alley, A" (Luks), 52, *53*
segregation, 123
sensibility, comic, 3–12, 18–28, 149–58; black, 28, 119–48

sequential art, 167n17
Seym, Louise, 100
Sharpe, Christina, 150–51
"Sherwood Sisters" (Glackens), 100
Shi, David, 13
Shinn, Everett, 9–10, 38, 44, 49, 56, 61–64, 163n32
Shinn, Florence Scovel, 9, 110, *112*, 153
SIA (Society of Independent Artists), 97
Singing Soubrettes (Glackens), 102, *103*
Sliced Nations game, 34, *35*, 162n21
Sloan, John, 9–10, 62, 94, 163n32, 170n8
slums. *See* ghetto fiction
smart magazines, 94
Smith, Shawn Michelle, 173n12
Smolderen, Thierry, 83
socialism, 169n51
Society of Illustrators, 97
Society of Independent Artists (SIA), 97
sociopolitical critique, 11
Sontag, Susan, 13
Spain, 38–39, *40*
Spanish-American War, 60
speech balloons, 70–71, *73*, 159n11
sports comics, *134*, 135–43, *138*, *140*, 144–45
stereotypes, 7, 11, 90
St. Louis Republic, 153, *154*
Strange What Difference a Mere Man Makes (Organ), 153, *156*
"Street Parade to Advertise Mose's Incubator Show, A" (Luks), 56–58, *57*
Strong, William L., 160n24
subjective humor, 6
"Such a Delicate Duck," 23
Sunday comic supplements, 35–36, 47, 67–74, *72*, 100, *101*. *See also individual publications*
superiority theory of laughter, 6
"Swallow-Tailer for Two, A" (Lessing), 86
Swan, Kate, 41
Swinnerton, James "Jimmy," 28, 121–48, 173n19; "And Sam Jes' Roared," 173n22; "Dear Reader, Please Permit Us to Present to You Sam!," *124*, 125; *Sam and His Laugh*, 28, 123, 125, 128, 132–33; "Sam as a Magician's Confederate," 126–28, *127*

Swinnerton, Louise, 131
syndicates, 95

tabloids, 49
"Take a Plunge the Water Is Fine" (Herriman), *140*, *141*
Tanguay, Eva, 152–53
technology, optical, 17
"Tempus Fugit" (Lessing), 171n29
tendentious humor, 6
Tenement Club, 160n24
theatricals, 99, *99*
3-D projection, 34
"Three Put Up a Better Argument Than Two" (Herriman), *139*, *140*
"Three Thousand Years Among the Microbes" (Twain), 31
Tisserand, Michael, 131, 133, 139
Titherington, Richard, 171n19
Töpffer, Rodolphe, 75
toys, 47
Trachtenberg, Alan, 74
Tragedy of Pudd'nhead Wilson, The (Twain), 30–34, *33*
"Tragic Rites of the Penitentes" (Luks), 41–42, *42–43*
"Training for the Football Championship Game in Hogan's Alley" (Luks), 50, *51*
translation: cultural, 74–85, 167n22; minoritizing, 88
tricksters, 128–29
"Trifle Light as Air, A" (Lessing), 88
Truth, 36, 44–47
"Tune in Court, A" (Hill), 106, *107*
"Turn About Is Fair Play" (Ladendorf), *37*
Twain, Mark, 6, 22, 25, 29–30, 64–65, 165n70; *The Comedy of Those Extraordinary Twins*, 30–32, 164n48; "Final Remarks," 32; "How to Tell a Story," 29; "Three Thousand Years Among the Microbes," 31; *The Tragedy of Pudd'nhead Wilson*, 30–34, *33*
twins and twinning, 47–54; *The Comedy of Those Extraordinary Twins* (Twain), 30–32, 164n48; *Hogan's Alley* (Luks), 50–52, *51*; *The Little Nippers* (Luks), 50–52;

"More Twins Born But There Are Others to Come" (Luks), 58, 59; *Mose's Incubator* (Luks), 56–59, 57, 59
Two Pair of Misfits: A Romance of Old Pavonda (Halitvack), 114
"Two Sketches of Human Driftwood" (Luks), 41

"Under His Nose" (Lessing), 94, 96
Unheimlichkeit, 158
University of Pennsylvania, 50
USS *Maine*, 60, 100

variety theater, 23
vaudeville, 22, 80–81, 161n48; blue performances, 23; boxing demonstrations, 141, 174n47
"Vaudeville Theater, The," 102, 103
Veblen, Thorstein, 153
Venuti, Lawrence, 88
Verdict, The, 62, 63
vernacular language, 77, 79
View-Masters, 34
visibility, 160n37
visual comedy, 94–106
Vorse, Albert White, 171n20

Wabe, Ashea (Little Egypt), 52, 53
wake time, 151
Walden, Daniel, 166n4
Walker, H. W. "Beany," 137
war correspondents, 36–38
Ward, Artemis, 6
Washington Bee, 120
Watkins, Mel, 126, 133, 149, 173n12
Watson, Fred B., 152
Waugh, Colton, 3
Waxman, Meyer, 166nn3–4
Weber, Joe: Mike and Meyer, 22–24, 81, 83; Pool Room Sketch (Weber and Fields), 22–23
West, Mae, 152–53
"When Yenkel Was King" (Halitvack), 114
white supremacists, 131
Wickberg, Daniel, 6, 29
Wiederseim, Grace Gebbie, 153, 154
Wiegman, Robyn, 160n37

"Wiles of the Wooer, The" (Kelly): *With a brewer-driver's huge hand between her two slender ones* (Glackens), 109, 111; rejected sketch for, 108–9, 110
Willard, Frank, 166n2
Willliams, Andreá N., 175n12
"Will the Military Spirit Have This Effect on Our Future?" (Luks), 60
Wilson, May, 100
Wirth-Nesher, Hana, 88
Wister, Owen, 86
With a brewer-driver's huge hand between her two slender ones (Glackens), 109, 111
With an expression of mournful resentment, he turned and left the room (Dirks), 94, 95
Woman and Macaw (Luks), 62
women, 152–57, 155
Wonham, Henry, 24, 31, 160n31
Woodman, Joe, 142
Woolf, Michael Angelo, 47
wordplay, 81
World Publishing Syndicate, 132
World War I, 152
Wuster, Tracy, 64, 161n2, 165n70

Yale University, 50
Yekl (Cahan), 88–89
Yellow Kid, the (Mickey Dugan), 26, 50–52, 71, 75; "Around the World with the Yellow Kid" (Outcault), 169n47; "Hogan's Alley Folk Have a Trolley Party in Brooklyn" (Outcault), 47, 48; "A Seeley Dinner in Hogan's Alley" (Luks), 52, 53; "Training for the Football Championship Game in Hogan's Alley" (Luks), 50, 51; *Yellow Kid's Diary* (Outcault), 163n44
"Yellow Kid? Ach, No! It's Only the Katzenjammer Kid—(and His Brudder)" (Dirks), 75, 76
yellow press, 20–21
Yiddish, 87–89
young doctor, A... (Glackens), 106, 107

Zurier, Rebecca, 102–4, 118

About the Author

Photo by Lia Finkelstein

Jean Lee Cole is professor of English at Loyola University Maryland, where she teaches courses in American literature from the nineteenth and twentieth centuries, book history and editing, and American visual culture. She is author of *The Literary Voices of Winnifred Eaton: Redefining Ethnicity and Authenticity* (Rutgers, 2002). She is also editor or coeditor of several books, including *Zora Neale Hurston: Collected Plays* (with Charles Mitchell; Rutgers, 2008) and *Freedom's Witness: The Civil War Correspondence of Henry McNeal Turner* (West Virginia, 2013), and is editor of the scholarly journal *American Periodicals* and former president of the Research Society for American Periodicals.

www.ingramcontent.com/pod-product-compliance
Lightning Source LLC
Chambersburg PA
CBHW070316240426
43661CB00057B/2657